Everyday Epiphanies

Everyday Epiphanies

A Collection of Columns and Other Writings

1999–2015

by

Daniel Oliver

Pax in Bello Group
Washington, DC

Inquiries should be addressed to:
Daniel Oliver
3105 Woodley Road, NW
Washington, DC 20008 USA

DanielOliver@PAXQB.com

ISBN 978-1-7357811-0-5 (cloth)
ISBN: 978-1-7357811-2-9 (trade paper)

1 2 3 4 5 6 7 8 9 10

For

Andrew Oliver

&

Ruth Blake Oliver

no longer travailing or heavy laden . . .

they loved to read,

and they loved to write,

and they passed those loves on to me.

—in grateful memory

Acknowledgments

My thanks to the proprietors of the following where this material originally appeared: *The American Conservative, American Greatness, The American Spectator, Breitbart, Claremont Review of Books, The Daily Caller, The Federalist, Fox News, Newsmax, Ricochet, Washington Examiner, Washington Times, and The Western Journal.*

I want also to acknowledge the contribution of the late Linda Bridges, copyeditor to the stars, including Wm. F. Buckley Jr. She was more than a copyeditor: she knew, and remembered, everything there was to know about conservatives and their musings, and made innumerable corrections to my fallible memory and understanding, and resultant copy.

My thanks also to Dara Ekanger who for the last few years has had the job of copyediting my pieces, and who has supervised the production of this book.

Contents

Introductions and Speeches

Preface

Writing for God . . . and Man

Why write at all?

I asked John O'Sullivan one night at dinner why I should bother to write columns. They take time (I have all the time that's left, as my father used to say). They are read only by thousands, and occasionally tens of thousands of people, but rarely, if ever, by hundreds of thousands. And who can tell what effect they have, if any? So why write?

"Write for God," John said, not offhandedly, but surprisingly quickly, channeling, knowingly or unknowingly (but, knowing John, most likely knowingly) Colossians 3:23. That was one of the best pieces of advice I have ever received. If you write, write for God. If you paint, paint for God. Whatever your talent is, *whatever talent you have been given*, don't hide it under a bushel.

And so I wrote (and still do). Unlike novelists I have talked to, who started writing when they were six or seven, I didn't start writing till much later: not really in college (except for the obligatory papers). I do, however, remember writing a paper in my sophomore year in college and getting a "C" with the comment from the TA (I went to a tony college) that said something like: "This is the kind of writing I would expect to find in *Life* magazine." I was thrilled.

Years later, I started writing paragraphs (off campus, so to speak) for *National Review* magazine. Eventually, Bill Buckley said that really wasn't working: I needed to attend the editorial meetings if I were going to write seriously. So I went to work for *National Review*, and after sending my first editorial up in the dumbwaiter that connected our floor to Bill's office a floor above, I received back an 8½×11" piece of yellow draft typewriter paper—standard for copy in those days—on which Bill had typed: "You are indeed a writer. The appropriate procedure is to kiss my ring." It was signed: "The Muse." Cloud nine.

That evening, as we gathered at 73rd Street (where Bill and Pat lived) for the fortnightly editorial dinner, Pat addressed me in a loud voice and said, "Dhanny, when Bill told me you could write, you could've knocked me over with a feather." Some things you never forget.

So I write. Okay, but why publish a collection? I'm glad you asked.

Publish for the record, assuming the book gets stored somewhere (The Library of Congress? The Library of Alexandria?) Perhaps—if the book burners don't get there first. But mostly, I think, publish for the grandchildren. They are my most dependable audience of the future. They have a stake in what I say—and more than they realize. They will be either proud or horrified by my writings—though perhaps (no!) just indifferent. But they will have the tie of kinship, and that is a stronger tie than almost anything else you, and I, can think of.

Man is born to create: my wife and I have five children. Those are our most precious, and only significant, creations. It is true that our thirteen grandchildren are not our direct creations, but they would have had a Hell of a time getting here without us.

One day they may get around to asking, or wishing they had asked, what did Grandpa *do*? (They know what Grandma does: *everything*!) Well, once upon a time, many years ago, he went to an office—but not during the memory of some of them, or the lifetimes of others. Hmm. Was he idle? I.e., Did he live in the Devil's workshop?

Nope. He wrote. And had fun doing it.

And I still do. And I hope that my writing makes God's world a better place, even if only a little better, for my children. And for my grandchildren. And for theirs. . . .

And for all of God's creation.

D. O.
Washington, DC
January 6, 2021

A Note on Organization

How should a book with two hundred or more separate pieces be organized? The are several possibilities: chronologically, by subject, by purpose, and perhaps others. I have decided to put all the columns first, in chronological order. Most of the columns are about domestic politics or culture, or both. And some, of course, are about more than one topic, making it difficult and perhaps confusing to group them by subject. Is a column about how good economic policies can help parents avoid sending their children to the government schools and do serious damage to the political poverty–welfare business a column about the economy, poverty, schools, welfare, or the Washington swamp? After the columns, I have put speeches and introductions I made in the same time period. Readers who simply have to know what I said about . . . X can look in the index, which is comprehensive.

Regulating Success

June 25, 1999

Success has a thousand fathers. It also has enemies. In the last twenty years there has been no domestic policy more successful than airline deregulation. Flying is cheaper. Life is better. Families take vacations to far-off places. People fly to visit relatives in towns you've never heard of. Ending the era of big government's interference in the airline business allowed the market to work its magic for consumers. Who says there's no such thing as a free lunch?

Now the lunch-busters are coming—the kind of big-government people who tried to nationalize medicine at the beginning of the Clinton administration. They propose to reregulate the airline industry. Only a graduate of the Hillary School of Political Smarts could have proposed such a truly awful idea.

The problem the government—in this case Department of Transportation—thinks exists and wants to solve is that the "major" airlines lower their prices too much or add too much capacity when they face competition from low-fare carriers.

Normally, of course, price cutting is good because it benefits consumers. However, antitrust law recognizes that sometimes—though rarely—price cutting can be predatory and work against consumers. That happens when a firm lowers its prices so much it drives competitors out of the market (losing money in the process), and then, having the market to itself, raises its prices above where they had been previously, recouping its losses and gouging consumers. That is what the Justice Department has accused American Airlines of doing.

Going after predatory pricing is a dangerous policy, though, because it tends to discourage price cutting by firms that are not predators. And the DOT's new rules would regulate capacity as well as prices. The new rules are sloppily drafted and if they become effective they will discourage competition. And clearly the Justice Department must think they are unnecessary—its suit against American Airlines makes no reference to DOT's new regulations.

DOT says it will scrutinize the responses (fares and capacity decisions) of "major carriers" to entry into a market by "new entrants" but not by other "major carriers" or carriers that are not "independent." DOT defines "new entrants" as those carriers that pursue "a competitive strategy of charging low fares," without defining "low" or the strategy, and DOT nowhere makes clear what kind of a carrier is considered "independent." How can matching fares or adding capacity be fair in response to one kind of competitor but not another?

DOT's proposed rule prohibits major carriers, in response to competition by a new entrant, from "adding capacity" and then selling "a large number of seats at very low fares"—without defining "adding capacity" (more flights? larger aircraft? seasonal adjustments?), "large," or "very low fares."

DOT's proposed rule says a carrier has engaged in "unfair" competition if, as a result of its strategic response to entry into a market by a competitor, it sustains lower profits or greater losses "than would a reasonable alternative strategy." What is going on here? Can it really be that government bureaucrats—risk averse by nature, without business experience, and steeped in post office economics— are now going to judge the reasonableness of the airlines' business strategies?

DOT's proposed rule prohibits major carriers from carrying more passengers at the new entrant's low fare than the new entrant itself carries. But how is the major carrier going to find out how many passengers the new entrant carries? No carrier, new or old, would be likely to reveal that proprietary business information to its competitor. That means the major carrier, not knowing how many passengers its new-entrant competitor was carrying but wanting to play it safe, would carry so few passengers at the new fare that it would not effectively compete with the new entrant, in which case— surprise—the new entrant could charge a higher price than it would if it faced competition from the major airline. How will consumers benefit from that?

And on and on it goes. The problem is, the people who produced these rules are the people who are going to judge the reasonableness of the airlines' business decisions—assuming the airlines will be willing to risk doing those things competition demands.

Hillary's husband told us the era of big government is over. It depends what he meant by "the."

Bridge Work
September 1999

It occurred to me, driving over Dyke Bridge on Chappaquiddick last month (thirty years after Senator Kennedy drove off that bridge— and one year after our attention from the lies President Clinton told us about Monica was distracted by his bombing of Sudan), that the era of mega-lying in American politics may have begun with Teddy Kennedy.

Curiously, we no longer seem to care when politicians lie about their personal lives, perhaps because we fear being labeled Puritans if we object to their bad behavior and perhaps also because we don't quite know where to draw the line between what is legitimately private and what the public has a right to know. But we have not been quick enough to see the effect of bad character on the polis. Bad character may be a good predictor of bad judgment.

When Teddy Kennedy explained the circumstances surrounding the death of the girl in the back seat of the car he was driving that night, he was widely perceived to be lying. But he became a liberal icon nevertheless. The country was spared having him as president, primarily because he had no answer to the television interviewer's question, "Why do you want to be president?" rather than because he lied to the nation about the girl who drowned. Teddy had set a new standard for lying (go on national television, and lie and lie and lie)—and by remaining a liberal icon tarnished the lamp of truth.

The lamp of truth is so dark now it can't reflect its own flame, blackened by undoubtedly the most lying couple in American history. President Clinton is a contumacious liar extraordinaire—he was recently held in contempt of court for lying and fined $90,000. His wife, Hillary, because of the statements she made in connection with the firing of the White House travel staff, the "losing" of her law firm's billing records, and her financial success in commodities trading, has no credibility whatsoever.

That Mr. and Mrs. Clinton are crooks and scoundrels isn't seriously disputed anywhere this side of the fever swamps of Democratic party hypocrisy—and the American Bar Association. Nevertheless,

Bill Clinton continues to enjoy the perquisites of office, unmolested by the hypocrites who would drive Republicans from office—who did drive Nixon and Packwood from office—because there is no shortage of people who say that character doesn't matter.

After all, the Left crows, the country is enjoying record prosperity (dishonestly they give all the credit to this administration). The rich are richer, as are the middle class. Even the welfare rolls are down, indicating that the poor are richer too. The tremendous growth of the economy has tended to marginalize government (Washington) and, the Right is pleased to say, the president's lack of moral authority has made it difficult for him to meddle.

But a president who lacks the authority to lead the country in the wrong direction is also likely to lack the authority to lead it in the right direction. US foreign policy is a shambles. Our errors in Kosovo have produced chaos and may turn into a winter disaster. Saddam Hussein must be laughing his rags off at us. We have no missile defense system to protect us in an increasingly dangerous world. And our culture is in free fall. This fall's television programming will set new standards of vulgarity (industry executives credit Clinton's escapades with making it acceptable): movies are so violent even Hollywood's friends are complaining, *Time* magazine invited Dr. Kevorkian to its seventy-fifth anniversary party, the American Bar Association asked the contumacious president to speak at its annual meeting, and the Miss America Pageant has lifted its ban on women who have had an abortion.

It turns out that character (of which telling the truth is one trait) counts after all—no, before all. That may be why the Republican Party is once again seen by the voting public (by a nearly two-to-one margin) as the party of values, and considered more trustworthy on a range of moral and ethical matters like honesty and knowing right from wrong. Character matters—and we will become increasingly aware of that if we drive over the bridge to the twenty-first century guided by the spiritual colleagues of the man who drove off that bridge on Chappaquiddick thirty years ago.

Incumbency Corrupts Too
November 1999

The campaign reform issue boils down to this: Does money corrupt? Or does money only seem to corrupt?

The difference is important because most of the "reforms" limit the freedom of citizens to participate in the democratic process. Limiting that freedom for the sake of appearances should make us nervous.

For money to corrupt it must do one of two things: (1) buy the vote of a sitting legislator, or (2) enable the wrong candidate, A, to get elected instead of the right one, B.

The first case—a legislator votes "yes" when, but for the contributions, he would have voted "no"—is clearly a corruption of the democratic system, but it is also almost certainly extremely rare. Every now and then a maverick will cross the aisle, but who can name one politician who in recent memory was thought to have done that for money?

The second case seems more troubling, but is not. To begin with, the candidate with the most money does not always win. Michael Huffington spent $30 million of his own money running for the Senate from California, but lost anyway.

But more important: who is competent to say, a priori, B should have won over A—other than tony newspaper editors, disgruntled executive directors of special interest groups, and incumbent politicians?

Trial lawyers, and a lot of other people, believe that lawsuits are necessary in a free market system to discipline the negligent and the reckless. The gun folk believe the right to bear arms—guaranteed by that Amendment which is closest to the First Amendment—is one of our essential freedoms.

If, say, the trial lawyers decide to spend a zillion dollars on the campaign of a candidate who will protect their franchise, they may be able to lure A away from whatever he is doing into a race for elective office. If A wins, of course he will protect their interests, but not because his vote has been bought, but because the way he is disposed to vote was why they supported him in the first place.

The question is, what's wrong with that? Isn't that what democracy is all about? Finding people who believe in what you believe and supporting them?

Democracy is about choice. But for democracy to work, voters need knowledge about the candidates. Candidates need money to communicate that knowledge, but challengers almost always have an uphill battle against incumbents.

Evidence presented in a pamphlet by former Reagan OMB Director James C. Miller III clearly indicates that most campaign reform proposals are nothing more than methods of protecting incumbents. We shouldn't be surprised. Incumbents are like businessmen: their goal is to achieve a monopoly position, not necessarily to nurture democracy. They hold five high cards.

Incumbents have free mail. In a recent election, eleven of the top twenty spenders in the House of Representatives "spent" more on franked mail than their challengers spent on their entire campaigns.

Incumbents can deploy taxpayer-funded case workers in their districts. In tight elections, incumbents increase their allocation of office funds to casework.

Incumbents tend to be better known. They hold "town meetings" and become celebrities in their districts.

Because incumbents can threaten (subtly) to vote for or against legislation that affects the economic fortunes of potential donors (everywhere in the country), it is easier for them to raise money.

And because incumbents tend to be able to raise more money more easily than challengers, but need to spend less, they can save some of the funds they raise for future campaigns—and for scaring off challengers.

According to Miller, during the past three decades the reelection rates in the House of Representatives have averaged between 92 and 94 percent—which prompted President Reagan to remark that there was more turnover in the Soviet Presidium than there was in the US Congress.

It is evident that the only campaign reform that would benefit the democratic process is one that would disproportionately disadvantage incumbents over challengers. That is not what existing laws do, and only a single one of the current proposals would do that—a proposal of Senator Mitch McConnell (R–KY) which would require candidates to use up all their campaign funds within six months following an election. All other proposals—whether they limit contributions, or provide free television time or public funding of campaigns—preserve or increase the natural advantages of incumbents.

Nothing validates the observation that new ideas tend to be bad ideas better than campaign reform. It is inherently anti-democratic because it is the handiwork of monopolists. What Congress should do is repeal all the existing laws except those that require disclosure of campaign contributions. All other proposals are just what you'd expect from incumbent politicians, which is why if "campaign reform" wins, democracy will lose.

Death of a Franchise
December 1999

Times are tough for injustice collectors. The great liberal franchise—poverty and welfare, education, and the environment—is losing its attraction to the customers.

The amazing American economy—one of Ronald Reagan's lasting legacies—is lifting people out of poverty so fast Bill Clinton's Census Bureau wants to revise the definition of poverty.

In September of this year, the Census Bureau reported that 1.1 million people left the poverty rolls last year. A year ago, the Bureau reported that there were one million fewer people living below the poverty line in 1997 than in 1996. And in 1997, the Bureau reported that in the previous three years, virtually all groups—non-Hispanic whites, blacks, Hispanics, and Asian-Americans—had seen poverty rates drop.

Much to the horror of the professional welfarists, more than 25 states have not spent their federal welfare grants. Three billion dollars out of the $12 billion made available last year are sitting in the federal treasury waiting for takers. Some state officials are afraid Congress will take the money back, which is not a bad idea.

But a better one is to give the money to parents of school children so they can send them to the school of their choice. What better welfare program is there than an education that leads to a good job? If that requires a change in federal legislation, Congress should change the law. But perhaps all that is required is an imaginative governor with a brave heart and buns of steel—or a good lawyer.

Meanwhile, the awful truth is that the poverty–welfare business is in grave danger, depending for its continuance in large measure on poverty statistics that so significantly misrepresent and inflate the number of poor people that they can fairly be called fraudulent. (Note to next non-liberal president: appoint someone head of the Census Bureau who can oblige it to yield honest numbers.)

The education franchise is also in serious trouble because vast numbers of the Democrats' core constituents—African Americans— prefer (the polls are unambiguous here) charter schools, vouchers, or any other form of privatized competition to the state-monopoly schools their children have for so long been consigned to by liberals. President Clinton, who rode off on a much-publicized poverty search during the summer, would have done better to look out his own window at the District of Columbia where the poverty rate, at 22.7 percent, is the highest in the nation, as is the out-of-wedlock birth rate (64 percent), and where the president's personal opposition to parents' having choice in education (that's poor African American parents, not rich white parents) assures that African Americans will continue to be ill-educated and poor.

The environmental business isn't going well either. Al Gore has staked out a position on the environment so far left it jeopardizes the movement's plausibility. In May of this year, a federal court of appeals overturned the Environmental Protection Agency's controversial and far-reaching Clean Air Act regulations, a major setback to the Clinton administration that stunned environmentalists. And Clinton has not dared to ask the Senate to ratify the Kyoto Protocol on global warming he negotiated, a treaty which his own Council of Economic Advisors estimated would cost between $7 and $12 billion a year but which a private firm estimated would cost closer to $300 billion a year.

Because the liberal franchise is losing its value, the liberals are pushing health care. And health care looks like a winner. Recent polls suggest that health care is a major concern of all voters. One poll asked people what was worrying them most. Among married couples with children, 72 percent were concerned about HMOs. Among people sixty-five years or older, 65 percent were concerned about HMOs, 65 percent about the elderly not getting medicines, and 62 percent were afraid of losing medical benefits.

But health care's real strength is strategic. Like much of the welfare pushed on the country by the Great Society firm of Johnson & Nixon, the more there is, the more is needed. The politician's trick is to hook his constituents on handouts, and then collect the votes. The more the government gets involved in health care, the worse it will get—which will seem to validate ever more government involvement. Health care policy will provoke the desire, but take away the performance. Canada's history with nationalized-socialized health care makes the case unassailably. But this country's history with health care makes the case too. It was government policy—letting employers pay for health care in lieu of increasing wages during the Second World War—that started the problem.

The good news is that the economy will keep on producing—the liberals will see to that because, like pushers, they will want their clients to have money for their addictions. But the bad news is that the injustice collectors have simply changed their field of concentration, and will try to do to health care what they did so successfully for decades to education and welfare.

Primary Democracy
February 2000

They laughed when America sat down to play Primary Time last year. And they complained: why should Iowa and New Hampshire— two of our least populated states—have so much power in the process of nominating a president? The people, the candidates, and democracy are the losers in such a system. However, as the Iowa caucus and the New Hampshire primary got closer, the real concern of some of the complainants became apparent. The primary season seemed to be bringing out the worst in the Republican candidates: their conservatism.

Before Ronald Reagan, the only Republicans "acceptable" to the liberal media were "moderate" Republicans, like Senator Javits and Governor Rockefeller of New York. Richard Nixon, too, tended toward big government in domestic affairs—though even that couldn't shield him from his opponents' hatred of his staunch anticommunism. President Reagan, however, not only legitimized conservatism; he moved the center over toward the right. But with Reagan only a distant memory now, the Left seeks to delegitimize the Right and enshrine the center, as they redefine it, because their center is, at least, left of right.

Liberals always recommend the middle of the road to Republican candidates. But democracy steers its own course. Even as journalists were preaching the necessity—the inevitability—of the middle way, George W. Bush was heading right. He wants to win, and he knows the right is where the competition, and the votes, are.

Steve Forbes had been hammering Bush on taxes and abortion. *Newsweek* said Forbes, who was winnowed out by Delaware, had a disproportionate impact on the presidential race for someone with so little chance of winning. Whatever Bush's real convictions on those two subjects are, his public stance—as front-runner—had been less than confrontationally anti-statist or pro-life. But as the Iowa and the New Hampshire contests drew near, his public positions became . . . clarified. In our system, you don't get a chance to become president of all the people until you satisfy some of them.

As one headline put it, Bush was "clarifying his abortion stand, again." He called the Supreme Court's decision in *Roe v. Wade* a "reach that overstepped the constitutional bounds." It was a prerogative of the states, Bush said, to decide on the legality of abortion, and he said "the court stepped out of bounds and usurped the rights of the legislatures." For liberals, that states' rights position is not acceptably middle-of-the-road either on abortion or as an interpretation of federalism.

Last fall, Bush seemed to be chastising Washington Republicans when he told a conservative think-tank audience, "Too often my party has confused the need for limited government with a disdain for government itself." In addition, Bush was coy—or careful—on tax cuts.

Now he says, "You mark my words: you leave money sitting around the table in Washington, Washington politicians will spend it." And, if tax money "goes to Washington, it will go to creating more government."

Ronald Reagan could have said that—and probably did. But because the Republicans are in control of Congress—quick: how do you tell?—and because people are feeling richer than they ever have before (thanks to Reaganomics), being anti-Washington and anti-tax may not be as powerful a campaign message as it was for Reagan. McCain was able to sweep New Hampshire on the character issue alone. But the message still has power, if not magic, and Bush will have to continue to deliver that conservative message if he is to prevail.

Meanwhile, Al Gore and Bill Bradley were having a food fight on the nation's front lawn. They accused each other of lying—on health care, abortion, and welfare—as they fought for votes in territory so far left you needed widescreen TV to see them. Gore charged Bradley with sounding like Ronald Reagan, and Bradley accused Gore of being a "favorite of the Washington lobbyists." It was a preview of the meanest presidential campaign the country will have seen in years.

The Bradley–Gore fight brought out the second worst fear of the liberal establishment: that the Democratic candidates would go so far left in primary time that neither one could win a general election.

The pundits say once the primaries are over, the candidates will scurry back toward the middle. Perhaps, but perhaps only if they really have no beliefs at all or no regard for the voters' intelligence— the ability to remember the positions taken by the candidates in the primary campaigns. That may be the game plan of Al Gore (a worthy protégé of Bill Clinton), but Bush, who knows that Reagan won, essentially, three for three, while his father was zero for one, may decide that the right—where some of his friends and many of the votes are—is the right place to be. McCain will continue to mine the character vein he discovered in New Hampshire. As a result, democracy appears to have performed better in this primary season than many people predicted.

Don't Give Up on Taxes
March 2000

It is not clear how well John McCain would have done if Bill Clinton were not such an awful man. But it is clear that fighting off the McCain boarding party took George W. Bush off message.

Until Iowa and New Hampshire, Bush was running on birthright, inevitability, a gazillion dollars—and a smirk to match. McCain relieved George W. of all four of those. Then Steve Forbes, who *Newsweek* said had a disproportionate effect on the campaign for someone who had so little chance of winning, made Bush into a tax-cutter-come-lately. But now, with Forbes gone, even conservative Republicans are saying even conservative Republicans will be neither seduced by, nor are even pruriently interested in, promises of a tax cut. Brother Safire says the conservatives' heavy tax-cutting is a "year out of joint." Where is Ronald Reagan when we need him?

Members of the vast right-wing conspiracy who want to know why the Reagan magic seems to have lost its attraction should read Bruce Bartlett's explanation in the December '99–January '00 issue of the Heritage Foundation's *Policy Review*. The problem is that in the new economy people don't just feel rich; they are rich. In the days of Jimmy Carter, inflation pushed taxpayers into ever higher tax brackets. Bracket-creep made people poorer, and made them welcome Reagan—who was not just the great communicator, but the great liberator as well. Today, the reverse is true. The growth in asset values makes taxes on incomes less important and the message of the tax cutter less compelling.

But the Reagan message wasn't about taxes alone. In fact, cutting taxes wasn't the main theme at all. Reagan's primary theme was the relationship between the people and their government. Reagan's promise was to alter that relationship by getting government off the backs of the people. His goal was to make the people freer. Taxes were only the details—and only some of them. Others had to do with regulation and military threats from abroad.

Reagan's main theme was freedom—and freedom is as threatened today by government as it was in 1980.

What Bush must do—and what McCain appeared to have no interest in doing, and Gore has absolutely no interest whatsoever in doing—is campaign for freedom. Not just reform (there's no point in reforming government so it can collect more taxes more efficiently)—but freedom.

Bush should talk first about the general principle: more government means less freedom.

Then he should make three proposals. First, he should push for a tax cut—the same percentage cut for everyone. That allows the people who earn the money to keep it. Cutting taxes for "the poor" but not "the rich" is simply more redistribution—a tax heist, not a tax cut. Yes, Bush has already talked about cutting taxes, but he must emphasize the freedom, not the cut.

Second, he should sign on to the campaign to pass a constitutional amendment that would require a two-thirds vote of Congress to raise taxes. And he should challenge Vice President Gore to join him. He won't, and then Bush can say that Gore is not willing to rule out a tax increase. Gore will say he would raise taxes only in an emergency—but in Washington there is not a single event that could come to the mind of man that would not be described by someone on the tax-collecting end of government as an emergency. You don't believe it? This year Congress decided that the Census—required by the Founding Fathers to take place this year—was an emergency. The two-thirds requirement is needed precisely to preclude even the robust in Congress from declaring that the rising of the sun and the going down thereof are emergencies.

Third, Bush should make the principled argument against the current income tax, the most offensive part of which is its structure of graduated rates. Graduated rates are based on the principle: "from each according to his ability," about which there is a whiff of something not wholesomely American. Equal rates are a freedom thing, and would get the government out of the business of treating people unequally. Graduated rates are unfair—and also complex—and the American people should be free of them.

Bush is no Reagan. But even a schoolboy who reads the Declaration of Independence aloud sounds eloquent, and could move voters. If Bush promises the American people more freedom, they won't even remember his smirk.

Internet Privacy
May 2000

Thank Heavens for little girls (and little boys too), the national nannies must be singing now. On behalf of "the children," the nannies persuaded Congress to enact the first internet privacy statute. That was only the beginning. The nannies hope that Moore's Law, which says the power of computer chips will double every eighteen months, will apply to internet regulation too.

Internet privacy is hot at the moment, in part because an internet advertising firm, DoubleClick, gathered "personal" information about people using the internet (name, address, age, shopping patterns) without their knowledge and sold it. The nannies didn't like that.

But in the 1960s, the nannies didn't like the ads sewing machine companies ran calling their machines "automatic." The nannies said consumers would think the machines made clothes without human intervention, and they got the Federal Trade Commission to prohibit the ads.

Now the nannies have a theory on privacy: that internet users have a privacy right that is violated when an organization collects data about them and their habits without their express permission. The nannies should stick to sewing—they'd do less harm to the new economy.

What is this thing called "privacy" anyway? People's names, addresses, and telephone numbers have been public for years in . . . telephone books. And people's buying habits have not traditionally been thought of as secret. They are known to at least one selling party in nearly every instance. A few souls, wary of the PC police, may sneak into back-alley stores to buy a pack of cigarettes. But that large lady in front of you at the drugstore doesn't seem the least perturbed that you see she is buying a pack of gum, a pack of Oreos, and a pack of condoms. Nor is her husband's purchase of a lawn mower or a Lexus likely to be known only to Deep Throat. Even if the information concerning those purchases were private (i.e., were private property), whose property would it be? The buyers' or the sellers'?

What's different today is that technology allows merchants to correlate lots of disparate information that was previously public but uncorrelated, and use the results to make their commercial operations more efficient. Sellers save money (and therefore can charge less) if they can target their advertising to people most likely to buy their products. That's why you want merchants to know as much as they can about you, from your taste in coffee (black, hot, and sweet) to your taste in music (Bach, gavottes, and suites). Consumers win when merchants have information that enables them to target their advertising because they get lower prices and spend less time searching for products. Poor consumers arguably benefit most because they have less time to search and less money to spend. The market works at least as well for the poor as for the rich.

The market is also working to provide security, which is to be distinguished from privacy. Of course we want to protect people's medical records and their financial transactions. It is also worth noting that the victims of commercial fraud on the internet tend to be merchants, who get stuck with any losses by the credit card companies. A customer's maximum exposure is fifty dollars. It may be that merchants will need more information about consumers, not less.

The market is also making it possible for people to surf the internet anonymously. Consumers today can block the "cookies" many websites send out by making simple changes to their internet browsers. Software vendors will enable internet users to send email anonymously. The market will provide more privacy, if that's what consumers want. Government regulation isn't necessary.

For the moment, the Federal Trade Commission agrees. It has concluded that self-regulation by the industry is sufficient to address whatever privacy concerns currently exist. That's good news.

Regulations tend to outlast their usefulness, if they are necessary even initially. If there is a privacy problem, technology—the market—will solve it. If there is regulation, it will be on the books for a lifetime. It was not until this year that Congress got around to repealing Depression-era legislation that reduced Social Security payments for older people who chose to work. That legislation was passed nearly seventy years ago. A lifetime.

Regulation could slow the growth of the internet for a lifetime too. But if we can resist the nannies' entreaties to have government oversee everything we do, there is infinite potential for the internet to grow and to serve consumers in the most amazing way.

Sweet and Low
June 2000

With Microsoft and the CD companies monopolizing the antitrust news, it's easy to forget that government is usually the enemy of competition, not its guarantor. That is quickly apparent from a blood-boiler of a case currently in the news involving a small company in the sugar business.

Heartland By-Products is a small sugar refiner in Taylor, Michigan, which imports a sugar syrup. In 1995, before starting to import the syrup, Heartland took the precaution of getting an advance ruling from the US Customs Service that the syrup it proposed to import was not subject to the tariff rate quota system of the domestic sugar program—a separate but related government scandal.

Relying on the Customs Service's favorable ruling, Heartland signed contracts, entered into leases, and invested millions of dollars in a new facility—none of which it would have done if it had known the syrup it was proposing to import would be subject to the exorbitant tariff.

In 1997, Heartland began importing the syrup from Canada. Not long afterwards, Heartland's competitors persuaded a group of congressmen to get the Customs Service to investigate Heartland to see if it was violating any Customs regulations. After conducting unannounced raids, Customs concluded that Heartland was not evading the tariff rate quota system. And in a memo a few months later, a Customs official noted that Heartland's operation was "perfectly legal."

Things weren't going well for Heartland's competitors, members of the Beet Association and the Cane Association, so they tried to get Customs to revoke its advance ruling. But a Customs official concluded that the ruling was "correct and should be affirmed."

In August 1998, a memo to members of the Beet Association stated, "We got a signal from Customs that some 'political muscle' in behalf of our petition might be welcomed by Customs officials."

A month later, twenty-two sugar-daddy senators (Republicans as well as Democrats) weighed in with a letter to the Secretary of the Treasury urging that Heartland's sugar syrup be reclassified—making it subject to the exorbitant tariff.

Customs complied and revoked the advance ruling that Heartland had relied on before starting its business. Heartland filed suit in the US Court of International Trade, which ruled that the Customs Service's revocation was "arbitrary, capricious, an abuse of discretion, and unlawful."

That decision is being appealed, but, not wanting to leave the issue to chance or the courts, the Beet and Cane crowd went back to their congressmen for a legislative fix. The congressmen were happy to oblige and tried to make the fix, in the form of an amendment to the Africa/CBI bill that would change the classification of Heartland's sugar syrup to make it subject to the tariff.

The great god of competition was smiling on consumers that day, however, and the congressmen were not successful. Nor did they fare any better when they tried to attach their amendment to the Agriculture appropriations bill. With luck, Big Sugar will lose this one big.

The Beet and Cane people have tried to portray Heartland's conduct as an end-run around the sugar program laws, laws that protect domestic sugar growers and keep the prices consumers pay artificially high. The product Heartland imports consists of refined beet or cane sugar mixed with water and molasses. Heartland imports the sugar syrup (which its competitors have dubbed "stuffed molasses") for the sole purpose of extracting the sugar.

When the law, which allows the importation of a substance with six percent or more of non-sugar solids (i.e., sugar syrup with a lot of junk in it), was proposed, Big Sugar was given a chance to object to it, but didn't. It's people were not foresighted enough to realize that someday technology would make it possible to extract sugar from that sort of syrup. Now that Heartland has discovered how to do that, Big Sugar wants the law rewritten, and has been successful in enlisting all too many congressmen on its side—and against competition and the consumers.

The federal government has just bought 150,000 tons of "surplus" sugar from farmers who have produced so much that prices have dropped 25 percent. A draft General Accounting Office report circulating on Capitol Hill estimates that the sugar program increases the costs of sugar to consumers by $2.2 billion a year—or something like $800 per acre for the domestic sugar growers. The sugar program scandal is the parent of the misery that has been afflicting Heartland.

The Power of Love
July 2000

If love means never having to say you're sorry, rich may mean never being truly bothered by government. As we Americans become ever richer, we may think we can insulate ourselves against the nuisances of excessive government. When the Dow reaches 36,000, we'll finally be free at last. Or will we?

Milton Friedman thinks not. After the celebration of the fiftieth anniversary of the Mont Pelerin Society (a group of free-market economists who first met at Mont Pelerin in Switzerland in 1947), Dr. Friedman wrote that although the lovers of freedom had won the war of ideas—central planning and nationalization are now in ill repute—we are doing rather less well in the realm of practice. Since that first meeting, government spending in the United States has gone from 20 percent of national income to 40 percent. And regulation has grown even more.

It's true we've had some spectacular successes in deregulating—most notably in the airline and trucking industries—but, as love means never having to say you're sorry, being a politician means never saying no to a regulation. In Washington, love means regulating your fellow man. And woman. And whosoever in Washington hath not love, hath not anything there, including a future.

There is a tendency among many of us to think that when politicians finish regulating this or that problem (which affects other people, not us), they will stop. When, finally, they succeed in banning cigarettes (I don't smoke) and guns (personally, I'm scared of them) and alcohol, and SUVs, and fattening potato chips—as well as fake-fat potato chips—then they will stop regulating.

Alas, no, Virginia. There is no end to regulation. In the name of health, safety, the environment, the old, the children—in the name of love—the politicians will try to regulate everything. And make each regulation seem imperative—including regulation of cell phones.

Regulating cell phones will prove irresistible because they are used by 86 million Americans—and what politician could pass up that much love? Cell phones will be targets because they may cause traffic accidents.

Robert Hahn and Paul Tetlock have written a small pamphlet, published by the American Enterprise Institute, in which they analyze the economics of regulating cell phones in vehicles. It's not a Sweet Valley High read, but it's a good primer on how to think about regulating.

Hahn and Tetlock estimate, on the basis of the meager evidence available, that cell phones are implicated in fewer than two-tenths of one percent of all vehicle accidents, and fewer than a hundred deaths a year. Now that's down a bit from 86 million, and even from 41,000, which is the number of people who die in vehicle accidents each year. But maybe there's still enough love for a hundred people to make regulating worthwhile.

Hahn and Tetlock's estimate of the cost of those accidents is derived from a study released by the National Highway Traffic Safety Administration, which counted primarily lost productivity and direct medical costs. Hahn and Tetlock added to that figure the value of a statistical life ($6.6 million—could a politician ever get away with that?), made other adjustments, and came up with a cost of accidents related to cell-phone use of $1.2 billion a year.

To determine the cost of a ban, they calculated the amount of money that would be necessary to compensate cell phone users, 60 percent of whose call time takes place while they are driving, "so that they would be indifferent to a ban." That cost they estimate at $25 billion—clearly not cost effective against a benefit of only $1.2 billion.

There are other studies which look at people in addition to numbers. One of these found no significant difference in "driving impairment" between using hand-held phones and hands-free phones. Any phone use may distract a driver's attention. Drivers who can't use phones at all may engage in other, and perhaps more attention-diverting, behavior—conversing, tuning a radio, eating, changing tapes, or even reading maps, which the NHTSA estimates may produce four thousand deaths annually.

Other wrinkles: enforcement of cell phone regulations might take resources away from more important police activities. And strict regulations would almost certainly reduce the prompt reporting of accidents on the highways.

Regulations are often justified on the grounds that there has been "market failure"—consumers fail to pay the full costs of risks they impose on others. But unless the market for automobile insurance is not working, the presumption should be that market failure is small. If the market is working, regulations are likely to make it less efficient. But the politicians tend to have less interest in efficiency than in the power that loving their constituents can bring to them. And that is why, despite the triumph of market economics, the regulatory state continues to grow, and to the disadvantage, primarily, of those who are least insulated by the Dow's journey towards 36,000.

Thanksgiving Enchantments
December 2000

This Thanksgiving we have a lot to be thankful for. Food is plentiful and cheap. Life expectancy is long. We are not at war. Political campaigning has stopped, for the moment. And pirating on the internet may kill pop music. By almost any measure, Providence has been extravagant, perhaps intemperate. Such good fortune made our Puritan ancestors nervous, and should make us wary.

Many may think politics is all economics. The slogan of the Clinton administration was, "It's the economy, stupid." But the Pilgrims didn't cross a sea whose waves were mighty and raged horribly for "the economy, stupid." They came to this unsettled land for something different, and found it—or rather created it. They came to build a godly society, where character was coin.

But prosperity set in and, almost three hundred years ago, Cotton Mather feared its debilitating effects. "Religion brought forth Prosperity," he observed, "and the daughter destroyed the mother."

Our great prosperity raises the question: would asking for

anything more be evidence we had been destroyed by greed? The answer is, it depends on whom we ask, and what we ask for.

Most political campaigns look to the future. Candidates promise to take us to utopia, generally by way of interfering with market forces and giving us other people's money. We should beware of candidates bearing government gifts. Most of our problems are caused by too much government. Consider medical care and education, two of the livelier political issues.

The problem with medical care is caused by the way it is paid for. The government has skewed the tax laws so it appears to patients that someone else is paying the bill. Hiding the real cost tends to reduce competition, drive up prices, and lower quality—all of which provides government with excuses to interfere again. The solution is to get the government out of health care and allow individuals to be responsible for their own care. People—patients—should buy medical insurance the way they buy homeowners' insurance. The market would provide them with quality products at competitive prices, and the health care "problem" would be solved.

The problem with education, the manifestation of which is that Johnny can't read, is that Johnny is required to go to the government monopoly school, which—especially in liberal Massachusetts, according to news reports—employs teachers who can't read either. The solution is to let parents choose where to send their children to school and get government out of the school business. The Clinton administration, whose leaders send their children to private school, opposes letting others have that same choice.

So as we gather together this Thanksgiving, one thing we should ask for is less: less government. And in keeping with that request, we may properly ask God to contrive the decriminalization of thanking Him for His bounty and asking for His grace—assuming He would deign to involve Himself in public policy.

The current rules interpreting the First Amendment's "establishment of religion" clause are the construct of arrogant civil servants (Supreme Court justices)—further proof that our most intractable problems are those created by government. Not only are those rules not in accord with, and insulting to, the wishes of most of our people; they are also clearly inconsistent with the practice and preaching of our Founding Fathers. On the day after the House of

Representatives passed the First Amendment, it passed, by a two-to-one majority, a resolution calling for a day of national prayer and thanksgiving. And George Washington, in his Farewell Address, told us that "of all the dispositions and habits which lead to political prosperity Religion and Morality are indispensable supports."

Those supports are gone now, at least from the city named after our first president. Cotton Mather might have been speaking to us when, concerned about the behavior of his contemporaries, he warned, "There is danger lest the enchantments of this world make them forget their errand into the wilderness."

We too have all but forgotten our errand: not to make our people rich, but to make them free. And free most especially from burdensome government. This Thanksgiving we should not only be grateful for His bounty but more mindful of our errand.

The Pessimists Were Wrong
January 2001

It's over now. The US Supreme Court dropped a neutron bomb on the Florida Supreme Court: its opinion destroyed the Florida judges, while leaving the courthouse standing. Many predicted that is the way it would end. Most said it was the way it should end: a court stepping in to provide the longed-for finality.

They were wrong. A better way was the pessimists' nightmare: having a legislature decide the election.

We were tipped off on the issue at the very beginning by Al Gore's spokesman, former Secretary of State Warren Christopher, who said he was shocked, shocked to find politics involved in determining the outcome of the election in Florida.

Politics is simply a synechdoche for democracy. Liberals, however, tend to be antidemocratic. That is why they like to keep the effects of their policies invisible (stealth taxes, cross subsidizations) and want final authority to rest with only their own—i.e., non-elected judges.

But the bane of the institutional arrangements of our system of self-government, especially over the last forty years, has been judicial activism—usurpation by judges of the functions of the legislatures. Starting, probably, in the early 1900s (the Lochner era) the Supreme Court became increasingly activist, as did other courts, federal and state. In this year's campaign, one of the most important issues for conservatives and liberals alike—perhaps the most important issue—was the future composition of the US Supreme Court. Would it remain somewhat restrained, following the appointments of Presidents Reagan and Bush (though Bush also appointed Justice Souter), or would it once again become the activist, antidemocratic court the liberals so badly desire—because they cannot always accomplish what they want through the legislatures?

We are conditioned constantly by our opinion elites to believe that courts are the final authority in our democracy. A recent *New York Times* editorial said, "The Supreme Court's willingness to rule on this dispute should . . . banish talk by Republicans of having Florida's legislature overturn election results." A law professor wrote that of four possible methods of settling the election (certification by Florida's "partisan" secretary of state, appointment of electors by the Florida legislature, resolution of the issue by the US Congress, or a court decision) "none would carry the kind of legitimacy that a decisive court decision can offer." Even William Safire listed as the least desirable of four methods of settling the issue "a divisive, embittering, party-line election in the House" of Representatives.

They are all wrong. The value of settling this election in a legislative body would have been to remind people that the ultimate power in our democracy is located in the people and their elected representatives, not in the courts. What better time to teach that—and how more visibly—than in deciding a presidential election?

How many people know that the US Constitution provides (in Article III, Section 2) that Congress may remove certain subjects from the Supreme Court's jurisdiction? The provision has never been used—and the possibility that it might be scares liberals even more than smoking—but its existence suggests that the Founding Fathers didn't see the judiciary as supreme.

Elections are political—especially in the sense of "democratic." At an earlier time in our history, some of the state legislatures voted for the president, not the individual citizens, who, having elected the legislators in the first place, were not thought to have been disfranchised by the arrangement. That is the powerful historical precedent for a legislative body granting us the finality we sought in this election.

The necessity to control the antidemocratic impulses of the federal judiciary was made plain the same day the Supreme Court heard oral argument in the final *Bush v. Gore* matter. A federal appeals court declared a Cleveland school voucher program unconstitutional because, the court claimed, it aided religion—another in a long line of incomprehensible federal cases that have made the First Amendment's "establishment of religion" clause look like a Jackson Pollock original.

All is not lost, however. There is at least a brass lining in having this election decided by the Supreme Court. The liberals, claiming that the Court reached a politicized verdict, are now in the uncomfortable position of having to profess doubts about the legitimacy of the Court's power.

But think how uncomfortable they would have been if the House of Representatives had had to decide this election, and had decided it—for Al Gore.

More Trade, Less Government
May 2001

While the conservative Philadelphia Society (whose members believe less government means more freedom) gathered in Philadelphia over the weekend of April 20–22 to discuss "The United States in the World Arena," representatives from thirty-four governments were meeting in Quebec City to promote the FTAA, the Free Trade Area of the Americas, the formal name given to the proposed extension of NAFTA (the North American Free Trade Agreement).

By any reasonable reckoning NAFTA has been a success. US merchandise exports to Mexico increased 90 percent during NAFTA's first five years, and exports to Canada increased 55 percent—a total of $93 billion in export growth. Jobs supported by US goods exported to our NAFTA partners were estimated to total 2.6 million in 1998. Trade in manufactured goods (over 85 percent of US–NAFTA trade) grew by more than 66 percent from 1993 to 1998. And because NAFTA eliminated some Mexican regulations, the United States is able to export to Mexico cars made in the United States instead of having to build plants there.

But not everyone is reasonable. Public Citizen Global Trade Watch, a subsidiary of former presidential candidate Ralph Nader, opposes the FTAA. Public Citizen isn't the only opponent. A cursory search of the internet turns up sixteen anti-globalization organizations, including Smash FTAA, Operation SalAMI, A22-Stop the FTAA, and Coalition to Shut Down the OAS/FTAA. Another group is the Anti-Capitalist Convergence of Montreal (in French, La Convergence des Luttes Anti-Capitalists, or "CLAC"). CLAC, which says it "fundamentally rejects a social and economic system based on the private ownership of the means of production and exchange," organized a Carnival Against Capitalism involving "conferences, teach-ins, workshops, cabarets, concerts, protests and direct actions" for the Quebec City meeting, and its leader, Jaggi Singh, managed to get himself arrested.

These anti-trade people tend to be the folks who want one-world government (run by them), not a world of free people, who are not necessarily united but who are freely tied to people in different lands by their own particular—and generally limited, generally commercial—interests.

Public Citizen's complaint presses all the buttons that fire up people who fear private enterprise and the market. PC warned in a website broadside, "The proposed FTAA agreement would: expand to a total of 34 countries NAFTA's legacy of undermining policies that protect workers, the environment, and public health; allow big business to sue governments for cash compensation for profit losses due to those public interest regulations ('investor to state' lawsuits); push to privatize education, water utilities, and other public services on which we all depend; and continue the 'race to the bottom,' where multinational corporations dump higher-paid union workers in the US and exploit sweatshop workers in Latin America instead."

Public Citizen says an FTAA agreement will have such effects as opening the door to greater corporate control and corruption, privatizing public schools and prisons in the United States, and also privatizing the postal service by transferring US Postal Service functions to a few delivery companies like FedEx, which could then send postal rates through the roof.

Clearly there are places in this land where neither light penetrates nor thought occurs, and there, in the offices of Public Citizen, you will find people, hunched over their word processors, who really think the US Postal Service (protected from price-reducing competition by a statutory monopoly) does a better job of delivering mail than FedEx. If they would step into the sunlight they might learn that FedEx has beaten the Federal Aviation Administration in developing a new airplane guidance system for its delivery planes, and has been hired by the Postal Service to do what it cannot. They might also learn that many people, especially black parents in Washington DC, would love to send their children to private schools—and would have had that chance if Bill Clinton, who gave corruption a bad name, hadn't vetoed the relevant bill providing them with that opportunity. And speaking of Clintonian corruption, why do the opponents of FTAA think markets are more corrupt than governments?

Big government enthusiasts claim the really important services must be provided by government—schooling, fire protection, air safety, etc. In fact, they have it backwards: some services are just too critical to be left to government. Markets work better than governments, as people all over the world are learning by looking at the United States. That is why the representatives of thirty-four governments went to Quebec: to continue hashing out another free trade agreement, which will limit the power of governments and better enable their people, like the citizens of the United States, to enjoy the blessings of liberty.

Educating Mrs. Atwater
June 2001

Gail Atwater, of Lago Vista, Texas, is not a happy citizen of her state—and there's a civics lesson in her unhappiness. She is the mother who, four years ago, was poked in the chest, yelled at, taken to a police station in handcuffs, fingerprinted, and jailed—all for not making her two children wear their seatbelts.

It is impossible not to sympathize with her—notwithstanding that she had been questioned about using seatbelts three months earlier. The policeman who arrested her behaved badly and should be punished (bring back stockades). And the law requiring seatbelts should offend anyone who cares about freedom and should be repealed—*pace* those who say that Mrs. Atwater, an adult, may be capable of assuming the risk of driving without a seatbelt herself, but should not be allowed to force that risk on her children. She built them, she paid for them, they're her children—and absent indications that she is a terrible mother, she ought to be free to choose what is in their best interest and presumed to know what that interest is better than any cabal of legislators.

Mrs. Atwater sued the city of Lago Vista for false arrest, but in April of this year, after a four-year battle, she lost in the US Supreme Court. In a 5–4 decision, the Court ruled that any driver can be taken into custody at a police officer's discretion, even for a minor infraction, without violating the Fourth Amendment's ban on unreasonable seizures.

The experience, not surprisingly, has piqued Mrs. Atwater's interest in political theory. "I started off as a liberal," she said, "and now I'm a conservative. I want to limit the government's power as much as possible."

Her husband was described as having, "in contrast," gone from being a conservative to being a liberal—but it seems clear that his liberalism is the anti-statist kind. When the local fire chief came onto Mr. Atwater's property while he was tending a small bonfire and ordered him to show some identification, Mr. Atwater refused and challenged the chief's jurisdiction.

Limiting the power of the state is the beginning of political wisdom, and we welcome Mrs. Atwater to our ranks. But it is important to understand the methods of limiting that power. One of the methods the Founders used was federalism, a concept Mrs. Atwater has still to learn. "A federal judge couldn't have jailed me for that violation," she said, "and yet a small-town policeman could." But that's just the point. Absurd seatbelt requirements have not yet become federal (i.e., "national") law and precisely because they haven't, Mrs. Atwater could move to a place where the laws—and the police—are less offensive.

But federalism means more than just not nationalizing our laws. It also means that states, because they can have different laws, can compete to provide better government.

The people who would like to have national seatbelt laws would also like to "harmonize" all laws (and especially tax laws) precisely to prevent people from escaping the imperatives of liberal statism by voting with their feet and going to live in a different jurisdiction. For years, people have chosen to live in New Hampshire instead of Vermont because Vermont has a huge income tax. A few years ago, businesses were racing out of California to Utah and Arizona because regulations governing businesses were less onerous there. They have shopped for, and found, better government.

New York State is currently in a panic because the auto insurance companies there may raise their rates 25 percent. One reason may be the architecture of the state's no-fault insurance law, which, by making claims easy to file, permits—and therefore encourages—fraud. In 1998, New Jersey passed legislation making it harder for crooks to file bogus insurance claims, and the thinking is that New Jersey's good legislation drove the crooks to New York. New York's law may have pandered, temporarily, to consumers (by making it easy to file claims) but seems now not to have benefitted them in the long run.

Because of federalism, however, drivers who can't afford insurance in New York can move to New Jersey, where the rates are lower. Mrs. Atwater also could move to New Jersey if she discovered that the seatbelt laws there were more reasonable and the police better behaved.

To most people, that might seem absurd. But Mrs. Atwater, who has been seriously bitten by Leviathan, may now, more than most of us, appreciate how federalism can protect her freedom.

Wednesday Morning
October 2001

Question 1. Interviews of structural engineers after the collapse of the two World Trade Center towers indicated both that steel loses its strength after reaching a temperature of about 1,500 degrees, and that that fact is well known to structural engineers. It would seem reasonable to us that a structural engineer would have known that the explosion of the jet fuel on the airplanes inside the towers would cause a fire in which the temperature would reach 1,500 degrees. Did any structural engineer warn the authorities in New York that the towers were likely to collapse after the fire had burned for a long enough time to produce sustained temperatures of 1,500 degrees? If not, why not? Had this information been acted on, none of the occupants of the first tower would have been sent upstairs instead of down, and the hundreds of rescue personnel who rushed into the buildings might not have lost their lives. That seems to us the most glaring after-the-fact failure of the day.

Question 2. Why was the second tower declared safe for occupancy after the first tower was hit, and after the authorities knew that a second plane had been hijacked? Is it asking too much of the authorities to say that they should have thought that there might be further danger (even of an unspecified nature) and to have continued the evacuation of the second tower?

Question 3. The transponders on the planes indicated that they took high-risk paths across other planes' flight paths, a maneuver which should have been apparent to air traffic controllers. Did they notice? If not, why not? If so, what, if anything, was done with that knowledge?

Question 4. Planes have buttons, we are told, that pilots can press indicating that a hijacking is in progress. The reports have indicated that those buttons were not pressed in three of the four hijacked planes. It is possible the public has not been told the whole story yet, but an obvious question is, why were the buttons not pressed? In the future, perhaps buttons should have to be pressed at regular intervals (every five minutes?) to indicate a hijacking is not in progress.

Question 5, for the future. Why not equip planes with devices that allow them to be flown remotely? In the event of a hijacking, or even a suspected hijacking, the on-board controls would be disabled, and control of the plane transferred to a remote source—to be determined—perhaps a plane sent up to escort and control it. Aren't planes mostly flown by computers already?

Question 6, for the future. Why are the doors to the cockpit so flimsy? What is the point of all the security if a large child could kick her way into the cockpit? Doors should be essentially impenetrable. If the crew is to be confined to the cockpit for the entire flight, the bathroom architecture will have to be altered.

Question 7 (a shocker). Why not allow some passengers to carry guns? The suggestion is sure to give the gun control crowd apoplexy. But already there are plans to have armed US marshals once again "ride shotgun" on all flights. That's a beginning, but the marshals will almost surely be easy for hijackers to spot, which will make them easier to neutralize. If hijackers knew it were possible that five or ten or twenty or even thirty passengers might also have guns, hijacking would become considerably more risky. The skeptic may ask, what about the passenger carrying a gun who has too much to drink? Yes, he's a risk, but if there's a sky marshal on board, he can deal with him. And there might well be ten others on board with guns who could deal with him as well. Besides, they could all be former law enforcement officials or government employees (i.e., people with established records) and the bullets could be non-fuselage piercing. A counter-terrorist force which is both distributed and covert (i.e., multiple anonymous passengers with guns) may be the best protection against hijackers.

Okay, we're not sure we like the gun idea either. The point is that Americans will have to think outside the box if they are to preserve their way of life. Yes, we could simply impose incredibly strict security measures, so onerous as to take the pleasure, and perhaps the usefulness, out of flying. But a free people should be allowed to do better, or at least to try to do better: to come up with imaginative solutions that address the problem while preserving their essential freedom. On Wednesday morning, it's time to play Wednesday morning quarterback, and ask the unaskable questions.

Who Lost the World Trade Center?
November 2001

As the nation pulls together to grieve, get back on its feet, and gear up for the coming struggle, pundits and politicians are saying we should not play the blame game. There are two reasons that is bad advice. One is that we need to take actions quickly—and some of those actions have been detailed in reports already written but ignored by people whose job it was not to ignore them. The other is that there are some people who are not up to the task of protecting the country—and some of them are still in the positions they have been occupying for a number of years. If we are to have new leadership, we must get rid of the old.

There are two sets of opinions about terrorism that are important to examine now. One, expressed until September 11, was that it couldn't happen here. Larry Johnson, a former State Department counterterrorism specialist, wrote in the *New York Times* in July, "Terrorism is not the biggest security challenge confronting the United States, and it should not be portrayed that way." The other set, expressed after September 11, is that there is nothing we could have done to protect ourselves. Michael Kinsley wrote that none of the recommendations in two reports on terrorism would have prevented the September 11 attack.

Not everyone was so wrong. Last year Senator John Kyl (R–AZ) said that after another World Trade Center bombing "everybody will be excited about getting something done, but the time to get excited is now."

Paul Bremer, the chairman of the National Commission on Terrorism, said last year, "We think there's a chance terrorists will try to stage a catastrophic event in the United State in the future. We're talking about something which will have tens of thousands of deaths."

Among the commission's recommendations was one to allow US intelligence and law enforcement officials to use the full scope of their authority to collect intelligence regarding terrorist plans and methods. The commission recommended that CIA guidelines restricting recruitment of unsavory sources, adopted in 1995 when the now-disgraced John Deutch (a recipient of one of Clinton's midnight pardons) was CIA director, should not apply when recruiting counterterrorism sources.

R. James Woolsey, a former CIA director and a member of the commission, agreed, saying the rule "deters people from recruiting the people they need. It's like telling the FBI they can recruit informants inside the Mafia, but they can't recruit any crooks." Robert Gates, another former CIA director, also agrees: "The problem isn't that headquarters will say no. It's the negative message it sends. People in the field will shrink from submitting anyone who might create a problem."

A former Clinton official disagrees. "I just don't see how serious, tough operatives are going to be deterred by a little paperwork," said Daniel Benjamin, who was a counter-terrorism official in the Clinton White House. But he misses the point. CIA personnel would worry, not about paperwork, but about losing their jobs (like the White House travel staff) if they hired people not thought "suitable" by their bosses.

Reports now, several weeks after September 11, indicate that the United States did indeed have considerable knowledge that an attack was imminent but not enough knowledge to pinpoint it. That suggests it is simply inaccurate to say that additional "human intelligence" could not have protected us.

The commission also recommended that the attorney general urge the FBI to exercise fully its authority for investigating suspected terrorist groups or individuals, including its authority for electronic surveillance. The commission's report indicated that, like the CIA, the FBI suffers from bureaucratic and cultural obstacles that hinder its obtaining information on terrorists.

Culture counts. That's one reason George Tenet, the current CIA director, should resign. (Michael Canavan, the Federal Aviation Administration's head of civil aviation security, was forced out, and he would seem to be less culpable than Tenet.) The CIA guidelines against recruiting unsavory sources are self-imposed. Tenet could have removed them at any time.

It may well be that no one action would have prevented the last attack or will prevent the next one. Cumulatively, however, prudent actions will make us more secure. But to adopt them, we have to look back and ask, Who lost the World Trade Center?

Ninth Circuit Obstinacy

December 2001

When Patricia and Robert Gentalas asked the city of Tucson, Arizona, for permission to hold an event with fellow Christians at a bandshell in Reid Park, their request was granted. But when they asked the city for a waiver (under the city's Civic Events Policy) of charges for various services—such as lighting and trash collection—worth

$340, the mayor rejected the Gentalases' request, stating, "We're not gonna get into prayer stuff." Funds were routinely granted to local non-profit organizations, but the city's policy was to refuse petitions when "an event is held to directly support any religious organization." The Gentalases held their event anyway and sued the city to make it change its policy—and their suit has now exposed the arrogance of the Ninth Circuit.

The suit was initially dismissed by the Federal District Court in Tucson, which found that the city's policy was supported by the Establishment Clause of the First Amendment to the Constitution.

On appeal, however, a three-judge panel of the Ninth Circuit overturned the district court's decision because, it said, Tucson had exercised impermissible "viewpoint" discrimination against the Gentalases. The court found that the Civic Events Policy was, itself, a public forum protected by the First Amendment, and cited the Supreme Court's decisions in *Rosenberger v. Visitors of University of Virginia* and *Lamb's Chapel v. Center Moriches Union Free School District*.

In *Rosenberger*, the Supreme Court overturned a decision by the Fourth Circuit Court of Appeals that had allowed the University of Virginia to discriminate against a student-run Christian magazine by withholding money from a fund (supported by mandatory fees) that subsidized printing costs for all other student magazines.

In deciding *Rosenberger*, the Supreme Court relied on its previous decision in *Lamb's Chapel*. In that case, the Court had overruled a decision of the Second Circuit Court of Appeals that had allowed a New York school board to deny after-hours school access to an evangelical group, Lamb's Chapel, that wanted to show a film about the media's undermining influences on "traditional, Christian family values," even though other community groups were routinely allowed such access.

Rosenberger and *Lamb's Chapel* made it clear that there was a constitutional principle of equal access to public facilities for religious groups.

But that didn't stop an eleven-judge panel of the Ninth Circuit from overturning the three-judge panel's decision in favor of the Gentalases. In an 8–3 decision, the Ninth Circuit validated Tucson's policy of denying funds to support the activities of religious organizations and dismissed the three-judge panel's definition of public funds as a forum, citing decisions that allowed discriminatory funding by the National Endowment for the Arts.

Now the Supreme Court has come to the rescue, sending the case back to the Ninth Circuit for reconsideration in light of the Supreme Court's decision last June in *Good News Club v. Milford Central School.*

In *Good News*, the Supreme Court overturned a decision by the Second Circuit that had allowed New York's Milford school district to deny the after-hours use of its facilities to the Christian Good News Club. Although Milford's policy gave access to any group teaching "moral and character development," such groups were forbidden to provide "religious instruction." According to Justice Scalia, Milford's policy had precluded the Good News Club from "independently discussing the religious premise on which its views are based—that God exists and his assistance is necessary to morality." The *Good News* decision was based on the earlier decisions in *Rosenberger* and *Lamb's Chapel.*

The Ninth Circuit's failure even to acknowledge *Lamb's Chapel*, a case that makes the Supreme Court's thinking on this issue reasonably clear, is troubling. The Ninth Circuit's obstinate refusal to follow the Supreme Court's set of precedents is even more troubling. However, there is now yet another case that says essentially the same thing as *Rosenberger* and *Lamb's Chapel*: government may not discriminate against religion when granting access to a public service. The Ninth Circuit had very little excuse for its disobedience last time, and has no excuse now.

Chef Zoellick and TPA

January 2002

Even veteran Washington sausage makers were feeling sick after President Bush managed to get the House of Representatives to vote in favor of Trade Promotion Authority (TPA). The last such authority, called "Fast Track," expired in the 1990s, and President Clinton was never able to get it reauthorized by Congress. TPA would give the president the authority to negotiate free-trade agreements with other countries and then bring them to Congress for a yes or no vote, with no tinkering allowed. Now President Bush has been successful in the House—but at what cost?

Four weeks earlier, a new round of global free-trade talks had been launched at a meeting in Doha, Qatar, but critics of that meeting—a different set of critics—were also asking, "At what cost?" The participants, ministers from more than 140 countries, agreed, remarkably, to discuss phasing out all farm subsidies, and the United States agreed, also remarkably, to put on the negotiating table its anti-dumping laws, which provide protectionist cover for an ailing, failing steel industry. In future trade negotiations the United States will be pressured to reduce its high tariffs on textiles and clothing.

The Doha meeting was billed as a triumph for US Trade Negotiator Robert Zoellick, who in addition to putting the US anti-dumping practices and reductions of textile tariffs on the agenda also agreed to permit greater access to generic versions of patent-protected drugs.

Washington's protectionists were not amused. After Doha, House Democratic leader Richard Gephardt (D–MO) said, "What they did in the meeting to me was negative in terms of getting agreement on trade promotion authority." Rep. Sander Levin (D–MI), a Democratic bigwig on trade, said Trade Promotion Authority was "even less tenable after Doha." Messrs. Gephardt and Levin voted no on TPA.

After September 11, Mr. Zoellick argued that TPA is important to the security of the United States as well as to its economy. He was accused of base-stealing, but a CIA-sponsored study on why states fail listed three primary causes, one of which was closure to world trade. That argument, and others, may have influenced the vote on TPA: the final count was 215–214.

But it wasn't arguments alone that carried the day. Whole herds of horses are rumored to have been traded—and then dumped into the sausage machine. In a letter to Rep. James DeMint, a Republican from the sovereign state of Textile (aka South Carolina), House Republican leaders promised to use "whatever means necessary" to cancel some of the export preferences Congress had granted Caribbean, Central American, and Andean nations. In the last few seconds before the vote DeMint changed sides, and TPA was saved. One White House official hinted that there were other costs too. (Don't even ask.)

Rep. Charles Rangel, ultra-Democrat of New York and a sponsor of the Caribbean Basin agreement (a proud achievement of the Clinton administration, designed to aid some of the world's poorest nations by letting them sell more of what they make, textiles and clothes, to the United States), said the letter to DeMint was "a betrayal of all the reasons we have trade"—but then proceeded to vote against TPA (so much for his commitment free trade). Mr. Zoellick said the concession to DeMint was "necessary to achieve a large good" and, chastising the Democrats, said that if a few more of them supported free trade it wouldn't be necessary to buy off recalcitrant Republicans.

Was the TPA victory really a disaster? Actually, no, for two reasons. First, the textile deals with the Caribbean and Andean countries are non-reciprocal, preferential agreements. Such agreements do not produce true free trade; in fact they are major departures from the basic GATT rules, and particularly the principle of non-discrimination. Second, according to the terms of the Agreement on Textiles and Clothing, the United States is going to have to phase out its textile quotas and move to tariffs anyway by January 2005. Tariffs make the cost of protectionism more apparent, and they are easier to remove. That's progress.

So in return for sacrificing only bilateral agreements and for giving the textile industry only a few more years to enjoy its protection, Mr. Zoellick has gotten (from the House of Representatives, at least) the authority to negotiate a new multilateral trade agreement— which is like giving up two pawns for a bishop. Or, to go back to the kitchen, what has come out of the sausage machine now looks more like chopped steak. And if the Senate goes along, it will look more like foie gras.

Beyond Enron and 9/11

March 2002

One consequence of the Enron debacle and the war on terrorism is that there's been little space for other news. Yet there are other political goings-on which require our attention, and more robust debate.

Any hope of getting an economic stimulus package died in Congress. Though President Bush pushed for a combination of tax and spending cuts, and the House of Representatives passed such a bill, Senate Majority Leader Tom Daschle (D–SD) killed the measure. As Senate Minority Leader Trent Lott (R–MS) put it, "The Daschle Democrats, in a cynical effort to score political points against this president, have chosen to fire a direct shot into a limping economy by killing" the bill.

The president called for an end to the partisan wrangling, saying, "We can't let politics dominate Washington DC." Maybe, but what's the point of winning an election if you don't get the voters to endorse your (partisan) philosophy? Though it was Sen. Daschle who ended any hopes for a stimulus package—and should be made to take the blame—the president's own package could have been more imaginative: big tax cuts, effective immediately. This could have sparked debate and prepared the ground for waging a congressional election campaign on a crucially important issue: the size of government, and how much it should take from a free people. What a debate!

When the president forwarded his 2003 budget to Congress, it received only a hostile reception from many. At issue were several of the president's proposed spending cuts, including a 28 percent reduction (agaahh!) in highway funding. Politicians from both sides of the aisle fainted dead away because the bill would have cut the federal highway budget by $9.2 billion. House Transportation Committee Chairman Don Young, a Republican from Alaska, called the provision "a drastic cut" (ooooh!) and proposed raising highway spending $4.4 billion.

Democrats harshly attacked Bush's plan to offer tax credits to some parents who enroll their children in private school. Though the president's proposal would offer a $2,500 refundable education tax credit only for parents whose children are in chronically failing public schools, Democrats objected. "Why did we spend all these months trying to improve public schools and then turn around and say, 'Here's some money, go off to private schools?'" asked Sen. Christopher J. Dodd (D–CT). House Education and Workforce Committee Chairman John A. Boehner (R–OH) contends that "low-income parents in disadvantaged communities with failing schools should have the same education choices that affluent parents have." There's a debate worth taking to the country.

Despite the partisan wrangling, Washington's politicians did manage to work together on a few issues—but politicians working together can be as dangerous as politicians not working together. The Senate approved a new cap on farm subsidies—$275,000 per farm—but it was largely cosmetic: it will save only .07 percent of the total cost of the bill. And even that may be bargained away when three Senators from the Northeast try to resurrect the nefarious dairy compact, which would raise the price of milk by as much as 26 cents a gallon. Even the Bush administration now supports farm subsidies. "This nation's got to eat," the president said. "It's in our national security interest that we be able to feed ourselves"—reason enough to keep the heavy hand of government out of the business.

Congress and the president also appeared close to a compromise on the administration's proposal for new charity legislation. "Government should not discriminate against faith-based programs," said Bush. Senators Joe Lieberman (D–CT) and Rick Santorum (R–PA) announced an agreement with the president that would provide funds for faith-based charities and tax incentives for charitable contributions. Although the proposal is farther away from the president's plan than the House version passed last year, Bush endorsed it, calling it a "great accomplishment." The bill would amend laws prohibiting federal money from reaching religious groups and would allow a $400-per-person charitable tax deduction for those who do not itemize on their returns. But the bill also includes increases in welfare spending and will cost $10–13 billion over the next two years. Nothing from Washington is perfect—but with Enron and 9/11 hogging the news these days, people aren't noticing.

Who's Who?
April 2002

One of the many consequences of the terrorist attack has been new interest in some form of national identity card for US residents. There is widespread belief that fake identification papers allowed at least some of the 9/11 terrorists entry into the country and may have assisted their planning and execution of the attacks. But the issue— sacrificing privacy—is hardly uncontroversial.

According to Larry Ellison, chairman of Oracle, an ID system, would likely involve cards embedded with digital fingerprints, retinal images, and perhaps photographs. These cards would allow security officials carrying portable fingerprinting kits or retinal scanners to perform on-the-spot identity checks. Additionally, it is likely that an ID system would require a sizeable central government database containing personal information on all legal US residents.

Most proponents of more efficient identity verification, such as Senator Richard Durbin (D–IL), deny the necessity of inventing an entirely new system. They favor, instead, modifying state driver's licenses. Durbin has already proposed legislation that would authorize a federal study of identification technology and develop new security standards for driver's licenses. "My bill is about making the driver's license, which some consider a de facto national ID card, more reliable and verifiable as a form of personal identification than it is today," Durbin told Congress last December.

If developed, the new driver's license system would probably be implemented in conjunction with the American Association of Motor Vehicle Administrators, which already works with all fifty state license bureaus on uniform license standards, and which, in January, petitioned Congress for $100 million to develop high-tech driver's licenses and a nationwide information database.

Some groups, such as the American Civil Liberties Union, oppose high-tech driver's licenses (as well as national ID cards), fearing they might facilitate violations of personal freedoms. In a letter to President Bush, the ACLU said a nationwide database would create "an unparalleled system of personal information sharing."

The ACLU found some unusual allies in Washington, including conservative House member Robert Barr (R–GA). "Let us not rush into a vast expansion of government power in a misguided attempt to protect freedom," Barr warned. "In doing so, we will inevitably erode the very freedoms we seek to protect."

Harvard University law professor Alan Dershowitz rejects these civil liberty objections. In an October 2001 *New York Times* article, Dershowitz said an identity card system would involve "a little less anonymity for a lot more security." He said ID cards would not violate constitutionally guaranteed privacy rights and "could actually enhance civil liberties by reducing the need for racial and ethnic stereotyping."

In addition to the philosophical issues, there is the question of the feasibility of such a system. Adam Thierer, a technology expert at the Cato Institute in Washington, says a national ID system "probably won't work." He claims that those operating the system "could be bribed or forcibly coerced into divulging information or producing fake ID cards. More realistically, hackers could invade centralized databases and distort or steal personal information."

Furthermore, several studies have found that large databases, such as the one proposed for a national ID system, are error prone. A 1999 Department of Justice study, which checked 93,000 Florida civil job applicants against the FBI's national criminal database, found that 5.5 percent of applicants with no criminal background were incorrectly assigned criminal records and 11.7 percent of those who had a criminal history escaped detection by submitting false information.

To date, no significant step towards a national identity card system has been taken. President Bush officially opposes such a system and Congress has limited its involvement to discussion. While much of the necessary technology may exist, practical and ideological questions surrounding the issue make swift adoption of a national ID system unlikely. Even—or especially—in this technological age, the land of the free is not yet ready for government always to know who's who.

Missing the Scandal
July 2002

The scandalette du mois is the discovery that the people who write the New York State Board of Regents examination required for graduation from high school have been "sanitizing" passages from literary works. Predictably there was a protest. Suddenly liberals were shocked, shocked to find censorship going on.

The changes were discovered by a Brooklyn woman, Jeanne Heifitz, who noticed the alterations in a passage familiar to her and suspected there were others. She went back over ten years of exams and found thirty quotes, nineteen of which had been significantly altered.

The figure seems startlingly high. After all, the bureaucracy itself had selected the passages for use. Which means the bureaucracy found it necessary to sanitize 63 percent of its own selections. Is 63 percent of American literature too gamy for high school seniors?

The nineteen passages reportedly had been stripped of virtually any reference to race, religion, ethnicity, sex, nudity, alcohol, even the mildest profanity and just about anything that might offend someone for some reason.

The work of Isaac Bashevis Singer, who wrote about Jewish life, was stripped of references to Judaism, and even the word "Polish" was deleted. Similarly, reference to race was excised from Annie Dillard's memoir, *An American Childhood*, though the passage was, precisely, meant to be about race and what she had learned as virtually the only white child visiting a library in a black neighborhood. A passage from a speech by United Nations Secretary General Kofi Annan praising California seafood and wine kept the reference to seafood but—hard to believe—deleted the reference to wine.

Some changes were political correctness taken to the point of silliness. "Fat" was changed to "large," "skinny" to "thin." A "hell" got changed to "heck." A "Gringo" woman became an "American" woman.

On the theory that predictable expressions of liberal indignation constitute news, reporters soon tracked down some of the authors to ask, "How do you feel about this?"

"I was just completely shocked," said novelist Frank Conroy, calling the changes "ludicrous" and grumping about political police.

"It is the practice of fools," said a Columbia professor who was not one of the authors misquoted.

Roseanne DeFabio, a New York state education official, tried to explain: "Even the most wonderful writers don't write literature for children to take on a test"—raising the question, why does the state test children on literature it claims is unsuitable?

More troublesome, if less remarked on, was that the test writers didn't notice that, because some of the questions were based on the authors' real (unaltered) views, they made no sense: students couldn't understand the questions after the alterations.

"This is political correctness run amok," said Arthur Eisenberg, legal director of the New York Civil Liberties Union, which seized the occasion to call a press conference and raise funds.

Mr. Eisenberg is right. But what we ought to ask is, Where did all this political correctness came from? That's easy. It was imposed by the political Left—invented by the student radicals of the 1960s and passed down to their own students since. Only conservatives fought it.

Look at the list of misquoted authors: Isaac Singer, Frank Conroy, Annie Dillard, Elie Weisel, Judy Blume, Anne Lamott, Albee, Chekhov, London, William Maxwell, Ernesto Galarza, John Holt, and, oddly, Kofi Annan.

Without being at all critical, we can observe that the list is not heavy with conservatives. Obviously these authors were chosen because they are acceptable to the liberal consensus and therefore considered safe to quote.

What have those of the authors still alive done about the threat to free speech posed by political correctness? Not much. In fact, some of them led the radical parade. For them to complain if their own handiwork now runs amok is hypocritical indeed.

The most troublesome part of this scandalette, however, is so obvious it tends to be unnoticed. The exam, and undoubtedly the curriculum, snubs the great American statesmen—historical figures, literary giants, legendary leaders, masters of prose.

Schooling in earlier generations would have used quotes, not from politically correct novelists, playwrights, and secretaries general, but from George Washington, Daniel Webster, Abraham Lincoln. No wonder children today have nearly no knowledge of American history or literature.

Beware of Treaties
August 2002

John Kreuttner, political cartoonist for *National Review* in its early days, delighted in drawing goofy liberal "talking heads" who spouted goofy liberal sayings. Then and now, liberal rhetoric could become so overwrought that it was hard to tell real specimens from Kreuttner's hilarious parodies. One memorable example: "When you question the loyalty of an electrician, you are attacking electricity!"

The same liberal illogic abounds to this day. Readers can no doubt call real-life examples to mind. ("If you question our demand to increase school lunch funding, you are starving millions of children.")

Just this week—honest, this is a real one, not a parody—the World Wildlife Fund announced that the world will end by the year 2050 unless we either "colonize two planets" or do everything the World Wildlife Fund tells us to do. (What it tells us to do, in case you can't stand the suspense, is to reduce our consumption to the level of Burundi, Africa—1/25th of present levels. Perhaps a better idea is for Burundi to increase its productivity and catch up with the world.)

Another instance of the effrontery of liberal rhetoric is "Women's Rights: Why Not?" by Nicholas Kristof in the *New York Times* (June 18). Mr. Kristof would like us to sign a "bizarre UN gender treaty" (as another writer described it) left over from the Jimmy Carter era.

Kristof began, "We now have a window into what President Bush and America's senators think of the world's women: Not much." Right. If you dare question the proposal, you hate women! If you doubt that its goal is worthy, or that its means are democratic, or that the United States should surrender sovereignty to a committee of UN busybodies with a leftist agenda, you hate women!

The treaty is "The Convention on Elimination of All Forms of Discrimination against Women," popularly called CEDAW. It dates back to the 1970s. So far, 169 countries have signed CEDAW, including such champions of women's rights as North Korea, Communist China, Saudi Arabia—which recently let 15 girls die in a fire rather than permit male rescue squads to get them out—and the recent, unlamented Taliban government of Afghanistan.

The United States is not a signatory. A cursory look at the treaty's provisions explains why we should keep it that way.

CEDAW, for instance, defines discrimination as "any distinction . . . on the basis of sex."

If we may put it so, there are two classes of people who are different from each other and do not wish to be lumped together: men and women. We wish to get together or not at our own speed, thank you, and not because UN police tell us to use the same restroom.

Another CEDAW provision orders signatories to "modify the social and cultural patterns of conduct of men and women, with a view to achieving the elimination of all . . . practices which are based on . . . stereotyped roles for men and women."

The United Nations was supposedly founded to promote peace. What business does it have ordering all the peoples of the world to change their customs and religious beliefs in order to conform to the views of a few totalitarian-minded bureaucrats? To push people around thus is to take away their rights while promising to do the opposite. After all, the Taliban "modif[ied] the social and cultural patterns" of Afghani women by beating and herding them with sticks. It is difficult to see how they were in violation of the language of CEDAW.

Let it be said: We are 100 percent for genuine women's rights—and men's rights, too. And so is President Bush. But it takes a whole different frame of mind—and framework of moral understanding and law—to achieve them. Why even give this silly UN initiative the time of day? Senate Democrats, ever searching for rotten legislation with which to embarrass President Bush, came across this 1970s clinker and brought it back. And that is why we meet Mr. Kristof pitching it in the *New York Times*.

The Democrats' thinking is: CEDAW says it is for women's rights so it must be a good thing. But CEDAW is a proven failure, it is obnoxious, and Mr. Bush and the Republicans must of course reject it, which in the mind of the goofy liberals will make them anti-women.

The truth is, this country has a marvelous record on the rights that matter: life, liberty, and property. Some of the signatories to CEDAW are among the worst rights offenders on Earth. In recent months women have been liberated from a brutal—and CEDAW-signatory—regime in Afghanistan. The treaty had nothing to do with setting them free. They were liberated by American bombs.

Smearing 101
October 2002

The Senate Judiciary Committee hearings on Priscilla Owen's nomination to be a judge on the Circuit Court of Appeals for the Fifth Circuit provided textbook examples of the fine Washington art of smearing. Justice Owen, currently serving as a justice on the Texas Supreme Court, was rejected by the Senate Judiciary Committee in a straight party-line vote, but only after the faculty of Smearing Studies had dissected her in class. Teaching that day were: Edward

Kennedy, Chappaquiddick Professor of Victimology; Diane Feinstein, Chairman of the Department of Smearing Studies; and Russell Feingold, a tenured member of the faculty.

Class opened with Prof. Kennedy making it plain that only the outcome of cases, not the law, mattered to him. "As I look at your cases," the professor began, "I see that you have a pattern of siding against the consumer or the victim of personal injury in favor of business and insurance companies." Undoubtedly, among the liberal professoriate, that passes for an indictment of a judicial candidate. But a person interested in a judicial nominee's qualifications would examine the holdings in individual cases rather than the cumulative score of who won and who lost.

Suppose, just suppose, that in the cases that came before Justice Owen the consumer-plaintiffs simply had no case? Should Justice Owen have engineered victories for them anyway? And of course it isn't even that simple. An appellate court's function is to review the decisions of lower courts. It might well be that a plaintiff with a terrific case, but a terrible lawyer, could lose in the lower court. But an appellate court's function is only to review the proceedings in the lower courts (trial, and perhaps appellate), not to try the case again from scratch. Only in Prof. Kennedy's world should judges ignore precedents and the law in order to manipulate the system for the benefit of "victims."

Justice Owen tried to explain the function of appellate courts to the professoriate in a discussion of her rulings in abortion cases.

Under certain circumstances a girl in Texas who wants an abortion can "bypass" the obligation to notify her parents. In order to get permission to bypass her parents, she must convince a trial court that she meets the law's qualifications. If she cannot convince the trial court, she gets another chance at the appellate level. If she fails again, she can appeal again to the court on which Justice Owen sits. The professors tried to blame Justice Owen for being the only person standing in the way of the few plaintiffs who were not successful in obtaining bypasses. The professors appeared incapable of understanding that before a case got to Justice Owen, the plaintiff seeking the bypass had lost in the trial court and lost again in a lower appellate court—and that Justice Owen's function was limited to reviewing lower court rulings.

Justice Owen was asked about a case involving health insurance coverage—and was blamed by Chairman Feinstein for depriving a family of benefits under their insurance policy. Feinstein was not pleased with Justice Owen's ruling. "[Y]our invalidation of the trial verdict completely threw out their entire reward. And, again—I mean, the law is there for little people," said the chairman of the Senate Judiciary Committee. It's not immediately clear that people who think there should be one law for little people and another for all the rest are qualified to judge the qualifications of judicial nominees.

In the case in question, the plaintiffs had not revealed to the insurance company that their children had suffered from jaundice all their lives and had a hereditary disease called HS. They sued to get extra benefits, which they would have been entitled to if, but only if, the insurance company had acted in bad faith in denying their initial claim. Justice Owen tried to explain that the only question before her was the bad-faith claim, and that given the circumstances—the family's not disclosing their children's medical conditions to the insurance company—the company was not unreasonable in denying their claim.

It transpired that the family for some reason (did they have a bad lawyer?) had never sued the insurance company for the policy benefits. But that was not Justice Owen's failure, nor was it hers to remedy.

Prof. Feingold asked Justice Owen why she had "lobbied" then Gov. George W. Bush for state funds for an evangelical prison ministry program. "Could you please explain," asked Prof. Feingold, "why you held this meeting in violation of the letter and the spirit of the Texas Code of Judicial Conduct?" It turned out that she had not lobbied for funds after all: the prison ministry was a wholly voluntary effort. But the smear had been accomplished, and, in due course, class was dismissed.

A Review of
Strictly Right: William F. Buckley Jr. and the American Conservative Movement
by Linda Bridges and John R. Coyne Jr.,
and
Cancel Your Own Goddam Subscription: Notes and Asides from National Review
by William F. Buckley Jr.

April 29, 2008

George Will called *National Review* the most consequential journal of opinion *ever*. It remade America by reinvigorating its spirit of enterprise and renewing its courage to resist and overcome Communism. Every fortnight, *NR* published good copy by good writers. It promoted Barry Goldwater and Ronald Reagan. But the key was Editor William F. Buckley Jr. who founded and nourished the conservative movement.

Bill Buckley died on February 27, 2008, at the age of eighty-two, at his desk, hard at work on tomorrow (in this case, another book—his fifty-sixth) yet more prepared for this day than anyone of his friends had ever known. His health was as dreadful as his spirits were cheerful—he had emphysema, diabetes, could barely walk, couldn't climb stairs, had fallen a few weeks before and broken his right wrist—but he worked on, almost compulsively. Why? "My father taught me that I owe it to my country. It's how I pay my debt," he said. For a book-length disquisition, see his *Gratitude: Reflections on What We Owe to Our Country* (1990).

Now his country owes *him* thanks, for the political movement he created that changed America and the world. By the late 1970s, the plain fact was that most practicing, effective conservatives were people who had been literally touched by Buckley—had received, so to speak, the "laying on of hands." They had met Buckley, either at their college (he spoke at more than five hundred colleges) or at his house in Stamford, Connecticut, or in New York at the offices of *National Review* or at his apartment, or at any number of appearances he made around the country during his public career. Buckley was everywhere. And so, increasingly, were his followers.

Buckley probably never intended to create a conservative movement. But he seems to have had a sense that organization was necessary—that organizations were necessary. And his planting hand can be seen in a number of them—the Intercollegiate Society of Individualists (now the Intercollegiate Studies Institute), the Philadelphia Society, Young Americans for Freedom, and the Fund for American Studies. But the most important organization, of course, was the magazine. *National Review* was not just a beacon. It was also the rallying point for conservatives: the conservatives' internet in the pre-internet age. In its pages writers could not only talk to laymen; they could also argue among themselves, honing the positions that, in time, would guide America into the *National Review* Age.

Buckley, as is now widely acknowledged, was the remarkable man behind it all—indeed, he was probably the most remarkable political man, certainly the most important intellectual political man, of the second half of the twentieth century. He was clearly one of the greatest of what is now sometimes called the greatest generation. *Strictly Right* and *Cancel Your Own Goddam Subscription* make that plain. *Strictly Right* is the storyline, *Cancel* provides us with some of the dialogue. Many of the now, er, mature movement conservatives know the Buckley story. But for many others, early (even middle) Buckley is ancient history. After all, *National Review*'s crowning success—the election of Ronald Reagan—took place twenty-eight years ago. Many may be familiar with some of Buckley's work, but they will not know the whole story of the precocious lad from—well, from a variety of places, a sufficient variety that his first language was Spanish, followed by . . . French.

Linda Bridges, *National Review*'s institutional memory (and former managing editor), and John Coyne, a former *NR* associate editor and writer, are fitting chroniclers. They were present, if not at the creation, then at least from about Deuteronomy on, so they have firsthand knowledge of the story they tell in *Strictly Right*, the story of a remarkable man and his time. Bridges and Coyne have given us a book that is both story and reference. They take us from WFB's life before *National Review*, through forging the conservative movement, Goldwater for President, the raging '60s, and on to, alas, all too close to the end: passing the torch. From their special vantage, they have written the biography of this great man, which is, therefore, part of the history of our time.

But the spirit of the man can be seen in the letters to and from him published in *NR*'s Notes & Asides, collected here in *Cancel Your Own Goddam Subscription*. The title is from Buckley's reply to an irate *NR* subscriber who wrote in saying, "Three cheers to Dr. Ross Terrill. He slashed you to bits as you have been doing to yourself for the past year. Cancel my subscription." Buckley's reply is vintage Buckley. And the book displays Buckley's vintage friendship, and shows how seriously he took friendship. In the first chapter of *Cancel*, he recalls getting a letter "claiming to come from a high-school student, so stunningly precocious I thought it phony." He published the letter and got to know young Edward Vazquez, who then wrote a bit for *NR*. When Vazquez went off to get a job, Buckley wrote a "To Whom It May Concern" letter of recommendation for him. "I know that he was accepted, and am sorry not to have had word from him since then, thirty-five years ago." For Vazquez's sake, I hope all these years he's been in an order requiring monastic silence. There is an exchange with Eric Sevareid who says, "My friendship is not easily given," to which Buckley replied, "My friendship, by contrast, is easily given, but does not preclude concurrent disagreement."

★ ★ ★

There was in Washington a number of years ago a prominent politician about whom it was said that even his friends didn't like him. In Buckley's case, even his (political) enemies did like him—John Kenneth Galbraith, Mike Wallace, and many more—though some may have been slower to come round than others. And with his friendly charm, Buckley captivated the legions of college students who became the conservative movement. Charm was needed, because his arguments were hugely politically incorrect, long before "PC" had been invented.

Though PC was not around in the '50s and '60s, vitriol flowed freely. Some of the letters in *Cancel* are stunningly vitriolic, a point worth pondering in this political season. In the last few months, the pundits have been wilting at charges hurled by the candidates at each other during the Democratic primaries. They have been shocked to hear former president Bill Clinton say nasty things about the young senator from Illinois. The impeached ex-president said that one of Senator Obama's claims was a "fairy tale." Ooo! Such ugliness the current American press has never heard. They should read *Cancel*.

From A. Ruesthe (1967): "You are the mouthpiece of that evil rabble that depends on fraud, perjury, dirty tricks. . . . I would trust a snake before I would trust you or anybody you support." From Richard Sharvy (1968): "You ridiculous ass. . . . [N]obody who matters pays any attention to clowns like you." From Carl E. Jampel (1970): "You are a hateful un-Christian demagogue and a fit associate for loudmouth Rusher. . . . I don't know whether the Lord should damn or save your little frightened cringing soul." And from John R. Owen (1972): "The convincer in my decision to quit buying *NR* was the disgusting appearance of Editor Bill Buckley on TV with his seedy-looking Schickelgruber-Beatnik hairdo and sloppy-collared shirts, along with a retinue of whiney-snively-militant-Sodomite-looking punks."

All that just fueled Buckley's fire. I doubt it bothered him a bit. Besides, he had an agenda: stopping centralism, collectivism, secularism, and Communism. That agenda required nurturing, man-aging, and protecting the right wing, and that meant separating, when necessary, the irresponsible ideologues from the conservative mainstream. Buckley's reading the John Birch Society out of the conservative movement (its leader said President Eisenhower was a Communist) was a major service to the conservative community.

Buckley also protected the anti-Communist Right by waging war with Linus Pauling. In 1963, Pauling, a Nobel Prize winner (later fa-mous for pushing Vitamin C as a cold cure) whom James Burnham had called a fellow traveler (because he was one) sued *National Review* for libel. Pauling had been making a living by filing libel suits against people who called him that, the defendants tending to settle because that was cheaper than defending. Not Buckley, who spent vast sums to defeat Pauling in court, putting him out of business and making it safe for conservatives to call fellow travelers "fellow travelers."

More skill, if less money, was required settling disputes among the in-house crowd. The question of whether to endorse Nixon in 1960 divided the senior editors of *National Review* about five to one—the one being not Buckley but James Burnham who favored, as always, what Buckley would later call the "rightwardmost viable candidate." Buckley crafted the magazine's editorial policy himself, neither endorsing nor rejecting Nixon, but saying either position was one a conservative could take—a high wire act that held the factions together. Nixon was always problematical for the Right, but Buckley thought he was incredibly bright. In 1967, Nixon told Buckley that he had learned two things from his race for governor in California in 1962 and from Goldwater's campaign for the presidency: that you can't win an important race with only the Right, and you can't win without it.

In 1973 Buckley again managed, even if he did not soothe, warring factions when he defended George Will ("a callow young columnist without a lick of sense," as Will later described himself—inaccurately) against the pro-Agnew crowd at *NR* and in Washington. Will had written a column for the magazine, "The Snicker Factor," which was not a flattering picture of the vice president. (Will had used the same analogy Buckley had used five years earlier: that Agnew was Nixon's insurance policy.) Some conservatives wanted Buckley to fire Will. Wisely, both at the time and, of course, in retrospect, Buckley refused to fire a fellow iconoclast, and one whose writing possessed, or was developing, Buckley's own grace and style.

* * *

It is easy to forget, given his many other facets, that Buckley was also a master journalist. He could sit down and write exquisite copy hour after hour, day or night, in his office or on the fly, before breakfast or after a long evening of entertaining guests; and fortnight after fortnight he produced a journal—determining the content, assigning articles, editing copy, managing the Letters section—that was the bible of the conservative movement. He saw his calling as popularizing the thinking that had been done, not doing the abstract thinking himself. The movement—and America, and the world—is lucky he didn't have a vanity that required a doctrine bearing his name.

In *Cancel* one finds no dreary doctrines but wit enough for a lifetime; and not just pretty little baubles in the air but wonderful instruction. Buckley was a born teacher (he once described his favorite occupation as correcting other people's errors), in a world where the reigning zeitgeist—central planning in its many guises—was one huge error. In a letter declining an invitation to appear on the television program *Laugh-In* he wrote, "I would rather be a comedian than a teacher, but it was not meant to be, and by dressing in the robes of the former, I diminish my usefulness as the latter." In the end, he relented, swayed, perhaps, by the size of the audience and the teaching opportunity. Years later, he volunteered to teach writing for two semesters at his alma mater, Yale.

His ongoing battles with the *New York Times*, perhaps *NR*'s Public Enemy Number One, reveal his polemical enthusiasm—though *Strictly Right* quotes the magazine's longtime publisher William A. Rusher's remark, that no one at *NR* ever believed anything until it was reported in the *New York Times*.

His lessons on the proper use of English are far more entertaining than Fowler's. To the correspondent who wrote, "Don't start a sentence with 'and' . . . I am beginning to wonder just how good (or bad) your high school was," Buckley replied, "Verses 2-26 and 28-31, Chapter I, Genesis, all begin with 'And.' The King James scholars went to pretty good high schools." And then to a subsequent correspondent, "But my point wasn't that the King James scholars correctly translated from the original, rather that they were the most influential writers in English history. The general rule is not to begin a sentence with "and"; the particular rule is that writers with a good ear know when to break the general rule." Or as Buckley used to say around the offices of *National Review*, "Let your ear be your guide." Uh-huh. Bet that's what Bach said, too.

Buckley wrote a memo to the *NR* editors and staff, complaining about an "epidemic of exclamationitis." "In the current issue, Mrs. Nena Ossa concludes her interesting essay on Chile, 'That would be the moment to pack and leave!' 'That would be the moment to pack and leave.' is, I submit, a much tenser way of suggesting that that would be the moment to pack and leave." There is a lengthy exchange with Hugh Kenner on the lead sentence in a piece Buckley wrote for *Esquire*. Buckley introduced the exchange with, "What follows is primarily of interest to syntacticians. How many of them are there? Not many. But—ah!—how many voyeurs?" Buckley describes his sentence as "springy and tight." Kenner replied, "Those aren't springs, they're bits of scotch tape. Have your syntactic DNA checked for mutations." It goes on and on. Not to be missed.

Though Buckley was not always right, he was always gracious. Eva Moseley corrected him on his insertion of a comma into "Wherefore art thou, Romeo?" What Juliet says, writes Moseley, is "'. . . wherefore art thou Romeo?' She isn't asking why he exists (nor, as some seem to think, is 'wherefore' a fancy Elizabethan word for 'where') but, in modern parlance, 'What did you have to go and be Romeo for?' It's names—especially Montague and Capulet, of course—that are the issue." Buckley replied: "Dear Mrs. Moseley: Quite right, and nicely corrected."

Running through the whole volume is a series of exchanges with Art Buchwald on which of them was being treated better by the Hertz rental car "frequent user" program. It's a great gag. And then there is the most impish reply, to the man who closed his letter saying that conservatives were still "attempting to force a square peg into a round hole." "The trick," replied Buckley after dealing with the other issues, "is to make the hole a little larger in diameter—and plop!, in goes the square peg." Exit cliché, pursued by a guffaw, dispatched by a grinning Buckley, irrepressibly young at heart.

Which is not surprising. In a *Vanity Fair* questionnaire, Buckley's answer to "When and where were you happiest?" was "Age five to seven." A couple of years later, Kalman Gabriel wrote, "Dear Mr. Buckley: I am a twelve-year-old boy from Oyster Bay, New York. If you could give me advice for life, what would it be?" "Dear Kalman: Don't grow up. Cordially, WFB."

* * *

Alas, it all came to an end. Buckley wrote on December 31, 2005, "I regretfully conclude that 'Notes & Asides' can't continue as a regular feature of *National Review*. The reason is: We aren't getting enough letters that qualify as 'N&A' material—inquisitive, zany, confused, annoyed, piquant." Maybe they all grew up. Maybe it was the end of the conservative movement. There is much grousing these days about its loss of direction. Without communism and, some say, without pre-Reagan levels of taxation to outrage and galvanize the

Right, it wanders, confused, in search of its mission, or a mission. Or a leader.

One view is that the conservative movement is over—that it ended in triumph when Ronald Reagan moved into the White House. Certainly the movement started out as a band of outsiders, who wanted primarily to influence the insiders who held the levers of power. When Reagan got elected, the conservatives took hold of those levers, which may not have been the original plan because, at least in the beginning, it seemed improbable. On the other hand, perhaps it was inevitable. Once inside the corridors of government, the conservatives became, if not corrupted by power, at least befriended by it, and whatever else happened, the conservative movement came to an end. A triumphant end, perhaps, but an end nevertheless. Now the conservatives, with their disparate interests, wander, not yet having found a new banner to march under. Hence the grousing. That's not Buckley's fault. He led them to the promised land. What they do after feasting on milk and honey is their responsibility. That view seems consistent with Buckley's comment about his life a few days before he turned eighty: "There's nothing I hoped for that wasn't reasonably achieved."

An alternative view is that only the creative stage of conservatism is over, but the movement goes on—which calls to mind A. P. Herbert's crack in *Uncommon Law*: "The movement of the law is clear, but it's not clear in which direction the law is moving." The conservative movement may not be over, but it's not clear to where it's moving.

Buckley was its prime mover: he helped create it—and he helped create the modern world as well. Communism is gone. And so, in many countries, are the high tax rates and other policies that are inimical to enterprise. In the nine freest and highest-income countries, the tax rate has dropped more than 30 percent since 1980—so pervasive has been the spread of free-market ideas, spread at least in part because of the Reagan Revolution, which was Bill Buckley's and *National Review*'s grand achievement.

People say it's not as much fun to be a conservative these days. That's partly because—whatever the election returns show—there just isn't as much *opposition* as there was when the movement was just setting out, when some of that opposition came from the Republican Party!

Now *every* Republican candidate wants to be considered a conservative. That's progress, though it may sully the brand, and confuse consumers.

It may not be as much fun, but there's still work to be done. Of the nine freest and highest-income countries, the United States has the highest corporate tax rate. And several countries in Eastern Europe have beaten us to a flat tax—countries whose new freedom, and more sensible tax regimes, were midwifed by the conservative movement. Most important—in this year when the first baby-boomer started collecting Social Security—is the need to teach the welfare society to nurture free-market entrepreneurship. Absent happy and productive entrepreneurs, America will be unable to pay the welfare society's bills, which are starting to come due with a vengeance. Solving that problem will be like . . . putting a square peg into a round hole.

Now that Bill is gone, who will teach us to make the hole a little larger?

Conservatism and Civil Rights: A Response to William Voegeli

October 9, 2008

As I read William Voegeli's piece on William F. Buckley Jr. and the civil rights movement, I thought, "Come on, Voegeli, make up your mind. Was Buckley right or wrong?" I concluded that Voegeli's answer would be, "Yes." Then I decided that, given the record, Buckley and the conservatives probably got a more balanced treatment from Voegeli than they would, and perhaps will, get from a lot of people.

No responsible person can regret the progress made by blacks since the civil rights acts. But even suggesting that there might have been a better—or perhaps just a different—way risks obloquy. Nevertheless, I think it useful to examine what I take to be Buckley's real position, because it reminds us of the limits of government, and remembering the limits of government is always useful.

In his essay, Voegeli quotes Buckley as saying in 2001 that he would vote for the civil rights acts if they were "out there today," and saying in 2004 that "federal intervention was necessary." But Voegeli overlooks the fact that only a few years earlier, in 1998, Buckley held that "the civil rights programs were a formulaic response to a real need and not by any means one that has proved as successful as an alternative means might have been." I think that statement is a better reflection of the position Buckley held through the years. Not much happened or was discovered between 1998 and 2001 that would have required a change in his opinion except, perhaps, just a little mellowing. He certainly mellowed in his opposition to state prohibition of tobacco: only last November, a few months before his death, he wrote that he would, if he had the authority, forbid smoking in America, notwithstanding that he would be violating his secular commitment to the free marketplace. He was dying of emphysema at the time.

Is it possible there was another way? We'll never know, of course, and Voegeli admits as much: "There is no way of knowing whether that train [Buckley's "organic" progress], running on those tracks, would have ever come into the station."

But what we do know is what the prodigious growth in government has produced. It is not too early to tell how blacks have fared since the onslaught of the Great Society programs, animated by the same government philosophy that produced the civil rights laws. The statistics on black illegitimacy and crime paint a grim picture. In 1960, the illegitimacy rate among blacks was 22 percent. Today, it's about 70 percent.

Voegeli quotes Jonah Goldberg, offering, in 2002, a "blunt" judgment on conservatives during the civil rights era: "Conservatives . . . were often at best MIA on the issue of civil rights in the 1960s. Liberals were on the right side of history on the issue of race."

Maybe so. But look at what Goldberg has to say today (in his book *Liberal Fascism*) about the Great Society programs:

The Great Society's racial meddling . . . yielded one setback after another. . . . In the decade after the Great Society . . . [b]lack-on-black crime soared in particular. . . . Economically, as Thomas Sowell has catalogued, the biggest drop in black poverty took place during the two decades *before* the Great Society. In the 1970s, when the impact of Great Society programs was fully realized, the trend of black economic improvement stopped almost entirely.

So: blacks seem to be doing badly and are angry. And whites are angry too, at least those who were victims of affirmative action or had to endure busing. Perhaps we should take another look at what "alternative means" there might have been. Is it conceivable that the "legitimate, organic progress" Buckley hoped for in 1960 could have produced a better result than the federal laws we got, "artificially deduced from the Commerce Clause or from the 14th Amendment"?

Even if the pathologies in the black community *are* the results of racism, isn't that a stronger argument for the position that you cannot change—because in forty years we have not changed—society by fiat, even constitutional fiat, but only by an organic process? There may be a finite amount of social adjustment government can get out of the people by running them through the federal wringer, their resistance in this case having been heightened by the manifest willingness of the liberals themselves to institutionalize racial discrimination.

In an address to the Conservative Party of New York in 1964, Buckley said the United States was "still reluctant to accept the state as a sacramental agent for transubstantiating private interest into public good. Have you reflected on the course of postwar American history?" he asked. "[W]ith all its power, the Establishment has failed in its efforts to ease over to the federal government the primary responsibility for education, or health, or even housing."

There's been a lot of easing over since 1964. George W. Bush's No Child Left Behind Act has inserted the federal government into education as never before. And we are now so close—oh, so close—to federalized health care you can smell the formaldehyde. In addition, of course, we've had a hailstorm of federal subsidies and programs—various community redevelopment programs; Urban Renewal (nicknamed by no less than James Baldwin "Negro Removal"); Aid to Families with Dependent Children; food stamps; the Special Supplemental Nutrition Program for Women, Infants, and Children; and on and on and on. That is the price we have *all* paid for altering the constitutional architecture Buckley sought to preserve—which should make us appreciate, at least somewhat, his hope in 1961 that "when Negroes have finally realized their long dream of attaining to the status of the white man, the white man will still be free."

If slavery was worse than Jim Crow (which it was) but Abraham Lincoln could countenance slavery to preserve the Union and still be regarded as our country's second-greatest president (or by some as our greatest president), why can't the early Buckley and his conservative colleagues, who were willing to countenance Jim Crow a little longer for the sake of not destroying the constitutional architecture, be regarded, not just as principled, as Voegeli regards them, but even just a bit . . . Lincolnesque?

Buckley's initial opposition to the civil rights acts made the liberals unhappy. His 2001 and 2004 positions supporting the acts made many conservatives unhappy. Perhaps a 2009 Buckley position might have made them both happy:

> I should have favored the civil rights acts given the real needs of 1964 and notwithstanding my contemporaneous misgivings concerning the possible damage to the constitutional arrangements. But in the light of what transpired I think rejecting constitutional decorum in the hope of progress not built on the good nature of the community would have been, unwisely, utopian.

That's the fusionist position.

Saving Senator Burris

February 27, 2009

Fellow Fairness Fanatics, you are invited to a Kaffee Klatsch ($1,000 per sustainably farmed, responsibly purchased organic cup) to show support for Senator Roland Burris, the Democrat who was appointed by Illinois Governor Rod Blagojevich to fill the seat vacated by Barack Obama.

The appointment of Senator Burris (the only black in the US Senate) was unquestionably legal even though, shortly after he made the appointment, Governor Blagojevich was impeached, because of, he says, his enemies' misinterpretation of the First Amendment.

The problem Senator Burris's detractors claim to have with the good senator is that he apparently gets confused when answering questions and filling out affidavits. He was asked whether he had been involved in fundraising for Gov. Blagojevich and he said, more or less, "no." And his friends may have to concede that he should have said, more or less, "yes," or at least a bit more of the "yes" and a bit less of the "no" than he actually did say.

But, hey, that's awfully technical. Like not paying the taxes you owe when you work for the International Monetary Fund. Or failing to report all that rental income you got from a luxury beachfront villa in the Caribbean. Or like getting a sweetheart loan from Countrywide Financial because you were a friend of the CEO, Angelo Mozilo, while you're serving on a congressional banking committee.

Clearly Senator Burris will fit in quite well with his new colleagues. So what's the problem? A quick look at his résumé tells us much.

The senator went to Southern Illinois University at Carbondale (where he was known as Trail Blazer, or just "TB") and he has a law degree from Howard University, which is only a little more than a "v" away from Harvard, where President Obama went.

The senator began his career as a bank examiner for the US Treasury Department (Barack Obama never did that) and has served as vice president of Continental Illinois National Bank (Wow!

Barack Obama never did that ["BONDT"]) and as president of the National Association of Comptrollers (BONDT) and of the National Association of State Auditors, Comptrollers, and Treasurers. Wow again. BONDT.

Impressive? Yes. But there's more. The senator was also a trustee of the Financial Accounting Foundation Board (BONDT) and served for three years on the Executive Board of the Government Finance Office Association of the United States and Canada. Double BONDT!

Let's face it: this guy knows something about banking and perhaps a lot more than most of his new "colleagues" who are up to their keisters writing bailout bills.

Senator Burris was also the first African American National Bank Examiner for the Office of the Comptroller of the Currency for the US Treasury Department. Wow! And his 1978 election to the first of three terms as Illinois state comptroller made him the first African American ever elected to an Illinois state office. The senator has also been recognized annually for sixteen years (!) by *Ebony Magazine* as one of the hundred most influential Black Americans. Wow again! Seriously wow!

As busy as he's been, however, the senator has nevertheless found time to give back to his community. Burris has served on non-profit organizations, including the National Center for Responsible Gaming (my god, he's a gambler! That means he might be better at rolling dice than Rep. Barney Frank), and he served on the board of the Auditorium Theatre of Chicago (my god, he's an actor! Like . . . like that guy who beat Jimmy Carter).

It is perfectly apparent that TB Burris is a very distinguished man, which is why he's listed in *Who's Who in America*, *Who's Who in Government*, *Who's Who in Law*, and *Who's Who in Who's Who*.

Let's face it: TB Burris has the talent. Let's face something else: TB's résumé is more impressive than President Obama's. No, seriously! TB hasn't just talked the talk, or walked the walk. He's hoped the hope, and changed the change.

Some people just can't stand competition, so now "they" want to get rid of TB, like a bad disease. This is a tough town.

The question Washington is asking today is, TB or no TB?

Help frame the answer. Come to our "Kaffe and Kash for TB" before his enemies cashier him out.

TB FOREVER.

Well, until the next election anyway.

Fighting Obesity is Best Left to the Individual
August 17, 2009

A report from the Centers for Disease Control and Prevention states that 65 percent of US adults are overweight and 30 percent are obese. The proportion of those who are obese has doubled in the last decade.

Last week the CDC held a conference in Washington, "Weight of the Nation," (I didn't make that up) to "provide a forum to highlight progress in the prevention and control of obesity through policy and environmental strategies." Thomas Frieden, the CDC's new director, reported, "Obesity and with it diabetes are the only major health problems that are getting worse in this country, and they're getting worse rapidly."

That's the progress he's highlighting?

Here's the frightening part. Frieden also said, "Reversing obesity is not going to be done successfully with individual effort." What does that portend?

The CDC says on its website: "American society has become 'obesogenic,' characterized by environments that promote increased food intake, non-healthful foods, and physical inactivity."

The message is: We are not responsible for our behavior. Advertisers are. That was, more or less, the thesis of John Kenneth Galbraith's "The New Industrial State," published almost a decade after the Ford Motor Co.'s unpopular Edsel model had refuted it. Two decades later, New Coke proved Galbraith wrong again.

According to the CDC, "The Division of Nutrition, Physical Activity, and Obesity (DNPAO) is working to reduce obesity and obesity-related conditions through state programs, technical assistance and training, leadership, surveillance and research, intervention development and evaluation, translation of practice-based evidence and research findings, and partnership development." Whew!

But as the CDC has already told us, DNPAO has not been successful. What appears obvious is that obesity cannot be controlled through "policy and environmental strategies" designed by government.

There is, however, one strategy that might work: Having people pay, out of their own pockets, for their health care and their health insurance and, presumably, paying more for it if they are overweight.

Eating is fun. Eating too much is more fun. Paying higher medical bills or insurance premiums for being overweight is not fun.

President Barack Obama's plan for socializing medicine will produce more of the "progress" the CDC and Frieden speak about. By socializing the cost of bad behavior, Obama's plan will increase it. As will having obesity recognized as a disability under the Americans with Disabilities Act.

We need a free-market health care plan, which would not only be less expensive and fairer but would also encourage the healthier behavior that has eluded the CDC's "policy and environmental strategies." Making people pay for their own behavior might also reduce the incidence of AIDS, vehicular accidents, and lung cancer.

Those are largely voluntary diseases and account for a huge proportion of America's health budget. The medical cost of obesity alone is about 9 percent of all US medical costs.

We Americans think of ourselves as being self-governing. But what does "self-governing" mean if we can't even stop stuffing ourselves?

And incidentally, or really not incidentally, why should government (or perhaps just "we the thin people") care if some people want to eat themselves into an early grave? We care, now, because we're footing the bill.

In the socialist paradise—some may call it Obamaland—no one is responsible for anything. But everyone pays for everything.

Once, a long time ago, on another continent, among a different people and for many decades, socialism was also tried on a grand scale. It produced poverty and scarcity. But not much obesity.

Richard Cohen's Wild Moose Chase

August 21, 2009

Liberals are getting worried now. *Washington Post* columnist Richard Cohen has played the McCarthy card against Sarah Palin.

Gov. Palin, expert moose hunter, is of course more than capable of looking after herself. But what does playing the McCarthy card say about the liberals?

There are three points to remember about McCarthy. But first: no one should discuss McCarthy who hasn't read M. Stanton Evans's seminal book *Blacklisted by History: The Untold Story of Senator Joe McCarthy and His Fight Against America's Enemies.* (See the *Weekly Standard's* review by the late Robert Novak.)

The truth—almost universally unacknowledged by liberals—is that McCarthy was right when he said there were communists in the US government. Liberals were quick to deny McCarthy's claim, but Evans shows why it should hardly have been surprising. The United States had just concluded a war in which the communists were our allies. Why was it so surprising, then, that the United States had not made an effort to ensure that there were no communists in the government?

Evans's second point is that the danger was not just from communist spies sending information to the Soviet Union, but from agents who were getting orders from the communists and attempting to influence US policy makers.

Of course, there were spies too. One of them, Alger Hiss, was a liberal darling about whose guilt there is now, finally, no doubt. But in January 1950, when Hiss was found guilty on two counts of perjury, liberals went into catatonic denial and marshaled every broom in the closet in preparation for the long witch hunt against anti-communists. Only a month later, Sen. McCarthy made his famous speech in Wheeling, West Virginia. The liberals have never forgiven him, even as they never forgave Richard Nixon for his role in nailing Alger Hiss.

The establishment liberals also went after McCarthy because he put his pants under the mattress to press them at night—remember the hard crease of the '50s?—McCarthy was so gauche. Hiss was so cooool.

Richard Cohen seems to have found a '50s broom in his closet. He describes McCarthy as "the Wisconsin liar, demagogue, and drunk." Now there is as little doubt that McCarthy came from Wisconsin as there is that JFK came from Massachusetts, so the barb must lie elsewhere. Politicians routinely lie, a failing Cohen may—must?—have run into at least, oh, three or four times during his long tenure in Washington.

And if McCarthy were the only demagogue Cohen has come across in his professional career he has led a sheltered life indeed.

No, it must be the drink. McCarthy drank. That must be the crux of it.

Still, we should ask Cohen whether he has routinely objected to other politicians' personal failings: JFK's, for example (whoring), Lyndon Johnson's (being a crook), or Senator Pat Moynihan's (the flatteringly sanitized version of which is that he was a "hard-drinking Irishman").

Ah, but that is to analyze a smear, the whole point of which is precisely to vilify in a way objective facts do not support.

And surely that is true in the campaign against Gov. Palin for her "death panel" comment about President Obama's health care plan. Gov. Palin objected that bureaucrats would be empowered to decide, for example, whether, based on her Down syndrome son's level of productivity in society, he was worthy of health care.

"Say what you will about any of the healthcare proposals," Cohen wrote, "not one of them suggests a 'death panel' empowered to withhold medical services from the aged or those with disabilities. To suggest that one exists is reprehensible. To state it outright is either boldly demagogic or just plain loopy."

What must Cohen think of the Senate Finance Committee which didn't just suggest a death panel existed or even state it outright, but actually *took action*? Alas, poor Cohen. Even before he'd had a chance to fetch his broom, the offending provision on consultations for end-of-life care had been dropped by the Senate Finance Committee from its proposed health care bill.

Who's loopy now?

Exit Cohen, broom in hand, pursued by a moose hunter.

What's Your Metric?

September 2, 2009

How do you watch freedom? How do you watch it grow? How do
you watch it shrink? What's the metric? What's *your* metric? What
do you think the metrics of your fellow citizens are? If you have no
idea what *their* metric is, how do you talk to them about freedom
with any sense of urgency?

Milton Friedman's metric was the percentage of GDP spent by
government.

Friedman said we could not be truly free in a country where
the government at all levels takes and spends 30 percent of GDP. In
Obamaland in 2009 government at all levels will spend 40 percent of
GDP (almost the level of World War II). That will go up, way up, if
the programs Obama is pushing get enacted. Perhaps to 50 percent.

But is that a valid metric, at least for most people? It's true that
government takes more of our wealth than it used to, but it's also
true that we can buy a lot more than we used to with what's left
over. As Bill Buckley used to note, you can buy all of Beethoven for
$10. How much more do you need? How do you measure wealth
anyway? To what extent is wealth a surrogate metric for freedom?

Another way to measure freedom, or lack of freedom, is by
counting the pages in (or weighing?) the Federal Register or the
Code of Federal Regulations, where the regulations that govern
virtually everything we do every day are listed. It's an imperfect measure because a one-page rule can be as burdensome as a 500-page
rule. Whatever the number, it will go up, and probably dramatically,
under President Obama.

A better measure is the cost of regulations. Federal regulations
impose a burden of more than a trillion dollars on the economy, almost as much as total federal income tax receipts. And of course,
states regulate too. How free can you be when there are a trillion
dollars worth of instructions telling you what to do each day? Slow
down. Stop smoking. Don't eat fat. Get off the couch. Put down
that soft drink.

Freedom House defines freedom as "the opportunity to act

spontaneously in a variety of fields outside the control of the government and other centers of potential domination." Quick: name a field that is outside the control of government?

How do Franklin Roosevelt's four freedoms (freedom of speech, freedom of religion, freedom from want, and freedom from fear) fare on Freedom House's measure? Not well.

Congress and the Supreme Court have substantially curtailed freedom of speech where it counts most: in political campaigns. And the Supreme Court has greatly limited freedom of religion with decades of rulings that prohibit people from praying or displaying religious symbols in a variety of circumstances.

Roosevelt and the progressives, and their heirs—today we call them (cover the children's ears, please) liberals—schemed to free people from want and fear by creating welfare programs. Today that array of programs—not just Social Security, Medicare, and Medicaid, but their cousins, state and municipal pension programs, among others—have become unsustainable, and people, especially the "little people" who pay taxes, are afraid. They see an aging workforce and a depleted tax base, and contemplate the fiscal ruin of the state and personal want in their future.

Perhaps freedom is just a state of mind. In that case, we might measure how our public figures value freedom by seeing how often they talk about it.

In President Obama's February 24 quasi-State of the Union speech to Congress, he mentioned freedom only once. In his Inauguration speech, he mentioned freedom only three times. In his Election Night victory speech, he didn't mention freedom at all.

In Ronald Reagan's first inaugural address he mentioned freedom eight times. In his first official State of the Union address in 1982 (1981 was a quasi-State of the Union address that was called in February and was only about economic recovery) he mentioned freedom six times. And in his acceptance speech in 1984 in Dallas he mentioned freedom six times.

In his D-Day address this year President Obama mentioned freedom only once. President Bush mentioned freedom four times in his 2004 speech marking the sixtieth anniversary of D-Day.

President Reagan mentioned freedom four times on the fortieth anniversary of D-Day.

Are those imperfect measures? Perhaps.

But then, what's your metric?

Laughing Gas
A Review of *The Death of Conservatism* by Sam Tanenhaus

October 1, 2009

With *The Death of Conservatism*, Sam Tanenhaus establishes himself as one of America's premier comic geniuses in the field of political commentary. There's a guffaw waiting for you on almost every page. And like a good showman, he saves the very best for the very last.

The Death of Conservatism is in a familiar genre: liberals telling conservatives what conservatism really is, or how to be truly conservative, or, sometimes, how to win elections. It's what the *New York Times* and the *Washington Post* do after Republicans lose an election. It's difficult to tell whether liberals really don't understand conservatives and conservatism, or whether they are just gloating after winning an election but pretending to be "responsible." Predicting the past is difficult. Predicting the future (especially in writing) can be folly. But that is the hook for *The Death of Conservatism*: "We stand on the threshold of a new era that has decisively declared the end of an old one. In the shorthand of the moment this abandoned era is often called the Reagan Revolution. . . . This moment's emerging revitalized liberalism has illuminated a truth that should have been apparent a decade ago: movement conservatism is not simply in retreat; it is outmoded." Conservatives, Tanenhaus writes, offer only nihilism.

In the amber of those lines you could hear the champagne corks popping on election night last year. The One has come; conservatism has gone; all will be well in the world! (Repeat three times.) We know better now, as Obama's job approval rating sinks in the polls and people already talk of a Republican resurgence in 2010. Even Tanenhaus knows better: "Of course conservatism has fallen on hard times before. . . ." Yet he can't resist this book.

Liberals often have problems identifying conservatism. It is common for them to conflate conservatives with Republicans, or

Wall Street tycoons, or big business as Tanenhaus does. But conservatives have struggled for years—decades—with Republicans (Eisenhower, Rockefeller, Lindsay, Goodell), Wall Street tycoons (Corzine, Bloomberg), and big businesses (pick any three—or three hundred).

Tanenhaus gives good marks to Presidents Eisenhower, Ford, and George H. W. Bush because they "respected the established boundaries of constitutional precedent, even if it meant carrying out actions imposed by hostile congressional majorities and adversarial courts"—not for them standing athwart history. He even calls Bush and Clinton genuine Burkeans and "the modern era's two true conservative presidents—and the two best." Ha ha ha. The Democratic Party's recent history, he says, is "choosing centrist, explicitly nonideological presidential candidates" like—are you sitting down?—Barack Obama. Ha ha ha. LOL

You gotta admit: that is funny.

Tanenhaus says the right defines itself by "what it longs to destroy: 'statist' social programs; 'socialized medicine'; 'big labor'; 'activist' Supreme Court justices. . . ." Well, yes. And why? Partly because conservatives don't accept Tanenhaus's analysis of Roosevelt's New Deal, "the boldly regulatory measures Franklin D. Roosevelt took to tame the furies of a ravaged economy through the proliferation of federal agencies and programs." Ha ha ha ha.

There were two problems with Roosevelt's actions. In his review in the *New York Times Book Review* (which Tanenhaus edits) of *The Forgotten Man*, Amity Shlaes's book on Roosevelt and the Depression, David Leonhardt wrote, "[Roosevelt's] economic meddling failed to accomplish his larger goal of ending the Depression." (Tanenhaus doesn't agree: "Rooseveltism worked," he writes.) FDR's programs also drastically curtailed people's freedom (e.g., among other actions, FDR outlawed the ownership of gold).

Much of the Roosevelt program *still* exists—which is why modern conservatives are *still* standing athwart history yelling, "Stop!" And now Tanenhaus's centrist hero, Barack Obama, is hitting the Roosevelt road again, trying to socialize American medicine.

Tanenhaus puts "socialized medicine" in quotes presumably to mock conservatives who call Obama's proposed health plan "socialism." Yet he quotes with approval Whittaker Chambers (whom he considers a true conservative for accepting the regulatory economics of the New Deal as the basis for governing in postwar America), who wrote to William F. Buckley: "The machine has made the economy socialist." If Chambers can use the term, why can't conservatives? The answer is, Obama's plan for 17 percent of the economy is socialism, and Tanenhaus knows Americans don't want socialism.

But Chambers was a pessimist: he thought by leaving communism he was leaving the winning side. In that he was wrong. Ronald Reagan won the Cold War, as he set out to do, and not, as Tanenhaus writes, by mere negotiation and compromise, but by outspending the Soviets on military hardware.

For Tanenhaus, conservatism is a mix of his understanding of Burke (maintaining equilibrium between conservation and correction) and Disraeli (advocating "policies the public demanded even though they might contradict the conservative leader's own ideological certitudes").

But what is the American public demanding now? Health care? Tanenhaus writes, "Obama's plan to extend health coverage to the nearly fifty million Americans who lack it is pure Disraeli." Ha ha ha ha. It is? Polls don't indicate Americans are demanding Obama's health plan—which is why, in desperation, the Democrats will likely change its name to KennedyCare. When that doesn't work, what'll they try next: JesusCare?

Tanenhaus says the American right "has missed the most salient fact about America today: the nation has entered a conservative phase, perhaps the most conservative phase since the Eisenhower years." Ha ha ha. Ha ha ha ha ha ha. That is funny.

Tanenhaus writes that Supreme Court justice David Souter "may well endure as the most authentic conservative in the Court's modern history." Ha ha ha ha ha ha! Ho ho ho ho ho ho ho. Isn't that rich?

"Culturally, too"—this is the best part, saved for the *very last* page—"these are conservative times. . . . [C]onservatives should savor the embrace of 'family values' by the nation's homosexual population, who seek the sanctuary—and responsibilities—of marriage and childrearing." Ha ha ha ha ha ha ha ha. HA HA HA HA HA! (Weep!) Ho ho ho ho ho! HO HO HO HO HO! HA HA HA HA! As the children say, you can't make this stuff up.

Ha ha ha ha ha. Ho ho ho ho.

What Tanenhaus does not seem . . . ha ha ha ha ha (sorry) . . .

What Tanenhaus does not seem to understand is that the right defines itself not just by what it longs to destroy, but by *why* it wants to destroy it. The right seeks to extend freedom—a word I do not recall seeing a single time in this book! (It's not in Tanenhaus's comic vocabulary, I guess.) Tanenhaus assumes (ha ha ha ha—sorry) that all the New Deal's statist interventions and depravations of freedom are here to stay—that accepting the entire New Deal, even extending it, is to be on the winning side of history.

Conservatives don't agree. Not to understand that is to have absolutely no clue what conservatism is all about. Even so, don't miss this book. It's a gas.

Nobody's Pluperfect
Speechless: Tales of a White House Survivor by Matt Latimer

December 14, 2009

Matt Latimer has written this year's most entertaining book about what goes on—or doesn't—in Washington. This is a laugh-out-loud book with a serious message, for those willing to hear it. It has also generated controversy.

Latimer was a geeky kid from Flint, Michigan, who set out for Washington (via law school and journalism school) determined to write for the president of the United States. America is a country where just about anyone can grow up to become just about anything—and that's just the problem, George Will said after Bill Clinton became president. Some Bush people feel that way about Latimer.

Latimer worked for a congressman and two senators before becoming a speechwriter for Defense Secretary Rumsfeld and then President Bush.

He is complimentary of Rumsfeld (as he is of Vice President Cheney), but he is critical of others, including some who helped him along the way. His treatment of President Bush is . . . frank.

Latimer has a gift for storytelling, but he's a bit unpolished at times (and he doesn't seem to understand the pluperfect). He says he had the feeling that White House Chief of Staff Josh Bolten "would stand at the window late at night to see who was still working," a snide comment he doesn't give any support for. He relates that in his interview with Secretary Rumsfeld, he told him about "all the long-winded speeches that senators gave to empty chambers, while their staffs praised them for their mediocrity." He says Rumsfeld "loved that observation." How does he know? "Rumsfeld seemed to like that observation" would have been better journalism, without any sacrifice of immodesty.

Latimer thought that working for the president would be the experience of a lifetime, and it was, but not in the way he had expected (that's the pluperfect). In the end he was disillusioned, but that's the way Washington is. Mostly. It wasn't for those of us who worked for Reagan.

In the final chapter he lashes out at "professional Republicans" who, he says, are only in it for being close to power for the sake of power, and who are more interested in keeping their lucrative contracts and cushy Georgetown houses than in supporting candidates who believe in Republican ideals. Yes . . . but. On Election Day, Latimer voted for Obama. Is the naïveté of voting for Obama better than the consultants' greed (that would be Latimer's term) in supporting McCain?

Latimer came in at the end of the second administration, and saw only the worn-out Bush, but he gives him full credit for the conservative actions he took: reducing taxes, supporting missile defense, and starting a discussion on Social Security. That's generous. It was not always great at the beginning. No tax cut could, or can, offset McCain–Feingold or Sarbanes–Oxley, both of which were enacted early on in the administration and neither of which President Bush vetoed.

Was Latimer disloyal to President Bush and to the others he worked with? That's the charge of my good friend Bill Bennett, who called Latimer a "worm" and has consigned him to the lowest circles of Dante's inferno which, Bill reminds those of us who haven't washed since college, is for "for people who are disloyal in the way this guy is disloyal, and at the very lowest point Satan chews on their bodies." Whoa! A lot of learning can be a dangerous thing too. Satan chewing on Latimer's body? Hell, Matt's so young Satan could suck him through a straw. Besides, they say the lowest circle has been *completely* renovated in compliance with Consumer Product Safety Commission standards (Charlie Rangel is rumored to have a still-un-reported income producing property there), and you can even hear Bill Bennett's radio show, when the furnace is low, but only if you also subscribe to the *New York Times*. Incidentally, what was Dante doing, slipping us the skinny on Hell?

The people whom Latimer criticizes, and their supporters, need to relax. Washington, after all, is a town where people don't take friendship personally. Or insults. Most of those whom Latimer criti-cizes are adults with considerable achievements, whose only damage will be to their egos—unless they make his criticisms a two-day story.

Latimer's a talented writer and could be a valuable resource for the conservative cause. Whatever his sins, a lot can be forgiven a man who reveals to us that President Bush said, "If bull—t was currency, Joe Biden would be a billionaire." Who has done more to rehabilitate the former president? Don't miss this book.

Operation Mainstreaming
January 17, 2010

Following the exhibition currently on display at the taxpayer-funded National Portrait Gallery ("Hide/Seek: Difference and Desire in American Portraiture"), the Smithsonian Institution in Washington DC is planning several additional exhibitions, including one in March on art and literature celebrating adultery, infidelity, and illegitimacy in America and one later in the year that will compare and con-trast adult/pubescent male relationships in the United States and in ancient Greece. The exhibitions are part of a ten-month-long explo-ration of "Cultural Anomalies in Modern American Life"—referred to by some as "Operation Mainstreaming."

Of course "Hide/Seek"-type exhibitions are hardly news. In 1989, an exhibition of Robert Mapplethorpe's photographs toured the country for several months before running into a buzz saw of oppo-sition just before arriving at Washington's Corcoran Gallery of Art.

Speaking for the Smithsonian Institution, Mr. Wall Plaque indi-cated that its museums must make way for controversial subjects.

Plaque stated flatly that we must be "committed to showing how a major theme in American history has been the struggle for justice, so that people and groups can claim their full inheritance in America's promise of equality, inclusion, and social dignity."

"Hide/Seek," the first of these exhibitions to be mounted, opened last October 30. According to Blake Gopnik, art critic for the *Washington Post*, the "Hide/Seek" show "surveys how same-sex love has been portrayed in art, from Walt Whitman's hints to open declarations in the era of AIDS and Robert Mapplethorpe's bullwhips. Amazingly, this is the first major museum show to tackle the topic."

Less amazingly, it received much unwanted publicity just before Christmas. The first group to object was the Catholic League for Religious and Civil Rights, which objected to a video containing an eleven-second clip of ants crawling over a crucifix. "Why should the federal government underwrite an institution that uses money to bash [Christianity], when it is unconstitutional for the federal government to underwrite the promotion of it?" the League asked. The segment was removed, but Martin Sullivan, the director of the National Portrait Gallery, got his licks in later in a National Public Radio interview by referring, if obliquely, to the League as among "the loudest and nastiest voices."

The Andy Warhol Foundation for the Visual Arts, which provided $100,000 in funding for "Hide/Seek," threatened to withdraw all future funding from the National Portrait Gallery if the eleven-second clip were not restored, which, to date, it has not been.

After the Catholic League's protest, others objected to the exhibition on the grounds that its attempt to mainstream homosexuality was inappropriate for an institution supported by the taxpayers.

Following the publicity over "Hide/Seek" and the public's learning of the two exhibitions scheduled for later this year ("Sex without Rules" and "Men and Boys: From Here to Antiquity"), other groups started gearing up to take on the Smithsonian. A Smithsonian official defended the exhibitions, saying: "America is a land where minorities can make it into the mainstream. We believe in, and we believe in believing in, inclusiveness. Achieving social dignity is part of the promise of equality."

The numbers are interesting. While only a small percentage of Americans are homosexuals (many put the number at around 2 percent), about 22 percent of American married men and 15 percent of married women are thought to have committed adultery.

"It's not just a numbers game," the official said. "It's about intellectual freedom, and sharing its fruits with the wider public. 'Hide/Seek' is about same-sex desire. 'Sex without Rules' will be about a common form of illicit desire. 'Men and Boys,' about a less common form. If you can have the first show, why can't you have the others? They all tackle themes outside of the cultural mainstream."

That cultural mainstream, especially regarding marriage (long considered vital to Western Civilization) has been significantly diverted in the last few decades. Recent Census Bureau data show that in 2009, for the first time, the proportion of people between the ages of 25 and 34 who have never been married exceeded those who were married. And the long-term slide in marriage rates has pushed the proportion of married adults of all ages down to 52 percent, the lowest count since records have been kept. The change in marriage habits has been most pronounced among those who lack a college education. Also, the country's overall illegitimacy rate is now 38 percent; the black illegitimacy rate, 72 percent.

The question for Smithsonian officials is, Should they be a force driving those cultural changes? Should they use their semi-governmental positions and expend their reputational capital (and taxpayer funds) to confer—or, more accurately, try to confer—"mainstream" status on behavior that most Americans think is aberrant and on notions of history that are decidedly on the fringes?

Ah, but when they hear the word "culture" they reach for their briefcases, and for them the discussion is over.

Note to reader: Only the "Hide/Seek" exhibition referred to in this piece is genuine. The others are fictitious, as are some of the quotes from "Smithsonian officials." (Martin Sullivan's quote and the quote from the plaque on the wall of the "Hide/Seek" exhibition are genuine.) When I showed the piece to several Washington friends, they were all fooled by my spoof. Even though "Sex without Rules" and "Men and Boys: From Here to Antiquity" are outrageous, my friends believed my account, and you may have too, because those exhibitions are—or would be—of a piece with the "Hide/Seek" exhibition actually on view. You are ready, and right, to believe anything about the Smithsonian because you have concluded, correctly in my view, that it has gone over to the other side in the culture war. That's the point of this piece.

Three Smooth Stones
January 25, 2010

How does David stay on message when he's opposing Goliath? That's the Republicans' double challenge this week. Even though a Republican won the special election in Massachusetts, the Democrats are dominating the news. They are very publicly plotting a comeback after their epic loss, and President Obama will take center stage on Wednesday night when he gives the State of the Union speech. Where are the headlines for the party of opposition—which is nominally Republican but which includes millions of Americans who think of themselves as independents?

David's modus operandi was, of course, inspired by the beautiful Bathsheba: KISS—which being translated means, keep it so simple even the mainstream media can't distort it.

Republicans, and particularly Scott Brown whose honeymoon will be shorter than David's love for Bathsheba, need to keep the focus on themselves and the simple solutions they can offer to the complex problems that have vexed the nation since the reign of Obama began.

One thing is plain: Obama has not succeeded, and the American people know it. The economy is stuck in a ditch, and the mega-health care overhaul has failed. What an opportunity!

Republicans should do three things:

One: Tackle the economic problem that is Americans' number one concern by proposing a simple (one-page?) bill to reduce taxes. There will be, of course, any number of suggestions for exactly which tax to reduce. But the key is to make the cut immediate, broad-based, and permanent. To Democrats and the mainstream media types who say the country can't afford a tax cut at this time, they reply simply: the country can't afford not to cut taxes at this time. Tax cuts produce jobs. Could we have the next slide, please? Economics professors by the dozens have recommended tax cuts, and Republicans will have no trouble rounding up legions of them, all armed with supporting graphs and charts, to saturate the talk shows.

Two: Repeal the stimulus bill. That will go part way to paying for the tax cut, and it will allow jobs to be created by market forces instead of crony politics.

Three: Propose a simple (one-page?) health care bill: a bill that fixes one or at most two problems with the current system. The bill could limit damages from medical malpractice suits, and put federal money into state high-risk pools so individuals with chronic conditions could be covered. Republicans should *not* try to fix everything. Americans are sensibly skeptical of grandiose plans to solve all ills. They will appreciate the modest approach. Republicans should confess publicly to not knowing everything, and should make a virtue of taking one small step at a time for the purpose of seeing how much improvement can be made by the market after a single legislative step. They should be publicly cautious about changing anything—as cautious as the American people are, remembering that the people are, by a huge majority, satisfied with their *own* medical plans.

How do Republicans announce these three steps? With a mega-media event that takes the PR ball away from the opposition. The Republicans should all gather on the steps of the Capitol—*all* of them—to announce the proposals: the tax cut on Thursday, the day after the State of the Union speech, the stimulus cancellation on Friday, the health care fix the next Monday.

They should claim the mantle of modesty and say they are attempting to limit Washington's interference in the lives of the people. They should say they are offering limited solutions to complex problems because limited solutions have a smaller chance of doing damage. The American people will understand that. They don't trust Washington— and who can blame them? The American people will understand the Republicans' modesty. And they will understand their proposals— which is more than the Democrats can say about their *own* proposals.

The Republicans should be quick and concise. Their power will lie in the simplicity of their proposals. Leave utopianism to the Democrats.

Throw only three smooth stones.

Goliath, whose height is six cubits and a span, won't have a chance.

Reloading
A Review of *Going Rogue: An American Life*
by Governor Sarah Palin

February 1, 2010

What's not to like about Governor Sarah Palin—for a conservative or a Republican? Her autobiography makes it abundantly clear why the liberal United Nations-hugging big-government socialist fascist gangster-capitalist atheist God-hating running dogs don't like her. But conservatives?

What are the three most important traits a conservative should look for in a president? A belief in God. A belief in a strong national defense. And a belief in the importance of the Tenth Amendment.

The Tenth Amendment?! Holy cow! (No, "holy cow" is not a multicultural sop to our friends in India. It's an old-fashioned expression meaning "Wow!")

Palin believes in God. So did the Founding Fathers, though not necessarily in precisely the way Palin does. Thomas Jefferson wrote: "God who gave us life gave us liberty." And also: "And can the liberties of a nation be thought secure when we have removed their only firm basis, a conviction in the minds of the people that these liberties are the gift of God?"

The United States has strayed far from that belief, or at least from the ability to express that belief in public, in no small part because of Supreme Court rulings so beloved by the liberal United Nations-hugging big-government socialist fascist gangster-capitalist atheist God-hating running dogs. Palin's belief in God is palpable—palpable being the operative word because periodically she holds her children's hands and prays.

There are other ways for believers to behave, of course. Crusty old-line Episcopalians, as well as old-fashioned Roman Catholics, tend not to like even to "do" the peace in church. But they shouldn't hold other Christians' practices against them. And if they have to choose between the aforementioned running dogs and Gov. Palin, it shouldn't be difficult.

Why is a belief in God important? Because, as Chesterton is said to have expressed it: "When men stop believing in God they don't believe in nothing; they believe in anything." Including progress (by which they mean the perfectibility of man), the wisdom of the state, and the need for big government (as the means by which the wise state, guided by a multiplicity of advisers who went to Harvard and Yale, can bring about the perfection of man). Palin: "The role of government is not to perfect us, but to protect us."

Protecting us is important for obvious reasons. And providing for the common defense is in the preamble to the US Constitution, along with establishing justice and ensuring domestic tranquility. Having a strong defense does not necessarily mean supporting the war in either Iraq or Afghanistan. But it does mean having a defense budget large enough to make our enemies quake. Palin: "America must remain the strongest nation in the world in order to remain free." At the peak of the Reagan rearming in 1986 our expenditures on defense were 6.2 percent of GDP. They are now 4.8 percent, and are projected to go down to 3 percent by 2019. Where is Palin (the proud mother of a son who went off to serve his country in Iraq) when we need her?

The Tenth Amendment is out of favor these days, but not with Palin. Writing about her campaign for governor of Alaska, she said, "I had great respect for the need for state government to preserve locally enacted policies. Likewise, I believed that national leaders have a responsibility to respect the Tenth Amendment and keep their hands off the states." And later: "Local government is best able to prioritize services and projects. That's the basis of the Tenth Amendment."

Palin is not the only Tenth Amendment enthusiast around. There are a couple of Tenth Amendment stirrings in the "lower 48," as Alaskans describe the rest of the states. In Arizona, there is a proposed amendment to the state's constitution to limit the power of the federal government to restrict "a person's freedom of choice of private health care systems or private plans of any type." In Montana, there is proposed legislation that declares that any weapon or round of ammunition made in Montana and remaining within state borders "is not subject to federal law or federal regulation, including registration, under the authority of Congress to regulate interstate commerce." (Roll over, *Wickard v. Filburn!*)

Palin believes in the Tenth Amendment and (or is it because?) she also believes in personal responsibility. In her first speech to the people of Alaska as governor, she said, "Take responsibility for your family and for your futures. Don't think you need government to take care of all needs and to make your decision for you. More government isn't the answer because you have ability, because you are Alaskans, and you live in a land that God, with incredible benevolence, decided to overwhelmingly bless." She was reminding them that their liberties are a gift from God. Amen.

This book is about public policy and campaigning, but it is also an intensely personal book—by, it has to be said, an amazing woman. Palin describes her childhood: striving at school, the physical pain of excelling at sports, learning to give her all and never to give up. "I realized that my gift was determination and resolve, and I have relied on it ever since." She writes about working, working hard, taking time off between semesters at college so she could afford the tuition. She had jobs by the dozens. Scut jobs, not soft-lighted muzak-muffled office jobs. She worked on the "slime line," slicing open fish bellies. You don't have to work the slime line to get to Heaven, but it helps you relate to millions of hard-working Americans.

She was part tomboy when she was young, but there were limits. Early one morning she went hunting with her father and he bagged a moose and began field-dressing it. "Here, hold these," her father said. "'I want to show them to my science class today.'" "I looked down to see the moose's eyeballs lying in his palm. . . . When he saw me wrinkle my nose and shake my head slightly, he set them aside." No wonder she wasn't afraid of Katie Couric.

If the story of Palin's discovering that her fifth child had Down syndrome doesn't bring tears to your eyes, you're reading the wrong magazine. She asked her husband if he had the same question she had: Why us? "He looked genuinely surprised by my question and responded calmly, 'Why not us?'" Sarah Palin is a mother extraordinaire, and she writes, "There is no greater service than mothering."

Are there other traits a president should have? Of course. Some executive ability helps. Let's see: who had more executive experience going into the last election, Gov. Palin or Sen. Obama? Palin describes rolling Exxon Mobil in negotiating the billion-dollar oil deal for Alaska. Exxon Mobil happens to be the largest company in the world. And while we're on the topic, who was our most recent compulsively executive presidential whiz kid? Right. Jimmy Carter. Case closed.

What about intelligence? Sure, intelligence helps—maybe. Quick, name one presidential decision made in the last sixteen years, i.e., during the Clinton (Yale, Yale, Oral Roberts) and Bush (Yale, Harvard) years that you think was either right because the president was intelligent or wrong because he was not intelligent enough. Okay, take your time (oh, and sorry, I meant oral sex, not Oral Roberts).

Time's up. Get the point? And remember what they said about President Reagan, who went to—how do you express a sneer in writing?—Eureka College? Now he's widely regarded as the best president of the twentieth century. (Roosevelt only won a war; Reagan won a war and saved the economy.)

Palin has a lot to say about the campaign: gracious words for Sen. McCain, and for some of the staff assigned to her. But clearly there was gross incompetence, followed by Super Bowl-sized blame-gaming by the grossly incompetent. When Palin tried to be Palin and do things off-script, they accused her of going rogue. Next time the rule will be: Let Palin be Palin.

Why did she resign the governorship? Because the liberals mounted a campaign of nonstop harassment. They made governing impossible by filing hundreds—hundreds!—of spurious Freedom of Information Act requests, ethics charges, and lawsuits. The problem can be seen plainly on the Alaska state web page under the heading "Who can file an ethics complaint?" The answer: "Anyone." From anywhere, which includes all the tutees of President Obama's mentor, Saul Alinsky. And in Alaska, because the governor has to hire attorneys at her own expense, Palin ran up legal bills of $500,000. She came to the conclusion that she could no longer serve effectively. In Alaska.

Is she quitting? Not likely. As her father said, "Sarah's not retreating. She's reloading." Praise the Lord. And pass the ammunition. (*Reloading* would have been a good title for the book too.)

Sarah Palin is still young, still blessed with the gifts of determination and resolve and true American grit. She has time to reload. And her best days, like ours, may be yet to come.

WBHO and WBHO FM in the Nation's Capitol

March 8, 2010

It may not be news that politicians dissemble. But that's no reason not to care about what a president says. Let us, therefore, unpack last Saturday's presidential radio address.

President Obama said he had met with some of the insurance companies two days earlier and said that "they couldn't give me a straight answer as to why they keep arbitrarily and massively raising premiums—by as much as 60 percent in states like Illinois."

Sixty percent! Could that be true? Actually it's not (see below), but let us examine the president's rhetoric first, because a clever rhetorician can, sometimes, hide his dissembling.

What does "states like Illinois" mean? Are there states like Illinois? Is Alaska like Illinois? Rhode Island? Michigan? Could President Obama have meant that there are other states in which insurance companies have also raised premiums by as much as 60 percent? Please. You know he didn't mean that, because if he had, he wouldn't have missed the chance to name them.

The proper formulation for what he *seemed* to be saying would have been that insurance companies had raised premiums "by as much as 60 percent in a number of states, including Illinois." His use of "like" was—sort of—shorthand for "including."

But "including" is also commonly misused (mistakenly or deliberately) to imply that there are more items on a list than those named, as when a person with two degrees says, "I have a number of academic degrees, including a BA and a PhD."

You could, properly, say, "a number of scandals engulfed the Clinton administration, including Whitewater, Troopergate, Travelgate, and Monicagate." You would not say (I hope), "Goldilocks had a run-in with some bears, including the Papa Bear, the Mama Bear, and the Baby Bear"—unless, perhaps, you were the president and your children's version contained a number of additional bears, including Smokey Bear, PC Bear, Hopey Bear, and Changie Bear.

Misusing "like" and "including" is not fatal. It's just careless

(English teachers used to take points off for it) or, in President Obama's case probably, deliberately deceptive.

But back to Illinois. According to the March 4, 2010, *Chicago Tribune*, "Consumers in Illinois who lose their jobs and have no other option but to buy their own health insurance will get socked this year with premium increases of up to 60 percent."

Whoa! The president went from that to "they keep arbitrarily and massively raising premiums—by as much as 60 percent."

What the *Chicago Tribune* is saying is that individuals who lost their *company* health insurance will have to pay 60 percent more for an *individual* policy than they had been paying (out of pocket) for coverage under the company's policy.

"Out of pocket" is important here: it is well known (even, one must assume, in the White House) that employers who pay for their workers' health insurance pay their workers less than they would if they were not paying for that insurance. Indeed, that has been a central point of contention in the health care debate. A worker is worth only so much. He can be paid either in cash or in benefits (often untaxed), or partly in each. According to the *Chicago Tribune*'s story, "Big firms commonly pay about $1,000 a month [for health insurance] per employee, with the individual employee paying about 20 percent to 30 percent of that amount."

Some employees may not focus on who's really footing the health insurance bill. Others may be well aware that their employer is paying 70 to 80 percent of the premiums, but know also that those funds are really wages that are being snuck out to the insurance companies without their having to pay income taxes on them.

Company health insurance policies are different from individual policies for a variety of reasons, and so their premiums will also differ.

What the president was doing was like comparing Goldilocks to Goldfinger. That's a good rhetorical trick, if you can get away with it.

Polls indicate the president can't. So do recent elections.

So when the president said in his radio address, "If you like the insurance plan you have now, you can keep it," people probably didn't believe him.

And when he said, "Doctors and patients will have more control over their health care decisions," people probably didn't believe him.

And when he indicated that his socialized medicine plan will prevent Medicare and Medicaid from sinking our government deeper and deeper into debt, probably no one believed him.

Except, perhaps, some White House bears, including Hopey and Changie.

Lash and Chain Morality
March 10, 2010

David Ignatius writes in the *Washington Post* that President Obama should try to shift the health care argument to what Ignatius calls the high ground: morality. He says that what is lacking is the sense that Congress must act because health care for all is a matter of social justice, "required by our moral conscience."

Ignatius cites the debate over "don't ask, don't tell" as an example of a policy debate that was finally decided on a moral basis. "By treating the issue as a matter of conscience," he writes, "the chairman of the Joint Chiefs of Staff altered the national conversation."

First: he has misread the "don't ask, don't tell" debate. The point of militaries is to win wars, not to promote social justice. If homosexuals mess up military morale and effectiveness by forming sexual *(eros)* relationships instead of comradely *(philia)* relationships, they shouldn't be allowed to serve. Whether homosexuals *do in fact* mess up military effectiveness is a factual question, not a moral one.

What actually happened in the "don't ask, don't tell" debate was that a number of military brass said that there were, in fact, no functional reasons not to allow openly homosexual personnel to serve in the armed forces. Whether that's what they really believed is difficult to know. In this administration it is almost certain, but at least likely, that any military person objecting to having homosexuals serve in the armed forces would be more likely to get a dead fish from White House Chief of Staff Rahm Emanuel than see another star on his shoulder. Political correctness isn't something that afflicts only college campuses.

Once the brass could no longer safely articulate a military reason for not having homosexuals serve, then but only then could they and the politicians start grandstanding on the morality question.

Second: Ignatius says providing basic health insurance coverage to all Americans is the right thing to do. Of course, by "providing," he doesn't mean just making it available; he means requiring (on penalty of fine or jail) people to have health insurance because that's the way of socialism. Oh, and also, it's part of Obama's plan.

Implicit in Ignatius's position is that a significant portion of Americans is unable to get health insurance today. That is simply not true.

The number of people without health insurance is said to be 45.7 million. But a little fact-checking of the kind we know Ignatius to be capable of reveals that many of those uninsured have chosen not to be insured. Ten million of those 45.7 million have incomes of $75,000 or more. Eight million have incomes between $50,000 and $75,000.

Suddenly, Ignatius's concerns seem less altruistic. Now we begin to understand why penalties are necessary to achieve full coverage. Those 18 million people tend to be young and healthy and least in need of medical care, which is why Ignatius would have them follow orders to buy health insurance. His morality hath taken on a strange hue.

The Census Bureau also reports that about ten million of the uninsured are not US citizens. Raising the question, how far must our morality extend? Must Americans cover everyone . . . including the bankrupt Greeks?

Fourteen million of the 45.7 million uninsured are poor and low-income people who are eligible for already existing government programs (Medicare, Medicaid, SCHIP), but fail to enroll in them.

So who's left? About eight million people, who can't get health insurance (the arithmetic is a bit fuzzy because there's overlap in the categories).

So: in order to provide health insurance to less than 3 percent of the population we must mount a moral crusade to change the entire American health care system?

That's not morality. That's madness. But madness is a medical term.

The political term is socialism. And if the twentieth century taught us anything, it was that there is nothing moral about socialism.

The Curious Incident at the *New York Times*

April 13, 2010

Europe and America have been rocked in recent weeks by the scandal of a Roman Catholic priest in Germany who molested children several decades ago and escaped serious punishment. But one detail has been missing.

The *New York Times* has run more than a dozen articles on the issue since the story first broke on March 12, under such headlines as "Memo to Pope Described Transfer of Pedophile Priest."

The most salacious part of the story has not been details of the sexual abuse (there have been few, there being, after all, only so many ways to molest) but the posited lack of interest of the miscreant priest's superior, then Cardinal Ratzinger, now Pope Benedict XVI. The gravamen of the story is becoming "What did the cardinal know and when did he know it?" Fair enough, perhaps. But we've been down this cover-up storyline before, when the *Times* went after President Nixon. It now appears the *Times* is trying to pin the Watergate cover-up tail on the Vatican donkey.

The real issue is limned not only by the *Times*'s headline, "Memo to Pope Described Transfer of Pedophile Priest," but also by a remark the Rev. Klaus Malangré, the Catholic Church's personnel chief in Essen, Germany, made to the Rev. Friedrich Fahr, his counterpart in the diocese of Munich to which the offending priest, Fr. Hullermann, was being transferred. Malangré suggested to Fahr that Hullermann could be allowed to teach religion "at a girls' school."

At a girls' school? Why would that be safe? Look up "pedophile" in the dictionary and you will find that it means an adult who is sexually attracted to young children. Wouldn't the pedophile Hullermann be sexually attracted to young girl children too?

Well, he might be, if he were only a pedophile. But then what would have been the point of Malangré's suggestion to Fahr?

Clearly, Malangré was warning Fahr that Hullermann was a homosexual. Of course, you knew that already, somehow. But that somehow was not because the *New York Times* told you. The word "homosexual" does not appear a single time in all the articles the *Times* has run since the story first broke.

Scotland Yard Detective Gregory asks Sherlock Holmes, "Is there any other point to which you would wish to draw my attention?"

Holmes replies, "To the curious incident of the dog in the nighttime."

Gregory responds, "The dog did nothing in the nighttime."

Holmes: "That was the curious incident."

Here are four possible interpretations of the *Times*'s curious omission of Hullermann's homosexuality. One, that the *Times* reporter didn't know that Hullermann was a homosexual and wasn't curious enough to find out. Two, the editors of the *Times* assumed all its readers would assume Hullermann was a homosexual. Three, the people at the *New York Times* thought the fact irrelevant. And four, the people at the *Times* are in thrall to the homosexual community and didn't want to disparage it.

One and two are implausible. If you could figure out Hullermann was a homosexual, so could a reporter for the *New York Times*. And since when did the newspaper of record omit an important fact just because many readers would know it anyway? Three is absurd: clearly the homosexuality of the offender would be one of the most important parts of the story.

Leaving the fourth reason: the *Times* made a choice to speak no ill of homosexuals.

But in fact, the third reason would probably be the one given by the *Times*. The people at the *Times* think or say they think that homosexuality is irrelevant to pedophilia. Bill Keller, the executive editor of the *Times*, wrote in March 2002 that "there is no known connection between homosexuality and pedophilia."

The *Times* may believe that, but other experts and probably most Americans would disagree. Besides, that's not exactly the issue. The issue is whether there's a connection between the homosexuality of the priests and the molestation of the boys.

The pedophilia story really begins more than forty years ago, when the Roman Catholic Church began accepting known homosexuals into the priesthood. The traditionalists objected, but the sixties were when enlightened, progressive, sophisticated life began. Like children who think they are the very first to discover sex, the sixties' liberals thought that any restrictions on what homosexuals could do must be wrongly discriminatory. For a liberal, everything goes. So, everything went, including homosexuals to seminaries.

In the years since then, we (the Catholic Church in particular, but all of us) really have reaped the fruits of what was sown in those turbulent years.

There are, in fact, at least three scandals here:. The first, that a priest molested boys thirty years ago, is scandal to be sure, but alas, hardly news now, given the number of such stories over the past decade including one in California that came to light only this past week.

The second, and underlying, scandal is that it's the homosexuals allowed into the priesthood in the sixties who have been causing most of the trouble.

Are all homosexuals child molesters? Certainly not.

Are most child molesters in the Catholic Church homosexuals? Almost certainly.

But try finding that story in the *New York Times*.

Isn't this the key question: Are homosexual priests *more likely* to molest children than non-homosexual priests? If we don't know, shouldn't we find out? Because if they are, wouldn't it make sense to pay special attention to the assignments given to homosexual priests?

In fact, wouldn't it make sense to pay special attention to the assignments given to homosexual priests until it was *certain* that they were *not* more likely to molest children than non-homosexual priests?

Not, apparently, to the *New York Times*. That would require it to be critical of supervisors who failed to identify priests who were homosexual and who assigned them to positions where they could abuse children. It's much easier for the *Times* simply to pile on after the abuses have happened, and write about a coverup.

What is the primary public-policy goal of a news story that exposes a coverup?

Presumably, to put future offenders (or their superiors) on notice that eventually they are likely to be detected and perhaps punished. The hope is that that knowledge might make those in positions of authority more vigilant in assigning, supervising, and punishing priests who might abuse children.

But wouldn't identifying the likely perpetrators, or a class of people likely to be perpetrators, and supervising them more carefully *before* they perpetrate be even more likely to serve the public policy of preventing abuse of children?

Again, surely yes.

And that is the third, and most serious, scandal. There is almost surely a coverup here. But it's a coverup by the *New York Times* of a group of people whose lifestyle the *Times* celebrates. The *Times* seems to be more interested in protecting its friends in the homosexual community than the youngsters in churches and in any other institutions where they might fall victim to predatory homosexuals.

One part of the "crisis" in the Roman Catholic Church is probably over. Abuses have declined since 1980, and the church has stopped letting known homosexuals into the priesthood. Scandals of this particular type won't be happening in the future, certainly not on the scale they have been. That is good news; although because of its cause (fewer, or no, homosexuals in the priesthood) you may not find it highlighted in the trendy papers.

But we shouldn't expect that the decline in scandals will persuade the *Times* to admit it was wrong. When the *Times* is asked in years to come why the abuse of children declined so precipitously in the Catholic Church, it will be all set with the perfect explanation.

Climate change.

Playing to Win
April 14, 2010

On April 21, 2010, the CEOs of several major US corporations will appear before a House Commerce Committee inquisition being staged by Chairman Henry Waxman (D–CA). The CEOs of AT&T, John Deere, Caterpillar, and other companies have, as is required by law, filed notices with the Securities and Exchange Commission announcing that their companies will be taking major writedowns (AT&T, $1 billion; John Deere, $150 million; Caterpillar, $100 million) because of the obligations imposed by Obamacare.

Rep. Waxman and his colleagues, relying on President Obama, the Congressional Budget Office, and the Tooth Fairy, thought (or say they thought) the cost of health care would go down under

Obamacare and profess to be shocked to discover that costs may rise instead. Hence the inquisition.

This, gentlemen of AT&T, John Deere, Caterpillar, and the others, is a moment not to be missed. Or muffed. The eyes of the nation will be upon you. You will have a unique opportunity to tell your fellow Americans about the true costs and consequences of Obamacare.

Here are ten points to remember, in addition to the obvious (don't fly in by private jet; don't stay in the biggest suite in the fanciest hotel; dress modestly—no French cuffs):

1. First and always, remember that Congress's positive rating for performance and ethics (according to Zogby) is less than 10 percent. Lower than lawyers. Lower than *O.J.*! Which means, basically, you've won before you begin. The public is on your side. Be brave.

2. Remember also that according to a Bloomberg poll, only four in 10 Americans support the Obamacare that these same congressmen who will be questioning you have just finished foisting onto the American people—which is one of the reasons Congress's negative rating is 90 percent.

3. Don't let them swear you in as a group. Remember the front-page photos of the oil-company executives taking their oaths in 2008? Or of the bankers in January of this year? Oh, yes. It's very traditional. Congress lines you all up at the table with your hands raised and makes you look like perpetrators. Don't let them do that to you. Probably the letter you have received from the committee informs you that you will be presumed to be under oath, in which case the oath the chairman wants to make you take is purely for show—to make you look like perps. Have your lawyers tell the committee that you'd like to be sworn in before the hearing begins, to save time. Or insist that each of you be sworn in separately standing right up in front of the chairman.

If you can't negotiate a satisfactory arrangement, tell the audience—the American people—about the chairman's manipulation before you begin your testimony. Remember, you are not the bad guys in this drama. They are. You employ people. They tax people.

4. Take command of the hearing. Watch the tape of Oliver North's opening testimony on July 7, 1987. North dominated from the beginning.

5. Have your team read what the committee members have said in the weeks preceding your appearance. They will have nothing new to say by the time the hearing comes along. That means you can rehearse your answers beforehand.

6. Bring your own visuals. This is theater. You need props. The cameras will love it. And test out your visuals on focus groups first.

7. Make the point that the law *requires* you to notify the SEC of the writedown. Teach the viewers that law and economics don't matter to congressmen. All they care about is politics. Ask one of your interrogators—Rep. Waxman, Rep. Stupak, one of the others—if he would be willing to indemnify you if you did not file with the SEC. Have a big white board with an outline of someone in jail, and movable photos of the congressmen, and ask any one of them if he is willing to go to jail instead of you—then move his photo to cover the cutout of the figure in jail. A guaranteed win on the evening news. (You can conceal this visual behind an incomprehensible graph when you walk into the hearing room.)

8. Don't sit passively when they ask you "Have-you-stopped-beating-your-wife" questions. When Rep. Dingell (Bully–MI) was questioning the Toyota executives, he said at the end of every question, "Answer yes or no." Take issue with that kind of behavior. Every time. Challenging the congressman makes him seem unreasonable. And it uses up his allotted time. You can respond to Rep. Dingell with, "Mr. Dingell: Are you going to try to bully me through the entire hearing? Please answer yes or no." Or your lawyer can say to the congressman, "My client will answer your question 'yes' or 'no' if that's appropriate. If it's not, he won't." Remember, the public sees through these congressmen (positive rating for performance and ethics, less than 10 percent). Let the mischief of their own lips fall upon their heads.

9. Don't take any guff from them. Remember how Caspar Weinberger, President Reagan's secretary of Defense, and James Baker, his secretary of State, handled obstreperous congressmen.

At a hearing in 1983, Sen. Donald W. Riegle Jr. (D–MI) denounced Weinberger, saying his "basic judgment is dangerous to our country."

Secretary Weinberger replied, "You have accomplished your principal purpose, to launch a demagogic attack on me in time for the afternoon and evening editions, and I want to tell you that I think that everything you've said is both insulting and wrong."

BIFF!

At a House Appropriations subcommittee hearing on February 24, 1992, Rep. Lawrence Smith (D–FL) accused Secretary Baker of not answering his question: "For you not to finish the answer is another attempt to try to reject any kind of significant intrusion . . ."

Baker replied, calmly, "No, Larry, I think I finished the answer."

Smith, boiling: "Well, sir, you did not finish the answer and it's basically the same way you want to deal with this subject."

Baker, ever so suave: "I finished as far as I was concerned, and I will determine when I have finished my answers, not you."

BIFF! BAM!!

When I was chairman of the Federal Trade Commission I appeared before a congressional committee and found it necessary to be a bit, er, cantankerous. After the hearing I called one of the committee members to thank him for the courtesies he had shown me, and I told him that testifying before Congress was my favorite indoor sport. The committee never called me back.

10. Remember that you will not often get a chance to play against such an unpopular team. Make the most of it. And have fun—so that you too can say, when it's all over, that testifying before Congress is your favorite indoor sport.

Freedom Worth Its Salt
April 28, 2010

The Food and Drug Administration has announced that it will soon require manufacturers of many food products to use less salt. They assure us that the changes will be calibrated so that consumers will barely notice them. That raises the question: Is there anything (other than sex) that the government can't regulate?

If people want less salt in their food, manufacturers will respond to their desires. As in fact they have already done. Stroll down your supermarket aisles and look at the number of products that come in a low-sodium variety. Soups. Juices. Peanuts. Crackers. Soda water. Cereals. Snacks. Cheese. Unsalted tops on Saltines! Frozen chicken Parmesan, cheese ravioli, chicken picatta. Chili. Vegetable enchiladas. Even sodium-free *salt*!

Why so many? Because consumers—the market—demanded them, and manufacturers responded.

But that's not good enough for Big Brother. He wants everybody to use low-sodium products, and he wants more of them. BB says it's healthy.

Maybe it is. But whose choice is it to be healthy? The individual citizen's or nanny government's? Ah, says BB, but some people are . . . well, you know, too stupid to realize that less sodium may be better for them.

The result is that we will all have to live in a society regulated for the stupidest among us. Is that really what America is all about?

And of course, requiring manufacturers to use less salt has to be just the beginning. The resulting product will be so easy to alter. Just—add salt! What will Big Brother do then?

He will outlaw salt, that's what he'll do. Perhaps not in the home, but in restaurants. You laugh? In New York City, Big Brother Bloomberg (the mayor) outlawed trans fats in restaurants in 2006. Two years later, California banned trans fats in all restaurants in the state. And this spring Assemblyman Felix Ortiz, a Democratic from Brooklyn, introduced a bill into the New York State legislature banning any and all salt in public eating places in the state.

You say you will bring your own? Please. Big Brothers Bloomberg and Ortiz will be waiting for you. It will be a misdemeanor to bring salt into a restaurant, as it is, even now, illegal in many places to take an open bottle of wine out of a restaurant. That was easy.

But what about private eating places—assuming the concept continues to exist in Big Brother's world? How will BB keep you from eating salt at home? Easy again. He will tax it. Look what BB did to cigarettes. Would $10 a pound cut into your salt habit? How about $20? Maybe $30?

The rationale is easy to understand—if you put yourself in the shoes of a bright young Harvard man who knows much more about everything than someone like us will ever know. He will look out for me and you. As a McDonald's jingle of the 1970s went, "We do it all for you-ou-ou."

Why does the government want to regulate our behavior? There are at least two reasons, one stated, the other not.

The stated reason will be that since the government is paying for our health care, it has the right to make us behave in ways that are healthy in order to keep our medical bills down. It isn't *fair* for us to burden our fellow taxpaying citizens because we don't behave properly—because we eat too much salt.

The other, and the real, reason is power: big-government types, like President Obama and his crowd, exist to control other people.

They have two goals: making the citizens utterly dependent on government (them), and managing every aspect of the citizens' lives. That is the leftist, progressive dream. And it is rapidly becoming a reality. In the land of the free.

Once upon a time, some people thought government might reach the end of regulating. Everything that could, reasonably, be regulated, would be regulated. Smoking prohibitions. Seatbelt requirements. Toilets that don't flush. Trans-fat-free restaurants. And the thousands of other regulations contained in the tens of thousands of pages of the Federal Register.

That is fundamentally to misunderstand the nature of Big Government People. There will never be an end to what the BGPs want to regulate. And as time goes on, the regulations will intrude more and more into the citizens' lives because the less intrusive regulations will already have been passed.

If the people *really* object to a regulation, the bright Harvard men will always fall back on the need to protect not just us, but also "the children," the permanent wards of that village Hillary the Lamp Thrower and her intern-molesting husband lectured us about.

Even if the bright Harvard men could protect us, the real question is: Do we want to be safe and healthy, or do we want to be free?

An old-fashioned American will answer, "Free." A progressive (a white-shoe socialist), having learned nothing from the history of the twentieth century, will prefer life in the Guiding State—especially if he is doing the guiding.

What can the freedom-loving American citizen do? When is too much regulation too much to take? When should civil disobedience begin?

Surely not over salt.

But salt is not the issue. The issue is freedom. If it's okay to be civilly disobedient to demand freedom for Blacks, why not also to demand not to have all of American life regulated, even if it's for the sake of the neglected children the progressives tell us it takes a village to raise? After all, the Civil Rights movement began because some lady wanted a different seat on a bus.

But of course that fuss wasn't about the bus seat. It was about freedom. Now Blacks can sit wherever they want on a bus. But soon they won't be able to eat salt.

In 1961, William F. Buckley Jr. expressed the hope that "when the Negroes have finally realized their long dream of attaining to the status of the white man, the white man will still be free."

He won't be, unless he pays more notice to the deliberately calibrated attenuation of his freedom.

News Quiz for Discerning
American Spectator Readers

May 6, 2010

In this contest, readers are asked to identify the bogus news item. All three items are "reported" in similar style, from *The American Spectator News Service*. Two of them record actual events reported by other news outlets. (Certain telltale aspects of the real stories have been altered in order to prevent sneaky contestants from finding the items on the web.)

Item 1

TAS NEWS SERVICE, MADRID (APR. 15, 2010): Antonio Tajani, the European Union Commissioner for Enterprise and Industry, has announced a new human right: taxpayer-subsidized vacations. "Traveling for tourism today is a right," Tajani said. "The way we spend our holidays is a formidable indicator of our quality of life."

The pilot project, which is to begin in 2013, could cost up to half a billion dollars a year. Tajani said he believes that subsidizing holidays for seniors, the disabled, young adults, and poor families will build pride in European culture, prop up resorts in the off-season, and bring north and south closer.

A Tajani spokesman said, "Why should someone from the Mediterranean not be able to travel to Edinburgh in summer for a breath of cool, fresh air? Why should someone from Edinburgh not be able to travel to Greece in winter?"

In a related development, Greece reached an agreement with other euro-zone countries and the International Monetary Fund for a three-year, €110-billion ($146.5-billion) bailout. "We have no other choices and no time, so accessing the bailout is inevitable," Prime Minister George Papandreou said, vowing that his government won't "allow the country to become bankrupt."

Item 2

TAS NEWS SERVICE, NEW YORK (APR. 20, 2010): The United Nations Economic and Social Council (ECOSOC) today announced the election of the Islamic Republic of Iran to a four-year term on the Commission on the Status of Women (CSW). The Commission is dedicated exclusively to gender equality and advancement of women. The election of Iran to CSW came one week after the country withdrew its bid to join the UN Human Rights Council.

In related news, a respected Iranian cleric, Hojatoleslam Kazem Sedighi, speaking on the record, said that "Many women who do not dress modestly . . . lead young men astray, corrupt their chastity, and spread adultery in society, which consequently increases earthquakes." The US Geological Survey, an unbiased, multidisciplinary US government organization that focuses on geography, geology, and geospatial information has offered no comment on the accuracy of Cleric Sedighi's statement.

Item 3

TAS NEWS SERVICE, WASHINGTON DC (APR. 30, 2010): The Democratic-controlled Congress today reauthorized the Opportunity Scholarship Program, which provides vouchers to poor students in the District of Columbia. The popular program, which was enacted by Republicans in 2004, provides scholarships of up to $7,500 a year to enable students to attend the school of their parents' choice. The per-pupil cost in the DC public schools is $14,400 on average, among the highest in the country.

Democratic Party Whip Sen. Dick Durbin of Illinois and Delegate Eleanor Holmes Norton (D–DC) worked tirelessly to reauthorize the program. Congress is thought to have been influenced by a recent

US Department of Education study that found that Opportunity Scholarship Program students are performing at higher academic levels than their peers who are not in the program, and are better off by virtually every important measure in their chosen schools. Teachers' unions concurred in the study's findings.

In a related development, President Obama has announced that he and Mrs. Obama are considering sending their two children to a yet-undisclosed Washington DC public school next year. The two children currently attend the exclusive Sidwell Friends School in Washington, where the tuition is $29,000 a year.

News Quiz #2
May 10, 2010

Degree of difficulty: Not too bad, but pay attention.

A number of the contestants in News Quiz #1 complained that it was insultingly easy. News Quiz #2 attempts to address that concern.

Contestants are invited to pick the bogus provision or provisions out of the following paragraphs which have been lifted (with some of the excess verbiage excised) from the Patient Protection and Affordable Care Act (PPACA), more colloquially known as Obamacare. The provisions have been separated into discrete numbered lines/paragraphs for ease of reading and identifying.

Time allotted: two hours. This is not an open-book, internet-research test, but you may discuss with other contestants.

1. In the case of food that is a standard menu item that is offered for sale in a restaurant or similar retail food establishment that is part of a chain with 20 or more locations doing business under the same name and offering for sale substantially the same menu items, the restaurant or similar retail food establishment shall disclose in a clear and conspicuous manner, in a nutrient content disclosure statement adjacent to the name of the standard menu item, so as to be clearly associated with the standard menu item, on the menu listing the item for sale,
2. the number of calories contained in the standard menu item, as usually prepared and offered for sale;

3. and a succinct statement concerning suggested daily caloric intake, as specified by the Secretary by regulation and posted prominently on the menu and designed to enable the public to understand, in the context of a total daily diet, the significance of the caloric information that is provided on the menu;

4. For the purposes of this clause, a restaurant or similar retail food establishment shall have a reasonable basis for its nutrient content disclosures, including nutrient databases, cookbooks, laboratory analyses, and other reasonable means.

5. The Secretary shall establish by regulation standards for determining and disclosing the nutrient content for standard menu items that come in different flavors, varieties, or combinations, but which are listed as a single menu item, such as soft drinks, ice cream, pizza, doughnuts, or children's combination meals, through means determined by the Secretary, including ranges, averages, or other methods.

6. This regulation shall not apply to items that are not listed on a menu such as condiments and other items placed on the table or counter for general use, or daily specials, temporary menu items appearing on the menu for less than 60 days per calendar year, or custom orders.

7. This regulation shall not apply to items that are not served in the restaurants or similar retail food establishments that are the subject of this regulation, except as the Secretary may by subsequent regulation determine.

8. This regulation shall not apply to any religious organization that provides any kind of nutrient substance as part of its religious observances, whether described in any written or spoken material of said organization as any kind of food or meal or otherwise.

9. In promulgating regulations, the Secretary shall consider

10. standardization of recipes and methods of preparation,

11. including but not limited to those listed in *Mastering the Art of French Cooking* by Julia Childs, *The Joy of Cooking*, *The Single Quaker Mother's Cookbook*, and *Low Calorie Cooking the Islamofacist Way*,

12. reasonable variation in serving size and formulation of menu items,

13. space on menus,

14. inadvertent human error,

15. training of food service workers,

16. variations in ingredients,

17. sunspots,

18. and other factors, as the Secretary determines.

Regulators Anonymous for the FTC
May 29, 2010

There's a proposal afoot to give more power to the Federal Trade Commission. That is never a good idea.

Last December, the House of Representatives approved a financial regulatory overhaul measure, Rep. Barney Frank's (D–MA), so-called "Wall Street Reform and Consumer Protection Act of 2009," which would grant the FTC faster rule-making procedures and stronger enforcement powers.

The bill is now being considered by the Senate where, so far, things aren't looking good for the FTC. The Senate might just get something right this year.

One of the provisions of Frank's bill—the "Give the FTC a Drink and Tell It to Go for a Drive Act"—would repeal some of the provisions of the Magnuson–Moss Act that were enacted in 1980. One of the provisions of that act limited the rule-making power of the FTC because the FTC had started behaving like a binge drinker of regulatory booze.

Congress found that "in many instances the FTC had taken actions beyond the intent of Congress." HIC! After one binge, the FTC considered imposing a total ban on advertising directed at children. Even the *Washington Post* said that would turn the FTC into the "national nanny."

The FTC's current chairman, Jon Leibowitz, argues for additional power (streamlined rulemaking procedure) on the grounds that it is "generally available to other federal agencies." As in, "Johnny can drink. Why can't I?"

Well, Johnny's family only serves beer. Most other regulatory agencies are limited to a single industry. The jurisdiction of the Securities and Exchange Commission is limited to the securities industry. The Commodity Futures Trading Commission regulates only commodity futures and option markets. The FTC, however—HIC!—regulates across most of the US economy.

Leibowitz has promised to use any new authority "very judiciously." ("I'll be very careful in delivering this bottle of Vat 69 to the Pope.")

Puhleeze. Does anyone really think that a man appointed by a president who has nationalized two car companies and the entire US health system will use any power "very judiciously"? And incidentally, raise your hand if you think "very judiciously" is a tighter standard than "judiciously."

Asked in a Senate hearing to enumerate the areas in which faster rule-making authority would be helpful to the FTC, Leibowitz replied he'd have to think for a while about what the commission wanted to do with it. (Don't they have lifelines at Senate hearings?)

Can it be that the chairman of the Federal Trade Commission, who has been a commissioner at the FTC since 2004, can't name a single area where the FTC would employ a new power? It is as likely that what he plans to do with the new power would scare even this Senate. As in, "I'm not going to tell you what I plan to do with this bottle, Senator." HIC!

The long history of the FTC is a sorry one: For almost its entire history, from 1914 to 1981, it muddled and meddled, and undoubtedly caused far more harm than good to consumers, the only people it was supposed to help.

The saving grace in the period from 1981 to 1989 was that it realized that the market doesn't have to work perfectly to work better than government.

One of the FTC's charges is to prevent practices that are "unfair," a standard the Supreme Court described as "by necessity, an elusive one." It is never a good idea to have independent regulatory commissioners, goaded on by grandstanding congressmen and campaigning attorneys general, wielding power based on an elusive standard. Especially when they can't even tell you what they plan to do with their power.

For that matter, it is never a good idea to have independent commissioners. I should know: I was one. I could not be removed by the president or by Congress (except "for cause"). No one in a democracy, except a member of the judiciary, should have such a position. In the twenty-second century we may understand that regulating is a psychological disorder. Until then, we should parcel out regulatory power to unelected, unremovable, regulatory commissioners very judiciously.

Alphaomegaizing the Conservative Movement
June 1, 2010

> *"For one thing, we learned that the modern conservative movement, which dominates the modern Republican Party, has the emotional maturity of a bratty 13-year-old."*
> —Paul Krugman, New York Times, Oct. 4, 2009

> *"The 'movement'—that began 50 years ago with the founding of Bill Buckley's* National Review; *that had its coming of age in the Reagan Years; that reached its zenith with Bush's victory in 2000— is falling apart at the seams."*
> —Howard Fineman, Newsweek, Oct. 12, 2005

In his recent book, *Speech-less*, Matt Latimer, one of George W. Bush's speechwriters, reports a conversation he had with Bush while they were reviewing a speech the president was to give to CPAC, the Conservative Political Action Conference. "What is this movement you keep talking about in the speech?" the president asked him.

"Well, the conservative movement," Latimer explained. "You know, the one that started back in the sixties, when conservative groups first took root."

The president leaned forward. "Let me tell you something," he said, "I whupped Gary Bauer's ass in 2000."

Conservatives have had a lot of fun with that remark at President Bush's expense. But think about it. His father and mother didn't understand conservatism, even after serving eight years with Ronald Reagan. They distanced themselves from the Gipper as soon as they could, promising to be kinder and gentler, which turned out to be a recipe for failure.

George W. Bush is clearly an intelligent man, but not perhaps a thoughtful man, or at least not a man who thinks about political philosophy. Henry Kissinger wrote that you have to do your thinking before you come to Washington. Once in power, politics is—has to be—about the exercise of power. There isn't time to think about philosophy. George W. Bush may have become seriously interested in politics at the national level in 1980, when his father became vice president (though he had already run for the House of Representatives in 1978), but probably only in the power part, which at that point was all his father had time for. And by then, the conservative movement had ended. And apparently, among the hundreds of books Bush read in his reading marathon with Karl Rove, he never came across one about the conservative movement—perhaps proving Kissinger's point.

(Yet . . . the remarks Bush read when he honored Bill Buckley and *National Review* on its fiftieth anniversary seemed to acknowledge, implicitly, the existence of the movement. Bush said Buckley had gathered an "eclectic group of people" to write for the magazine and that it was hard to imagine that there was once a time when the only conservative game in town was Bill Buckley and *National Review*.)

"Look," Bush said to Latimer, "I know this probably sounds arrogant to say, but I redefined the Republican Party." Yes, Mr. President, you did. You redefined it right out of power because you didn't understand how it had gotten into power, because you didn't understand conservatism. Or the conservative movement.

When did the conservative movement begin? How do you tell, exactly? And does it really matter? The most plausible date is November 1955, when William F. Buckley Jr. launched *National Review*. Why then? Because the Conservative Movement—we'll dignify it now with initial caps—was a small intellectual movement, all of whose exponents could fit into a phone booth. One of its goals, of course, was to win elections. But it was mostly about ideas—ideas that were worth defending even if they did not win elections. No one really expected to win elections right away.

National Review was not the first conservative voice in postwar America. *Human Events* had been around since 1944. *The American Mercury*, which had changed hands several times since its founding by H. L. Mencken and George Jean Nathan in the 1920s, had been a conservative political journal since about 1946. And a group of classical libertarians, led by Henry Hazlitt, John Chamberlain, and Suzanne La Follette, revived Albert Jay Nock's *Freeman* in 1950. Buckley wrote occasionally for all three of them, and worked briefly as an editor at *The American Mercury.* But *National Review* had something the other journals didn't: a leader.

Bill Buckley was the only articulate, enthusiastic, combative conservative intellectual with national stature, and even that came really only after his campaign for mayor of New York City in 1965. After that race, his nationally syndicated column, "On the Right," took off, and he started his television program, "Firing Line." By then, he had already had a hand in launching conservative organizations like Young Americans for Freedom, the New York State Conservative Party, the Philadelphia Society, the Fund for American Studies, and the American Conservative Union (which, annually, brings us CPAC, Mr. President).

Buckley started making it safe to be a conservative. Before that, it was . . . not safe. It's not that it was risqué, as being parlor pink had been (eccentric, but also effete and not dangerous). It was much worse. Being a conservative was not "nice," not politically acceptable, and not socially acceptable. So conservatives tended to keep their heads down.

Buckley fixed that, with his band of conservative writers, gathered at *National Review*, sending out the encouraging words, first weekly, then fortnightly, to readers throughout the land. Eventually these writers and their younger successors were to be found at colleges and other institutions. Twenty-five years after the launching of *National Review*, being a conservative was no longer like having the plague, and Ronald Reagan, a professed conservative, a proud devotee of *National Review*, a personal friend of Bill Buckley's, was elected president—and running against an incumbent.

Conservatives were everywhere. Conservative organizations were everywhere. Conservatism was everywhere. Not everyone was a conservative, of course. But it was no longer accurate to say that conservatives were not mainstream, not nice, not acceptable. That didn't stop left-wing ideologues from saying it, of course, but they had lost their power to derogate conservatism. The battle was over. The Movement had won.

And so the Movement ended.

Now there are conservative journals galore, for the public, for students. (There are more than one hundred college newspapers in

the Collegiate Network run by the Intercollegiate Studies Institute.)
More than 100 think tanks. Radio programs. A television network.
Columnists. Speakers. Speakers' bureaus. Dating services! That's not
a movement. That's an avalanche. A tsunami. A major portion of
intellectual, political life in America.

In 2008, Eric Alterman wrote (in the *Nation*) about the early days of
the Conservative Movement: "If you look at the great thinkers of the
conservative movement, they wrote books. Not only Friedman and
Buckley but also Russell Kirk, Friedrich Hayek, Whittaker Chambers,
even Allan Bloom." That seems to be all the conservative writers he
could think of, but that's exactly the point. He could name them all.
Well, maybe not all, but the leading lights. Now there's a galaxy of
writers, and you can see, weekly, fortnightly, monthly, and quarterly,
advertisements for their books in the conservative publications.

Today, there are so many active conservative intellectuals around,
you couldn't squeeze them into all the phone booths in America.

Movements are particular crusades with limited goals. The
Oxford Movement, which started the Catholic revival in the Church
of England, began, according to John Henry Newman, one of its
participants, with John Keble's Assize Sermon on National Apostasy
in July 1833. A more or less agreed-on date for the movement's end
is 1845, when Newman converted to Rome.

One could argue when the civil rights movement in the United
States began—a plausible date is 1955, when Rosa Parks refused to
give up her seat on the bus—but there is little question when it
ended. According to Steven Hayward in volume one of *The Age of
Reagan*, a "top aide to Martin Luther King remarked in August 1965
that 'there is no more civil rights movement; President Johnson
signed it out of existence when he signed the voting rights bill.'"

Does the cause of promoting civil rights continue? Yes, of course—
though it has now de-scended to political-football status with the extension, for twenty-five years, of the
federal government's power to disapprove of state actions involving changing precinct boundaries, polling places,
legislative districts, ballot formats, and other voting procedures.

The "Conservative Movement" is also over. Conservatives
won. Conservatism is now a national intellectual, and political,
force. To speak of conservatism today as a "movement" belittles

it, marginalizes it, which is why it makes sense for liberals like Krugman and Fineman to use the term. But why would conservatives? The term sets conservatism back, back to the days when Bill Buckley had the phone booth nearly to himself. And the government-sponsored monopoly AT&T had all the phone booths to itself.

Now we've had a generation—a whole generation!—of deregulation, privatization, and tax cuts. With *New York Times* editorials frothing all the way. You never hear them complaining about Rosicrucians. And the Soviet Union is on the ash heap of history, exactly where, nine years before it got there, President Reagan predicted it would be, and where *National Review* sought to consign it when the magazine was launched in 1955.

Curiously, perhaps, the end of the movement is not signified by the number of people in the country who call themselves conservative, which is now 40 percent but in 1968 was only three points lower. What counts is the number of intellectual operations there are, because they set the tone and shape the zeitgeist (not to be confused with immanentizing the eschaton).

Are we winning all the elections? Not on your obama, we're not. But that's politics. In the intellectual world, which was where the movement began, conservatism has succeeded.

Of course there's work to be done. Young people to be taught. Old-timers refreshed. New problems addressed. As Bill Buckley said in 1964, in an address to the Conservative Party of New York State: "Modern formulations are necessary even in defense of very ancient truths. Not because of any alleged anachronism in the old ideas—the Beatitudes remain the essential statement of the Western code—but because the idiom of life is always changing, and we need to say things in such a way as to get inside the vibrations of modern life."

After the last election it became clear that we need new formulations. But we always need new formulations. We always need to rebuild. Now at least we have a foundation.

Nostalgic conservatives, seeing old age, may long for the Movement. After all, those were glory days. We were young. We had stomach for the fight. We were going to change America. And maybe the world. But the odds were long, and the money was short.

Younger conservatives (living in easier times?) may long for the fellowship of movement politics and covet the honor of its success.

The struggle, the hopes, the fears, the disappointments. And some day, dawn. Maybe. How do we prove to our fathers, and our children, that we're strong? How do we prove it to ourselves?

Perhaps you can't blame them, young or old. They see America threatened, and they want to defend their country—want to band together to serve and protect their country.

Terrific! Conservatism lives! Of course there are battles still, and unlimited battles ahead—and there always will be: but now there are warriors to match.

But the Movement—Bill Buckley's Movement, the struggle of the few, the happy few, the band of brothers—is over. It ended in 1980, when Ronald Reagan was elected president.

Here's the real test of whether the Conservative Movement still exists. To how big a crowd can you give a St. Crispin's Day speech before it stops being a St. Crispin's Day speech?

Barack Obama's Square Box

June 14, 2010

When John F. Kennedy Jr.'s plane crashed into Atlantic Ocean off the coast of Martha's Vineyard, Massachusetts, in July 1999 some observers said he had gotten himself into a "square box," meaning that he had run into the limits of his experience and his imagination.

Barack Obama is in a square box, and observers are now beginning to talk about his inevitable crash.

There was some question about JFK Jr.'s flying experience. There's no dispute about Barack Obama's executive experience: he has none. In fact, he is the least qualified person ever to be elected president.

Prior to being elected, he had done almost nothing. Certainly nothing requiring, or teaching, executive ability.

He served in some capacity as a "community organizer," which Sarah Palin might say is like running a Sunday-school picnic, but without the kids.

He worked as a civil rights attorney, whatever that means. And he taught at a law school, which may be why he always sounds as if he's lecturing to twenty-somethings.

He served in the Illinois legislature for a few yeas, but spent most of his time voting "present." Then he served in the US Senate, but for only two years.

Would the directors of any mid-sized company have asked him to be its CEO? He wouldn't even have qualified for—in Ross Perot's memorable phrase—middle management.

He is a man without significant executive experience in life.

He also seems to have little imagination. His supporters say he is tremendously brilliant. Maybe. But how do we know? Obama has never released his college or law-school grades, and, given the educational institutions he attended (Columbia University and Harvard Law School), we are entitled to assume he may have been an affirmative-action admittee. As he was to the White House.

Besides, the relationship between brains and imagination is not clear. Harvard brains are obviously not a necessary condition for a fertile imagination. President Reagan went to Eureka College. But he had the imagination—the vision—to reduce taxes and win the Cold War. He inspired America and was the most successful president of the twentieth century. (Roosevelt only won a war. Reagan won a war *and* saved the economy.)

Certainly nothing Barack Obama has done since becoming president shows much imagination. He is a complete knee-jerk liberal. Not a single action he has taken makes you say, "Wow, that was clever."

His economic policy is straight from the FDR-progressive mold. And although, like Roosevelt's, it has failed miserably (skyrocketing deficits, persistent unemployment), he lacks the imagination to try something else. Even his speeches are turning into liabilities. Exhibit A (or are we up to Exhibit Q now?): his Oval Office speech on BP, which his *friends* panned.

His foreign policy is now a Washington joke. Rude to America's friends, obsequious to her enemies, he leaves people wondering what disaster will be next. He got off to an awful start by taking the wrong side in the Honduran crisis. The good guys threw out the bad guy, and Obama backed . . . the bad guy.

It has only gotten worse. Iran seems set to get the bomb. Israel is friendless in this administration, even when it seeks to keep the bad guys out of Gaza, Israel's Cuba. In Europe he is known as "Obama the Impotent." The president of France wonders out loud if he is "weak." Obama has even dissed our best allies, the British, repealing (to the extent one man can) the long-term "special relationship." And much, much more.

Some people are suggesting that if the Republicans win big in November, Obama may make a midterm course correction, as President Clinton did. But Clinton was a man of experience. (He was also a Rhodes Scholar.) Before he became president, he had been elected governor of Arkansas, defeated for reelection, then reelected two years later. He figured out what people wanted and gave it to them. He even realized that America wanted welfare reform, although he didn't.

Clinton, George Will said, was not our worst president; but he was the worst man ever to become president. Obama is not the worst man ever to become president. But he is certainly the most incompetent—as Americans, watching this weak community organizer flail impotently against the BP oil spill, are now coming to realize.

Obama's performance will not get better, because Obama lacks the experience and the imagination to make it better. His crash now seems inevitable.

Mayday!

A Separate Peace?

June 28, 2010

At just the moment when Barack Obama, firmly at the controls of Dodo Bird One, is plummeting towards Earth, some conservatives are making a separate peace with the New Deal.

The country seems to be on the cusp of a new beginning. Anti-incumbent fever is running high. Tea Party activists are talking the language of the Founding Fathers. The incompetence of the president is noted by everyone, including his friends. There's a sense that Americans may, after all, be able to take back their government and their destiny from the progressive, liberal, big-government, anti-freedom statists.

After more than sixty years of veneration of Franklin Roosevelt's New Deal by left-wing academics, books have finally been written that challenge their version of history. In 1948, John T. Flynn wrote *The Roosevelt Myth*, but it couldn't be a bestseller in those days. So it fell more recently to Amity Shlaes, Burton Folsom Jr., and others to tell the truth about the myth of the Roosevelt years.

How perverse of history, then, to deliver the country at just this moment to a new set of Rooseveltian progressive politicians.

Maybe not. Maybe this time the progressive statists can be defeated for good. Well, never for good, but maybe for a generation.

But to do that, conservatives (the regular militia) and the Tea Party activists (the reserves) need to go back to the conservative movement's roots.

Or perhaps back to its root: William F. Buckley Jr.

Buckley, the *young* Buckley, the "enfant terrible" Buckley, started *National Review* (and the conservative movement) with a call to "stand athwart history, yelling Stop." But that wasn't all he said.

Steven Hayward has recently questioned (in the Winter issue of the *Claremont Review*) the reach of Buckley's command. "Neither Chambers nor the conservative movement as shaped by Buckley ever explicitly challenged the Left's idea of progress, or the terms in which the Left understood human advancement. . . . [R]emember the *National Review* rallying cry: to stand athwart history yelling 'Stop,' rather than grabbing hold of history and sending it in a different direction."

Hayward strikingly ignores two of the magazine's stated credenda, published in that same first issue in which the line about standing athwart history appeared. One of those was:

> The century's most blatant force of satanic utopianism is communism. We consider "coexistence" with communism neither desirable nor possible, nor honorable; we find ourselves irrevocably at war with communism and shall oppose any substitute for victory.

For thirty-four years, *National Review* spent a fortune on paper and ink fighting communism and opposing any substitute for victory. And when the fighting was over, communism was gone, and history went off in a different direction. If that isn't grabbing hold, what is?

But Buckley's rallying cry wasn't solely about standing athwart history yelling "Stop." He also wrote about those who had not "made their peace with the New Deal." How else to interpret that except as a challenge to the Left's idea of progress?

"Among our convictions," wrote the young Buckley, is that "the growth of government—the dominant social feature of this century—must be fought relentlessly. In this great social conflict of the era, we are, without reservations, on the libertarian side." And, he added, "The profound crisis of our era is, in essence, the conflict between the Social Engineers, who seek to adjust mankind to conform with scientific utopias, and the disciples of Truth, who defend the organic moral order."

Wow! No one's writing like that anymore. Today we're Norma Desmonds. We think it's the pictures that got small. We need to re-read, perhaps fortnightly, *National Review*'s opening call, and marvel at its clarity and its courage.

Hayward is correct, however, in part. Too many conservatives have made peace with the Left's idea of progress, which may be why the Tea Party activists have taken up the cause of small government.

Reviewing Lee Edwards's biography of Buckley in *National Review*, James E. Person Jr. writes: "And lest the reader come away with the understanding that Buckley held to a Pickett's Charge brand of conservatism, it is useful to remember that he believed, as Edwards notes, 'that if conservatives in politics wanted to be successful they had to steer a middle course between the ideal and the prudential.'"

Person writes, "Thus Buckley could on one occasion write, to the dismay of a few on the right, 'What conservatives are going to have to get used to is that certain fights we have waged are, quite simply, lost. It is fine, in our little seminars, to make the case against a federal Social Security program, but it pays to remind ourselves that nobody outside the walls of that classroom is going to pay much attention to our Platonic exercises.'"

Ramesh Ponnuru, reviewing William Voegeli's new book, *Never Enough: America's Limitless Welfare State* (*National Review*, May 17, 2010), writes: "Voegeli is oddly emphatic in writing that ending the welfare state should not be even a distant goal of conservatives. They will never undo the election of 1936. He is perfectly aware that almost no Republican politicians and very few conservative voters seek any such goal; that is part of why the goal is too utopian to be maintained. Perhaps a lingering suspicion that conservatives still harbor the goal impedes their political success. But what more would Voegeli have conservatives do to dispel that suspicion?"

But what is prudential in politics changes with time, and people who would be successful in politics must change also.

A question for conservatives today is, Is Buckley going to be remembered for saying that "certain fights we have waged are, quite simply, lost," or that conservatives should stand athwart history yelling "Stop" and should make no peace with the New Deal?

Of course, the New Deal was younger in 1955, when *National Review* was founded, and perhaps seemed more vulnerable. After the Lyndon Johnson years, on the other hand, it may have looked permanent.

Until now.

For the new reality is: Social Security is doomed. And probably other parts of the New Deal along with it. Buckley didn't live to see the new reality, but he had an intuition, back in 1955.

Social Security is doomed for the reason expressed by Herb Stein, chairman of the Council of Economic Advisers under Presidents Nixon and Ford: "If something cannot go on forever, it will stop."

Modern, enlightened countries, like Chile and New Zealand, have better social security systems than the United States. And there isn't any reason the United States can't move to a better system too. Indeed it will have to, because the current system cannot go on forever.

So, it turns out that we do not have to make peace with the New Deal. The New Deal was a failure. And it is time to repeal it.

If ever there was a time to stand athwart history yelling "Stop," it's now. But that's not all. We must remember that the often-quoted "yelling Stop" is synecdochic for all the other battle cries listed by the young Bill Buckley in the first issue of *National Review*.

The progressive impulse towards ever bigger government, described by Buckley as "the dominant social feature of this century," will always be with us, because it is rooted in man's desire to control his fellow man. It was the great social conflict of the era of *National Review*'s founding, and it remains so today.

It will *always* be necessary to stand athwart history. And *always* necessary to make no peace with, indeed to make war on, social engineering in whatever guise it manifests itself.

It is fashionable in certain parts to say that it is no longer possible to leave to our children a better world than the one we have lived in. Rubbish! We (and our parents) have lived for the most part in an increasingly socially engineered world, utopia bound, callous towards human freedom at best, more often contemptuous of it.

What we offer our children now is hope, at least (as the social-engineering projects begin their final crumbling), and, if we are successful, a life of freedom.

Rand Paul and Halitosis

July 12, 2010

Now—while the body of Senator (and former Exalted Cyclops) Robert Byrd (KKK–WV) is still as warm as a smoldering cross on a black family's lawn, and the memory of his record-length service in the US Congress as fresh as a clean white sheet on a Grand Imperial Wizard—now is a good time to take a cold look at the comments on the Civil Rights Act of 1964 made by Kentucky senatorial candidate Rand Paul. (See https://tinyurl.com/sybdrth.)

What is most surprising about Dr. Paul's comments is how he barely said that a private establishment should be allowed to discriminate against black patrons.

What he did say (in an eleven-minute interview with Rachel Maddow) was that he would have marched with Martin Luther King Jr. and that it was sad that the South wasn't desegregated until 120 years after transportation in Boston was desegregated. He said that there had been "incredible problems" in the South, which had to do mostly with voting, schools, and public housing; in other words, with "governmental racism" and "institutional racism." He said that that was what the Civil Rights Act largely addressed, and that he largely agreed with it. He pointed out that the Act had ten titles, and nine of them addressed institutional racism. He then asked, If you support nine out of ten things in a law but you think the tenth is misguided, do you just vote for it or do you work to modify it?

He also said, "I'm not in favor of any discrimination of any form. I would never belong to any club that excluded anybody for race." But he said we should ask the question: What about freedom of speech? Should we limit speech by people we find abhorrent? Should we prevent racists from speaking?

He said, "I don't want to be associated with those people, but I also don't want to limit their speech in any way, in the sense that we tolerate boorish and uncivilized behavior because that's one of the things freedom requires is that we allow people to be boorish and uncivilized, but that doesn't mean we approve of it."

He couldn't have been referring to former President Bill Clinton, who, in a eulogy for Senator Byrd, excused the senator's association with the Ku Klux Klan on the grounds that he was just "a country boy from the hills and hollows of West Virginia" trying "to get elected." Paul couldn't have been referring to Clinton's comment because Ex. Cy. Byrd hadn't died at the time of the Paul interview.

Then Paul has some fun at the liberals' expense: "[R]ight now . . . many gun organizations are saying they have a right to carry a gun in a public restaurant because a public restaurant is not a private restaurant. Therefore, they have a right to carry their gun in there and that the restaurant has no right to have rules to their restaurant. . . . So, you see, when you blur the distinction between public and private, there are problems."

But not for liberals, because they care as much for property rights as they do for a first edition of *The Fiery Cross*. Liberals could easily decide that there is no popular consensus that property rights are fundamental and for them popular consensus, not the Constitution, is what governs. See the recently decided gun case *McDonald v. Chicago*.

Finally, the obviously frustrated moderator Rachel Maddow says, "But I think wanting to allow private industry—private businesses— to discriminate along the basis of race because of property rights is an extreme view, and I think that's going to be the focus nationally on your candidacy now and you're going to have a lot more debates like this."

Maddow's second thought was probably correct, but it's worth noting that the statement about wanting to allow private businesses to discriminate is hers, not Paul's.

Nevertheless, the issue prompts some observations.

1. It is always useful to consider the effect any piece of legislation has on property rights (of course, it is individuals who have a right

to property, not the property that has rights). Liberals tend not to be fastidious about property rights, but conservatives, and Tea Partiers, and probably most Americans, are. Liberals tend to subordinate individual rights to the dictates of the state.

2. It is always useful to remind people that it was Republicans who made passage of the Civil Rights Act of 1964 possible. As *Time Magazine* observed (Feb. 21, 1964), "In one of the most lopsidedly Democratic Houses since the days of FDR, Republicans were vital to the passage of a bill for which the Democratic administration means to take full political credit this year." (A bottle of champagne and an autographed copy of the new book by *The American Spectator* editor Bob Tyrrell goes to the first ten readers who guess correctly how Senator Byrd voted on the bill and whether he engaged in the second longest filibuster in history, taking up 86 pages in the *Congressional Record*.) Remarkably, the Democrats are still taking credit for the Act today, at the same time that they and their Main Stream Media colleagues excoriate, on matters of race, the party that enabled it to pass. (For a superb history of the period, see Bruce Bartlett's *Wrong on Race*.)

3. It is interesting to note that black progress stopped at about the time of the Civil Rights Act. Of course, that was also when the Great Society programs were introduced. Thomas Sowell has made the point that the biggest drop in black poverty took place during the two decades *before* the Great Society which was also, of course, before the Civil Rights Act. In the 1970s, Sowell says, "When the impact of Great Society programs was fully realized, the trend of black economic improvement stopped almost entirely."

Or was it the impact of the Civil Rights Act? That may be a rude question, but to ask it requires liberals, who are feverishly trying to enact new Great Society programs, to come up with *some* explanation for why black progress stopped after the Civil Rights Act was passed. Global warming? Maybe, but back in 1964 liberals worried about global cooling. Or running out of water. Or oil. Or anchovies or something, *anything* that required the impositions of big government.

4. The useful question, for today, is not whether the Civil Rights Act should have been passed in 1964, though that is an interesting historical question, but whether, given the conditions that exist *today*, it

would be appropriate to enact it *today*. That is an interesting question and one that Dr. Paul should have mercilessly hectored the moderator with for two reasons.

First, if the Act does impinge on property rights and is not needed today because the conditions that existed in 1964 no longer exist and there are no new conditions that warrant it, then it should be repealed, because impinging on property rights for no reason is not acceptable (unless, perhaps, you're a liberal). To say it should be repealed is not to say, liberals please note, that it should not have been enacted in 1964.

Second, if, in the forty-six years since the passage of the Act, conditions have changed so little that it *is* still needed, it can plausibly be said that the Act failed, and that a different approach e.g., allowing change to happen organically, as was argued by some of the Act's opponents, might have been a more successful method of achieving the societal integration the Act was supposed to midwife.

5. Finally, there is good authority for the proposition that to every thing there is a season. A media interview during a senatorial campaign is not a good season for an honest discussion on the advisability of the passage of the Civil Rights Act. That is like a bridegroom announcing to his bride, as he carries her over the threshold, that she has halitosis. Dr. Paul probably knows that now. We will see in November if "now" was time enough.

News Quiz #3
July 16, 2010

In this contest, readers are again asked to identify the bogus news item. All four items are "reported" in similar style, from *The American Spectator News Service* (some minor details have been slightly altered). Three of them record actual events. Readers of previous quizzes have been a bit snippy in complaining about the ease of detecting the bogus item. Nevertheless, in News Quiz #2 very few people actually guessed the correct answer. Better luck this time. (And no cheating by looking on the web!) A bottle of bubbly and an autographed copy of the new book by *The American Spectator* editor Bob Tyrrell goes to the first three readers who correctly identify the bogus paragraph.

Item 1

TAS NEWS SERVICE, HORSENECK BEACH, MASS.—A few transgendered women caused a stir over Memorial Day weekend by going topless on Horseneck Beach. According to police, complaints were received after several individuals removed their tops and revealed their surgically enhanced breasts. They covered up before the police arrived, but even if they hadn't, they were doing nothing illegal, the police chief noted. Because they have male genitalia, they can't be charged with indecent exposure for showing their breasts.

Item 2

TAS NEWS SERVICE, MANCHESTER, UK—A transsexual has won a legal battle over the backdating of a pension. The sixty-eight-year-old claimant was named Robert when he was born. The claimant underwent a "gender reassignment" operation ten years ago and sought a state pension the following year, upon reaching the age of sixty, the age women are eligible for pensions.

Relying on the Recognition of Gender Act 2004, which requires married transsexuals to divorce before the government will recognize their newly acquired gender, the government pensions minister ruled in January 2008 that the claimant was allowed to receive a pension only from the male retirement age of 65. But the couple, who had been married for thirty years, did not wish to divorce.

The government declared that under the Act the claimant was not entitled to be recognized as female while still married to his wife, because one woman could not be married to another.

The groundbreaking decision from the Lord Justices, however, found that the pensions minister was wrong to treat the claimant as a man for state pension purposes, and that the denial was in breach of the claimant's human rights.

Item 3

TAS NEWS SERVICE, WASHINGTON, DC—Following complaints by high-school students and college-age adults that the free Durex condoms offered by the city are not big enough and not of good enough quality, DC officials have decided to start distributing Trojan condoms, including the company's super-size Magnum variety.

"If people get what they don't want, they are just going to trash them," said University of the District of Columbia student T. Squalls.

"We thought making condoms available was a good thing, but we never asked the kids what they wanted," said DC Council member David A. Catania, apologetically.

Officials have also begun to authorize teachers or counselors, preferably male, to distribute condoms after they have completed a thirty-minute online training course called "WrapMC"—for Master of Condoms.

The city, which has six hundred thousand residents, expects to hand out more than four million condoms this year, an average of more than six per person.

"We want to support the regularization of condom use city-wide," said Shannon L. Hader, director of the city's HIV/AIDS Administration. "We are promoting this idea that using condoms is healthy . . . to try to destigmatize condom use."

Durex condoms cost the city 5.7 cents each, but the Trojans will cost six to nine cents each (depending, of course, on size).

Item 4

TAS NEWS SERVICE, ROCHESTER, NY—Charges have been dropped against a forty-three-year-old gym teacher, Louis Andrews, who was accused of incest, a Class E felony in New York. Subsequently, Monica Andrews, his daughter, bore a child and claimed Andrews was the father. Because the alleged event occurred one week after Monica's eighteenth birthday, Andrews was not also charged with having sex with a minor, police said.

During the course of the paternity suit brought by Monica to prove that Andrews was the father of her child, Andrews's attorney's wife, Joan Tyler, a gynecologist, while discussing the case with her husband, made an interesting discovery. Andrews's blood type is A. The blood type of Andrews's wife, Sharon, is B. The baby's blood type is A, but the blood type of the baby's eighteen-year-old mother is O.

Fans of detective fiction will quickly spot the problem: Monica could not possibly be the child of Louis Andrews, because a child must inherit his or her blood type (A, B, AB, or O) from the mother or the father. Thus, if a child's blood type differs from the type of both the mother and the man alleged to be the father, the man could not possibly be the father of the child.

Sharon Andrews, upon being confronted with the impossibility of Andrews's being Monica's father, confessed to having had an affair that resulted in the birth of Monica.

News Quiz #3 Report Card
July 30, 2010

In Quiz #3, contestants were asked to identify the bogus paragraph. Although takers of earlier quizzes complained that they were too easy, they would have done better to study harder. In order to give a passing grade to a decent number of the takers of Quiz #2, it had to be graded on a curve so steep it looked like an excuse, about something, from the Obama administration.

Quiz #3 was a bit livelier in content, and had more takers. The first three to identify the bogus paragraph were, interestingly, the first three to hand in their papers: MoneyMatters, Monty.Crisco, and Bill Lannon, though MoneyMatters had read the story about the students' complaining about substandard condoms, which takes a little luster off his success. They will each get a bottle of bubbly and an autographed copy of Bob Tyrrell's new book—but only if they send us their real names and addresses.

Jameson Campaigne guessed item #3 because, he said, "The rest read like daily dispatches from the *New York Times*, so they must be true." That's exactly the point, of course, as R. Martin noted: "You've made your point: when it comes to government behavior it's hard to distinguish believable from unbelievable."

Maddox made a similar comment: "I say they are all true because the world we now live in is absolutely crazy! None of theses stories are more absurd than what we read every day about actions taken by our dear leader and his crowd of crooks." Just so, Maddox.

Bill agreed that "all of the stories are entirely plausible" and he agreed with Eric Cartman that the transgendered bikini-wearers wouldn't have put their tops back just because the cops showed up. Excellent point! In Washington it's always the cover-up that gets you into trouble. And for the record, it was Rehoboth Beach in Delaware, not Horseneck Beach in Massachusetts.

Ray thought item #2 was bogus, arguing that "two different mandatory retirement ages based on gender? Yeah right, and I have some oceanfront property for sale in Arizona."

Yeah, right. You can't make this stuff up because some government crazy has beaten you to it.

Ray was joined in his guess by pump shoes who said he (she?) was going with number 2, "because, even in the UK, I doubt there is a Recognition of Gender Act." Ah, but there is, pump shoes, though it is actually called the Gender Recognition Act.

But then Ray handed in a second blue book: "I've Chengdu my mind, it's the INTRO that's bogus! Here's what tipped me off: 'A bottle of bubbly and an autographed copy of the new book by *The American Spectator* editor Bob Tyrrell goes to the first three readers who correctly identify the bogus paragraph.' Well, there's your bogus paragraph. A bottle of 'bubbly,' as if!"

C'mon Ray, don't be such a cynic. The champagne will be on the way to the winners as soon as we get their addresses. But, you, for your doubting, will have to be the very first with the correct answer next time in order to get the bubbly. Second place will get you exactly what you think the winners of Quiz #3 are getting.

And for all the paternity lawyers, congratulations on spotting the flaw in the bogus paragraph.

Well, that's the recap. Thanks for participating.

Oh, and please note: all participants, indeed all readers, are invited to send in genuine news items for future quizzes. Anyone whose item is used in a quiz will get an autographed copy of Bob Tyrrell's new book (or, if they prefer, one of his previous books)— except Ray, who will have to send in two items.

Corn vs. Coronary Bypass Surgery

July 25, 2010

It is argued here and there that President Obama is not a social-ist. But with the incredible recess appointment last week of Dr. Ronald Werrbick to head the newly created American Center for All-American Food Excellence ("American CAFÉ"), the charge of socialism is becoming difficult to refute. Dr. Werrbick will direct an agency that oversees all food production and distribution in the United States. Even though the food industry may account for a slightly smaller portion of US GDP than health care, it is arguably far more important.

Half the population spends little or nothing on health care, while 5 percent spends almost half the total amount. Food, on the other hand—and obviously—is a requirement of all people, at all times.

Werrbick is clearly a socialist, and it is fair to assume that Obama thinks Werrbick's views match his own. Why else appoint him? And why else take over two of the three automobile companies, and take effective control of the banking industry? If that isn't socialism, what is?

Because the president's recess appointment will deprive the American people of the chance to learn of Werrbick's views through Senate confirmation hearings, it is worth taking a close look at what Werrbick has said about food policy. The following are excerpts from speeches and articles by Dr. Werrbick over the last few years.

"I cannot believe that the individual food consumer can enforce through choice the proper configurations of a system as massive and complex as food. That is for leaders to do."

"You cap your food budget, and you make the political and eco-nomic choices you need to make to keep affordability within reach."

"Please don't put your faith in market forces. It's a popular idea: that Adam Smith's invisible hand would do a better job of designing food policy than leaders with plans can."

"Indeed, the Holy Grail of good food for all in the United States may remain out of reach unless, through rational collective action over-riding some individual self-interest, we can reduce per capita costs."

"A progressive policy regime will control and rationalize financing—control supply."

"The unaided human mind, and the acts of the individual, cannot assure excellence. Food production and distribution is a system, and its performance is a systemic property."

"Food is a common good. We need to move toward a single payer, speaking and buying for the common good."

"For-profit, entrepreneurial providers of fruits, vegetables, meat, and dairy products, for example, may find their business opportunities constrained."

"I would place a commitment to excellence—standardization to the best known method—above production and distribution autonomy as a rule for food."

"Food production and distribution has taken a century to learn how badly we need the best of Frederick Taylor [the father of scientific management]. If we can't standardize appropriate parts of our processes to absolute reliability, we cannot approach perfection."

Wow! Head for the hills.

Actually—and fortunately—there is no American Center for All-American Food Excellence, and there is no Dr. Ronald Werrbick. I made them both up.

But there is a Dr. Donald Berwick, who has just received a recess appointment to the Centers for Medicare and Medicaid Services (CMS), an agency that has a bigger budget than the Pentagon. Berwick's decisions at the CMS will shape American medicine the way "Dr. Werrbick" would have been able to shape the American food industry.

The quotes from "Dr. Werrbick" were actually excerpts from articles and speeches by the real-life Dr. Berwick, with appropriate substitution of food terms for health-care terms. The original quotes can be found in Daniel Henninger's must-read piece in the *Wall Street Journal*, http://online.wsj.com/article/SB10001424052748703792704575367020548324914.html.

What is striking about the quotes from "Dr. Werrbick" is how much more outrageous they sound when applied to the food industry than to the health-care industry. That is, in part, because our philosopher-king guardians have encouraged us for years to think socialistically about health care, but not yet about other industries, like food production and distribution.

But if our guardians succeed in socializing medicine, who can think they will not try to socialize the food industry, which, it can be easily argued, is far more important than health care? After all, which is more often more important to more people: corn or coronary bypass surgery?

Is Obama a serious socialist? Of course he is, as the term is broadly used these days. What still gives cause for encouragement is the fervid denials. This administration, however socialist it is, knows that the American people are not socialist, and knows also that "socialist" is a dirty word in American politics.

Risking a confirmation fight in the US Senate over a committed socialist like Dr. Berwick is something only a capitalist would do. That is why President Obama, no capitalist he, slipped the socialist Berwick in by a recess appointment.

Mau-Mauing the Free Press
August 3, 2010

Lee Bollinger, president of Columbia University, host to Iranian President Mahmoud Ahmadinejad, and newly appointed head of the New York Federal Reserve Bank, says government should get into the business of subsidizing journalism. Like other Obama appointees, he says he is concerned that, with the changes in the financial structure of journalism, Americans might be deprived "of the essential information they need as citizens."

It's not difficult to imagine that one of those "needs" would be a more "balanced" view of President Obama. Can anyone doubt that an administration that was willing to Madoff General Motors' bondholders in favor of its own union supporters would not exercise maximum bias in subsidizing the press? Mr. Bollinger, practicing the glib and oily art to speak and purpose not, is a harbinger of Venezuelan-style gangster journalism.

Bollinger writes, "American journalism is not just the product of the free market, but of a hybrid system of private enterprise and public support." It is?

"In the 1960s," he writes, "our network of public broadcasting was launched with direct public grants and a mission to produce high quality journalism free of government propaganda or censorship."

Is there anyone in the room who thinks NPR (National Public Radio, supported by the US government) is not an organ of the liberal intelligentsia?

Is there anyone who does not understand why liberals agitate for the return of the "Fairness Doctrine"? That's the government regulation that used to require radio and television stations to broadcast as much liberal programming as conservative programming.

The problem for liberals was, and is, that liberal programming is not popular, which is why a liberal radio station, Air America, couldn't survive in the broadcast marketplace. Conservative talk radio, on the other hand, is hugely popular. Whatever the effect of the Fairness Doctrine when it was first promulgated in 1949, the point of reinstituting it now would be to hobble conservative radio. Because stations would have to broadcast as much unpopular (i.e., money-losing) liberal programming as popular (i.e., money-making) conservative programming, it would make sense not to broadcast either kind, and to use the time instead to broadcast popular programs that had no ideological content. *Everyone*, roughly speaking, knows that. The Fairness Doctrine was—and may be again—an example of brazen government manipulation of the media.

Who can think it would be any different if the ideas of people like Lee Bollinger were put into effect to subsidize print journalism?

Bollinger writes: "There are examples of other institutions in the US where state support does not translate into official control. The most compelling are our public universities and our federal programs for dispensing billions of dollars annually for research."

We must hope this man Bollinger is only naïve. When I was general counsel of the Department of Education in the early '80s, we sought to have an open competition for the awarding of millions of dollars to organizations that did research on educational issues. When Congress found out about the proposed competition, it blocked it, and required the department to continue to fund the organizations that had been awarded grants by the Carter administration. In other words, the point of the program was not research. It was payola, to favored constituents. Is it really possible that a university president doesn't understand that?

Government financing without government influence? It can't be done. Who decides which organizations get the money? What are the odds Bollinger and his colleagues would have financed William F. Buckley Jr.'s upstart magazine, *National Review* (described by George Will as "the most consequential journal of opinion *ever*") or its modern-day equivalent? About the same as finding a chaste maid in Cheapside.

Bollinger writes: "Trusting the market alone to provide all the news coverage we need would mean venturing into the unknown—a risky proposition with a vital public institution hanging in the balance." Come again?

It would be comforting to say that this is the most extraordinary statement from a government official we have seen in a generation.

Alas, it is not so. Dr. Donald Berwick, who, in a recess appointment, has just been made head of the Centers for Medicare and Medicaid Services, has said things just as extraordinary. Daniel Henninger collected a great swatch of them in a piece for the *Wall Street Journal*, which I referred to in my own piece on Berwick.

Said Dr. Berwick: "I cannot believe that the individual health care consumer can enforce through choice the proper configurations of a system as massive and complex as health care. That is for leaders to do."

And: "Please don't put your faith in market forces. It's a popular idea: that Adam Smith's invisible hand would do a better job of designing [health] care than leaders with plans can."

And this: "A progressive policy regime will control and rationalize financing—control supply."

There are many more Berwick quotes—Henninger's piece is one of the most important to be published this year—and they clearly demonstrate the mindset of this administration and its cronies, and, no doubt, of the experts who would be involved in "designing" journalism for the American people.

Berwick, of course, is talking about health care, which is important: it is one-sixth of the US economy. But is it as important as *journalism*? Surely not. Journalism is what permits a democracy to function in any polity larger than a village. That's why the Founding Fathers included freedom of the press in the First Amendment.

All the more reason, then—for socialists like Berwick and Bollinger and Obama—to have government finance the press. That will enable the leaders of a progressive policy regime to design the proper configuration of the free-press system, which a free market has failed to do.

Besides, putting government in charge of the press may be the only way to get Obama's popularity numbers up.

On the other hand, that hasn't worked for Hugo Chávez in Venezuela.

America the Generous
August 15, 2010

Forty billionaires have just pledged to give away at least half their wealth to charity, concerning which a few observations.

Scripture says it is easier for a camel to pass through the eye of a needle than for a rich man to enter the kingdom of Heaven (capitalized because, as Ralph de Toledano pointed out, it's a place—you know, like Scarsdale). We could note in passing, but will not, that there is no suggestion that a rich woman would be similarly challenged.

Viewed from Scripture's vantage point, the forty billionaires may simply be taking the necessary steps to make the needle's eye larger or the camel (and their riches) smaller.

Is it fair—is it accurate—to say that these people who are giving away billions are being generous?

During the 1968 presidential campaign, William F. Buckley Jr. remarked that the Democratic candidate, Hubert Humphrey, had already promised the American people everything and that, since beyond everything there is only nothing, Humphrey was now promising the people exactly: nothing.

There's a bit of that here too. If we assume that even half a billion dollars is more than enough to live on, indeed more than enough to satisfy the dreams of avarice, then any additional wealth can mean nothing to him that possesses it; in which case what these generous people are giving away is also: nothing.

At least nothing that means anything to them. Which again raises the question: What is generosity?

But perhaps that's just being churlish. How *is* a rich man supposed to be generous? What *can* he do? Is it *possible* for him to sacrifice? Perhaps it is best just to understand that that's his business.

There are other miscellaneous points. One of them is that the donors will get tax deductions for their gifts, the meaning of which is unclear since they have so much money that taxes have no impact on their lives—which, not incidentally, tends to diminish their resistance to high taxes, which is not good for the rest of us.

Another point is that it is almost certain that the country would be better served if these billionaires kept their money and continued to invest it. Investing is an activity at which they have proved to be exceptionally skilled, and their investments would be far more likely to produce jobs and products—real benefits—than anything any charitable institution could possibly do with the funds.

A third point is the curious collectivity of the operation. Why did they get together to make a joint announcement? Why not just make their decisions in the privacy of their privy chambers? Were they looking for glory (which would suggest that having billions is not satisfying), or setting an example (for whom?)?

There is at least one potential significant benefit of the gifts: the funds will be deployed by private people, not government, which would surely waste it. But this is only a potential benefit: most of the donors are liberals, and it is possible, even likely—perhaps certain— that the money will go to the usual left-wing causes. With good luck, it will be wholly wasted; with bad luck it will do significant damage to limited constitutional government (the only real hope of the poor). The relevance of either scenario to generosity being—what?

Still, the gifts do focus on one aspect of modern democratic life that the big-government types like to avoid. The donors are private people who will be fulfilling their *own* obligations to the poor.

It is part of liberal dogma that "we must look after the poor," by which, of course, liberal politicians mean they will take our money by force and deploy it in ways they see fit.

Joe Biden, Exhibit A, spoke in 1988 of "changing the attitude of Americans about what their responsibilities are to the poor, about what their responsibilities are to other people."

What is this man talking about? Americans are an exceedingly generous people, as has been amply documented by Arthur Brooks in his book *Gross National Happiness* and in a piece he wrote for the American Enterprise Institute, of which he is the president.

Here are some of the points he made:

- "In 2006, Americans gave about $295 billion to charity."
- "Charitable giving has generally risen faster than the growth of the American economy for more than half a century."
- "Most estimates place the percentage of American households that make monetary contributions each year at 70 to 80 percent, and the average American household contributes more than $1,000 annually."
- "About a third of individual gifts go toward sacramental activities, primarily supporting houses of worship. The rest goes to secular activities, such as education, health, and social welfare."
- "No developed country approaches American giving. For example, in 1995 (the most recent year for which data are available), Americans gave, per capita, three and a half times as much to causes and charities as the French, seven times as much as the Germans, and 14 times as much as the Italians."
- "Tax deductibility is actually irrelevant for most people. IRS records show that only about a third of people who file tax returns itemize their deductions."
- "When we measure monetary giving as a percentage of income in order to ascertain the level of one's 'sacrifice,' we find a surprising result: it is low-income working families that are the most generous group in America, giving away about 4.5 percent of their income on average. This compares to about 2.5 percent among the middle class, and 3 percent among high-income families."
- "Self-described 'conservatives' in America are more likely to give—and give more money—than self-described 'liberals.'" (Isn't that delicious!?)

It is apparent that Americans have not needed the example of billionaires to teach them how to be generous.

If we think there are questions about the generosity of billionaires' giving away their own money, what are we to make of politicians giving away *our* money?

The question becomes increasingly urgent as the ability of government to spend money diminishes relative to the budgets of the faux-eleemosynary programs the politicians concoct.

It is not possible to count quickly the government programs that give money to the poor; they are, roughly speaking, innumerable: food stamps; children's health insurance; the Women, Infants, and Children Program; college student aid; Temporary Assistance for Needy Families; federal foster care; et cetera; et cetera; et cetera.

What we have discovered is that it is as difficult to stop the politicians from taking money from the productive sector and giving it to the nonproductive sector—in the name of charity—as it is for a camel to pass through the eye of a needle. That is becoming, or has become, the central problem of our time.

Of course, "in the name of charity" (or any similar formulation, such as meeting one's "responsibilities to the poor") is congressional nonsense. The recipients of federal grants can be charities, but the taxpayers aren't being charitable because they are acting under coercion; and Congress isn't being charitable because the funds don't belong to Congress.

If the acts of the forty billionaires serve to remind us of the inescapably individual nature of charity, their gifts will be worth trillions, and our debt to them inestimable.

A Review of *Signature in the Cell: DNA and the Evidence for Intelligent Design* by Stephen C. Meyer
December 1, 2010

Signature in the Cell is a wonderful read, particularly at Christmas, and while you read you hear the cracking of the liberals' icy-cold objection to allowing God in the public square.

Stephen Meyer makes a compelling case that life did not come into being because of random collisions of atoms in the prebiotic soup, but rather because an intelligent designer—an intelligence or "mind"—created it.

A few quick points, in an attempt to give a flavor of Meyer's five hundred pages of argument:

First: Meyer says the "odds of getting even one functional protein of modest length (150 amino acids) by chance from a prebiotic soup is no better than 1 chance in 10^{164}" (p 212). That's 10 with 164 zeros after it. Then Meyer says the probability of producing "all the necessary proteins needed to service a minimally complex cell" is 1 in $10^{41,000}$ (p 213). That seems like a very small chance—indeed, the argument sounds conclusive. But wait a minute: didn't those proteins have a long, long time, a billion years in fact, to play the odds? Yes, but . . .

What are the odds of flipping a coin ten times and having it come up heads every time? Small: $(1/2)^{10}$, or one out of 1,024. But suppose you were to do ten flips ten thousand times? Well, that makes it more likely you could get at least one series of ten heads in a row. Meyer calls those ten thousand flip-units the "probabilistic resources."

So one question is, what were the probabilistic resources for the proteins? How much time, how much opportunity, was available for their development? Meyer computes the answer at 10^{139}. Or rather, *only* 10^{139}, the point being that the probabilistic resources were *magnitudes* below the odds (1 in 10^{164} or 1 in $10^{41,000}$) of development by chance.

Second: Suppose you buy a roulette wheel and start spinning it in your living room and the ball, improbably, lands in 16 red ten times in a row. What do you conclude? You conclude the wheel is defective. You examine it and you discover a flaw, a nick or a ridge or some other imperfection, that causes the ball to land in the same slot every time.

But suppose you're a croupier at a casino and one of the players, Tim Geithner, say, bets on 16 red and the ball, also improbably, lands on 16 red ten times in a row. Now what do you conclude? You conclude, HE'S CHEATING! (Of course, readers of this magazine knew that already.) The improbability of ten 16 reds is no greater than it was in your living room, but the conclusion is different because there's an intelligent consequence, a functional significance, to the ball's equally improbable behavior: Geithner wins money. (IRS please note.)

But the development of life isn't actually like roulette. In roulette, the ball has to land somewhere. But DNA, which is actually an information package, didn't have to develop into a package that conveyed any useful information at all. Its development was more like scattering Scrabble letters on the floor. You could scatter all day and it is not inevitable that they would form even multi-letter words, much less a sentence like, "In the beginning was the Word," a sentence that contains information and conveys meaning. And if the Scrabble letters did form a sentence, you would fall down in surprise (with practice, landing on your knees) and say, "Somebody did that!"

That somebody is the intelligent designer, by whatever name you choose to call him, her, or it.

There is much, much more to *Signature in the Cell*. But here's the real significance of Meyer's book and the argument for intelligent design. Charles Murray argued in his 2009 AEI lecture that in the next two decades or so, science, specifically the findings of the neuroscientists and the geneticists, will shatter the two central myths of liberalism, which Murray labels "the equality premise" (when different groups achieve different results in life it's because of bad human behavior and an unfair society) and "the New Man premise"("human beings are malleable through the right government interventions").

Likewise, the argument—the argument from *science*—for intelligent design will cripple the liberals' ability to deny the role of intelligent design. You can call that intelligent designer God if you choose, but you don't have to. But if it's okay to conclude, through science, that "god" exists, it will be okay to teach it in the public schools. And if it's okay to allow a scientific god into the schools, it won't make much sense to exclude a religious god. From the schools or from the public square.

The liberals' interpretation of the First Amendment, which never made any sense, will become implausible. God will return to the public square, in Scarsdale, in 90210, and in your town as well. And, Deo gratias, to a Supreme Court near you. Merry Christmas.

Note to reader: In his review (in TAS September 2009) Dan Peterson uses the figure 1 in 10^{74} as the probability of a protein's developing "by chance." But as I read Meyer, he puts the probability of development by chance at 1 in 10^{164} for one protein and 1 in $10^{41,000}$ for "all the necessary proteins needed to service a minimally complex cell."

As important, when I read Peterson's review, I didn't think he explained Meyer's point about "probabilistic resources" adequately—and that was *one of the reasons I read the book myself. Peterson mentions a billion years as the time available to the proteins for developing. But without knowing how long it takes a protein to develop, we have no way of knowing whether a billion years is a long time or a short time, a lot of opportunity or a little opportunity. A billion years, after all, is a gazillion nano-seconds (and two gazillion demi-nano-seconds). If a gazillion turns out to be $10^{1,000,000}$ then there's plenty of "time" (opportunity) for a protein to develop if it can develop in a nano-second. Meyer addresses that issue by saying that the probabilistic resources are only 10^{139}, and it is that information that is needed to make the case against random development convincing.*

That's one of the reasons I wrote this piece. And also to make the point that parallels Charles Murray's point.

Reading the Constitution
January 12, 2011

The formal reading of the Constitution in the House of Representatives is one of those events that bring a knowing smile to the face of sophisticated liberals, the sort of people who curl up next to an eco-friendly fire on Sunday morning with their hard-copy *New York Times Book Review* while their partner reads the *New York Review of Books* and most Americans are taking their children to church clinging to their Bibles and (if they're lucky enough to live in the right state) their guns too, though ammunition was in short supply last autumn.

The *New York Times* called the exercise an "empty gesture." Rep. Jerrold Nadler (D–NY) called it a "ritualistic reading" and said that it was "total nonsense."

Those and other sophisticates are the heirs of Woodrow Wilson, who once compared the Constitution to "political witchcraft." "Living political constitutions," Wilson wrote, "must be Darwinian in structure and in practice." For Wilson, the Constitution was "one thing in one age, another in another."

The Constitution as Darwinian is the essence of the progressives' position on constitutional government, which is why they find the public reading so . . . quaint.

But the reading may focus the nation's attention on an astounding fact: we actually have a constitution, and it has or had a purpose.

And not only do we have a constitution. We also have a Constitution Day.

Constitution Day (September 17) is actually an official federal holiday, though it is not observed by granting time off from work for federal employees which is a shame because the less they do the freer we are, or as Milton Friedman used to put it, we should be glad we don't get all the government we pay for. The act creating Constitution Day requires each educational institution receiving federal funds, which is, roughly speaking, 99.99 percent of them (though some put the figure at 99.999 percent), to hold an educational program on the United States Constitution for its students on that day, and it might be useful for one of the incoming Tea Partiers to ask Arne Duncan, the secretary of Education, how rigorously his department monitors the faithfulness of the 99.99 percent, and, as the followup question, why the department hasn't been more rigorous in enforcing the law's requirement, assuming that its current level of enforcement is above the level of rigor mortis, but only for the purpose of embarrassing the feds and not with the intention of having them further impose their own considerable incompetence on the grantees.

Of course, not all liberals abjure the Constitution. The American Civil Liberties Union, calling itself the "nation's guardian of liberty," says it works "daily" to defend and preserve the individual rights and liberties that the Constitution guarantees, notwithstanding that the first issue the ACLU lists on its website is the death penalty, which, even though specifically referred to in the Constitution, the ACLU seeks to abolish.

Still, the ACLU's position on the rights of the accused has not been wholly mistaken and should be considered carefully by those who believe in limited government, which includes most of those cheering the reading of the Constitution in the House of Representatives.

The point of the constitutional protections for people who have been accused by the state is to make sure that the state proves its case. And if it can't, then the accused goes free even if she's guilty. The reason is that the Framers, like the Tea Partiers, feared government and its power more than they feared random lawbreakers. The state is a far larger threat to our liberties than any mere criminal could possibly be. That is a point conservatives need to remember. (Of course, that is not true of terrorists: they do threaten us every bit as much as the unrestrained state, which is why we treat them as enemy combatants, not as mere criminals, and don't accord them the same constitutional protections.)

So, as the Tea Partiers and the liberals line up to trade punches, they should each pay attention to their opponents' positions. In the field of criminal law, liberals, like conservatives, do value limits on state power after all.

The *New York Times* also said last week: "The new House leadership says this [reading] is necessary because the health care law and other measures that Republicans do not like have veered from the Constitution. But it is the judiciary that ultimately decides when a law is unconstitutional, not the transitory occupant of the speaker's chair."

Yes, but: The Supreme Court may have the *last* word on what is constitutional, but Congress has the *first* word, which means that if it pays attention it may greatly limit the scope of the judiciary, which may cause distress over at the *New York Times* and among the sophisticated liberals with the knowing smiles, but even good public policy has a price.

All That Gold
January 24, 2011

As Republican politicians look frantically for ways to solve the country's financial problems, they should not overlook the mountain of gold towering before them. That mountain is the accumulation of federal regulations that now occupies more than 82,000 pages in the Federal Register.

No one knows for sure what the cost of all those regulations is, but it is probably at least $1.75 trillion, or 14 percent of US national income. By comparison, the income-tax burden is about $2.3 trillion.

The current Congress is not likely to be successful in repealing much of anything, given the veto power of the liberal progressive in the White House. But the House of Representatives could at least set the stage for massive repealing in preparation for the Republicans' taking control of the government in 2012.

High on the list of regulations that should be repealed is the Occupational Safety and Health Act (OSHA), enacted in 1970 with, alas, President Richard Nixon's enthusiastic support. OSHA was just one reason, and a good one, why conservatives suspended their support of Nixon—until Watergate.

The mandate of OSHA is to protect workers from job-related injuries and illnesses. Its regulating is fanatically intrusive, and is estimated to cost around $65 billion a year. Its existence is justified in the literature with phrases like, "Since the 1970 enactment of OSHA, workplace injuries are sharply down." Yes, and since the 1970 enactment the tides have been going in and out too.

In fact, despite all that oppressive regulating, the record indicates, remarkably, that OSHA has had no effect at all. A graph published by the Cato Institute shows that the decline in workplace fatalities was steady over a sixty-year period that began long before OSHA was created. Looking at the graph, it is impossible to point to the moment when OSHA commenced its massive meddling. The graph of non-fatal workplace injuries, on the other hand, is almost flat, also indicating that OSHA has made no difference.

What the science shows, therefore, is that OSHA has been completely ineffective. But who cares about science?

In theory, this administration cares about science. On March 9, 2009, President Obama signed an executive order that said, "Science and the scientific process must inform and guide decisions of my Administration on a wide range of issues, including improvement of public health. . . ."

But in practice, this administration has already indicated it doesn't care the square root of π about science—which is certainly taking a back seat when it comes to regulations put out by the Department of Transportation.

As reported by Holman W. Jenkins Jr. in the *Wall Street Journal*, Ray LaHood, the secretary of Transportation, is on a campaign against "distracted driving" caused by cell-phone use, which he labels an "epidemic."

But there are problems with Secretary LaHood's campaign, especially in an administration that says it wants to restore scientific integrity to government decisionmaking.

What does science tell us about using cell phones while driving?

The Insurance Institute for Highway Safety reported that a study by researchers at its affiliate, the Highway Loss Data Institute (HLDI), found no reductions in crashes after laws that ban texting by drivers took effect. A previous HLDI study had found no reductions in crashes after bans on handheld phones had taken effect. In fact, crashes increased in three states after texting bans were imposed. No one knows why yet, but one theory is that drivers' attempts to be clandestine in using their phones may cause accidents.

Secretary LaHood, a man undistracted by science, should be exquisitely tortured in the appropriate congressional hearing. But his campaign is a mere Pinto, or Lada, compared to the war waged on business by the Occupational Safety and Health Administration.

Is there any indication that bureaucrats are capable of learning from science? Very little. In 2009, the District of Columbia cancelled safety inspections of automobiles, having discovered that states that did not require inspections did not have higher accident rates than states that did. A 2005 report by the District's Department of Motor Vehicles "clearly showed there was not a positive effect of safety inspections on traffic safety" in the city.

Lest you start having fuzzywarm thoughts about DC bureaucrats and think they were concerned about the inconvenience that inspections caused the citizens of the city, you should know that the District discovered it could save $400,000 a year by cancelling the inspections—raising the question: If the city fathers knew in 2005 that there was no benefit from the inspection program, why did they wait until 2009 to cancel it? But we digress.

Or do we? Like the DC inspection program, OSHA has not done what it was supposed to do, and instead of $400,000 a year, it has cost billions. It should be abolished now. Why wait?

Abolishing OSHA is an idea whose time must be advanced. It would have tremendous support from the business community, especially small businesses, for which the epidemic of regulations the country has been suffering for the last half-century are a far greater burden than they are for big businesses.

The Republican House should start laying the groundwork immediately. It could appoint a commission (a Team B?) to study regulations—en masse, not just OSHA—and recommend wholesale repeal. The commission should consist of people from the think tanks, who would not be beholden to any pressure groups. They would assist the House in holding the necessary hearings, now, to prepare for wholesale reform later. They could move quickly because much of the research has already been done.

All that gold. The mountain towers. And waits.

State of the Union: Probably as Bad as Obama's Speech

January 27, 2011

Even President Obama's own cheering squad thinks he flubbed the State of the Union speech, which they find all the more amazing after his performance in Arizona. The country faces a single serious problem (and many lesser ones, of course), but the president failed to address it seriously.

Barack Obama's State of the Union address had some of the familiar features: the emphasized antithesis: "What comes of this moment will be determined not by whether we can sit together tonight, but whether we can work together tomorrow."

And the ritual dishonesties: "Thanks to the tax cuts we passed . . ."—what do you mean "we," Kemosabe?—". . . and these steps, taken by Democrats and Republicans. . . ." Yes, but how many Democrats had to hit their drug of choice before voting to maintain the Bush tax cuts?

There was the ridiculous simile about the airplane without an engine: "Cutting the deficit by gutting our investments in innovation and education is like lightening an overloaded airplane by removing its engine. It may make you feel like you're flying high at first, but it won't take long before you feel the impact."

Similes have to work to be effective. How do you "feel like you're flying high at first" in an airplane that has no engine? How did it take off? Was it launched from the White House lawn with a giant rubber band made from domestically grown rubber trees stretched by ten thousand illegal but unionized immigrants who went to the DC public schools that President and Mrs. Obama won't send their own children to?

Then there was the nod to the stimulus: "So over the last two years, we've begun rebuilding for the twenty-first century, a project that has meant thousands of good jobs for the hard-hit construction industry." Except that even the president has confessed that the shovel-ready jobs were an illusion.

But there was more wrong with the speech than the president's rhetorical clumsiness and dishonesty. There are substantive issues that should trouble us. The president said: "[Students] come here from abroad to study in our colleges and universities. But as soon as they obtain advanced degrees, we send them back home to compete against us. It makes no sense."

The president may be right about that, but not for reasons he would give. He was linking foreign students, here on F-1 and M-1 visas, with the children of illegal immigrants. He was stealing a base in order to promote amnesty.

The real question is, Why do we have a student-visa program? Foreign students receive a high percentage of the doctorates awarded every year in the physical sciences and in engineering, and we should ask what the US gets out of it. According to George J. Borjas, the Robert W. Scrivner Professor of Economics and Social Policy at the Kennedy School of Government, a large percentage of all permanent-residence visas granted to foreign students "have nothing to do with 'exceptional skills' or 'high job demand,' but are granted because of family connections."

So the real question is not, Why do we send them home, but Why do we let them come in the first place, if it's not the best ones who stay?

On foreign trade, the president said, "To help businesses sell more products abroad, we set a goal of doubling our exports by 2014—because the more we export, the more jobs we create here at home." True, but then he said, "Now, before I took office, I made it clear that we would enforce our trade agreements, and that I would only sign deals that keep faith with American workers and promote American jobs."

What he is really saying is that we will limit imports that threaten American jobs—what else could "keep faith with American work-ers" mean? The problem is that exports are related to imports. In Econ 101 you study charts that show imports and exports moving up and down together. It's not difficult to understand why: the majority of US imports are used by domestic firms as intermediate goods in their production, some of which is then exported. Cut off imports, and you cut off exports.

Here's a doozie: "We are living with a legacy of deficit spending that began almost a decade ago. And in the wake of the financial crisis, some of that was necessary to keep credit flowing, save jobs, and put money in people's pockets."

To say that only "some of that was necessary" is an obvious slap at President Bush for having gotten the country engaged in the Iraq War—the bad war, as opposed to Obama's good war in Afghanistan.

There are two problems. First, the numbers don't support Obama's claim. From 2003 through 2008, the Iraq War cost $554 billion (by comparison, federal spending on education during that same time was $574 billion). The deficit for the period 2003 through 2010 was about $4.3 trillion.

Second, President Obama himself took credit for a successful conclusion to the war in Iraq later in his speech:

> American leadership has been renewed and America's standing has been restored. Look to Iraq, where nearly 100,000 of our brave men and women have left with their heads held high. American combat patrols have ended, violence is down, and a new government has been formed. This year, our civilians will forge a lasting partnership with the Iraqi people, while we finish the job of bringing our troops out of Iraq. America's commitment has been kept. The Iraq war is coming to an end.

So: he blames Bush for getting us into the war and racking up huge deficits, and then takes credit for winning it. Some people thought you had to go to Harvard *Business* School to learn how to diss your predecessor.

Finally, talking about the deficit commission, he said: "And [the] conclusion [of the bipartisan fiscal commission] is that the only way to tackle our deficit is to cut excessive spending wherever we find it. . . ." This is more difficult and, alas, way above the pay grade of this president, which is why even his supporters have complained about his speech. We can never, *never* cut the deficit (by which is meant cutting it substantially, perhaps even balancing the budget) by cutting only "excessive" spending, for two reasons. First, we will *never* all be able to agree what's excessive. And second, to balance the budget we may have to cut expenses that we *all* agree *are* important.

Johnny needs braces on his teeth. He *really* does. Unfortunately, in the real world, we have to buy food and homeowner's insurance first.

To some extent, the president may be the victim of his own success. His address in Tucson was widely acclaimed. He was said to have had perfect pitch.

It was never true. He received the accolades only because until then he had been so bitingly partisan, and because being so bitingly partisan was precisely what he had advertised himself during his 2008 campaign as not being.

For one brief—shining?—moment he stopped. He went to a funeral. He didn't bash his opponents. People said he was terrific. He may even have believed it.

But it wasn't true.

Egypt and the Realpolitik of Violence and Freedom

January 31, 2011

President Barack Obama's Friday evening statement on the situation in Egypt reminds us of George Orwell's comment that sloppy writing leads to dangerous political thinking.

"Good evening," said the president (ritually, if, under the circumstances, inaccurately). "As the situation continues to unfold, our first concern is preventing injury or loss of life." Our *first* concern?

Egypt has been our most important ally in the Arab-speaking world. The United States gives $1.3 billion in military aid to Egypt *annually*, and has given $28 billion in economic aid since 1975. We've done that for a reason. The Middle East is a metaphorical salad of dominoes waiting to fall and a powder keg waiting to blow. Islamist extremists plot, and live to plot, the end of the Great Satan and its consequence, chaos. Egypt has been a realpolitik force in opposition to that plotting.

But according to the president, our *first* concern is preventing injury (sprained ankles?) and loss of life. Maybe that's just a sop to the vegans and animal rights folks (the 2012 election looms). But a president facing the prospects of Armageddon starting, and in the nature of Armageddon, ending, on his watch might nudge other concerns into first place.

The president called on the Egyptian authorities "to refrain from any violence against peaceful protesters." The mind reels. What could the president have meant? Had he not seen the coverage of the riots in Cairo? How do you have a peaceful riot? How do you have a peaceful riot in the Middle East? These folks are not the Women's Christian Temperance Union—and come to think of it, there was nothing peaceful about the WCTU or its most famous member, hatchet-wielding Carrie Nation.

"At the same time," continued the president, "those protesting in the streets have the responsibility to express themselves peacefully. Violence and destruction will not lead to the reforms that they seek." A few minutes later, the president said, "Violence will not address the grievances of the Egyptian people." The White House press secretary, Robert Gibbs, had sounded the theme earlier in the day: "There's no situation that this is certainly not a situation that will be solved by violence."

Where to begin? Either the protesters will succeed, however success is defined, and therefore will have succeeded by resorting to violence, or the Mubarak regime will survive, however that is defined, because its violence was more violent than the violence of the protesters.

Whether the situation is "solved" depends on where you're throwing your bombs from. Whoever wins this struggle will have succeeded through the use of more or better targeted violence. "Now ultimately," said the president, "the future of Egypt will be determined by the Egyptian people." What did he mean by that? "*Should be* determined by the Egyptian people"? Maybe. But "will be"? It hasn't been for decades if ever. Ultimately, as Keynes remarked, we're all dead. And for a lot of Egyptians this week, "ultimately" may come rather sooner than they had expected.

What should the president have said? There were two options. One is: nothing. Never underestimate the advisability of saying nothing. The United States has few good options in this situation. Keeping quiet may preserve whatever our best option is.

The second option would have been to teach, but the president is not good at teaching, as he demonstrated in his State of the Union speech. And teach whom? He could have outlined, for the American people, the dilemma: realpolitik vs. idealism. Kissinger vs. Bush. Perhaps Kissinger vs. Bush for Dummies. But how likely is it that that lecture would help the United States win the hearts and minds of whoever wins the tanks and guns in Egypt?

Besides, the president may not have thought through that dilemma (after all, his State Department took the wrong side in *Honduras*!), so he's coasting on liberal shibboleths. Violence is bad. Violence is counterproductive. Floss after every meal. But that is dangerous thinking, which, *pace* George Orwell, can proceed to, as well as from, sloppy writing.

To think that violence is always bad is not to know—as American soldiers know, along with millions of people in far-off lands whom their bravery has liberated—that violence can be the handmaiden of freedom.

Freedom for the Egyptians, however, is still years away, as it is for millions of their pitiful fellow Arabs, whatever is midwifed by the current violence. And however great the interest of the Egyptian people is in their own freedom and human rights, it is eclipsed, even if they don't realize it, by the national security interest of the United States.

Getting Serious about Regulations—NOT!
February 2, 2011

In a January 18, 2011, op-ed in the *Wall Street Journal*, President Obama wrote that he wants to ensure that federal regulations "protect our safety, health, and environment while promoting economic growth." He made a similar claim in his State of the Union address.

Before anyone starts calling him the "deregulation president," it's worth taking a closer look at his op-ed. Hidden in the fluff, of course, is a lot of nonsense; even points *he* must think are nonsense: "We have, from time to time, embraced common sense rules of the road. . . ." Only "from time to time," Mr. President? You are *so* right!

How about this: "Over the past two years, the goal of my administration has been to strike the right balance"; the right balance, that is, between "placing unreasonable burdens on business—burdens that have stifled innovation and have had a chilling effect on growth and jobs" and "meet[ing] our basic responsibility to protect the public interest."

What does he take us for? The past two years have been a time of unrelenting regulating without any attempt whatsoever to strike a balance, let alone "the right balance."

Mr. Obama says he is ordering a government-wide review of the rules already on the books. Really? On December 31, 2010, the Federal Register, where those rules are hiding in plain sight, was 82,589 pages long. Raise your hand if you really think Mr. Obama's people are going to review a significant portion of them.

"Where necessary," he writes, "we won't shy away from addressing obvious gaps . . ." including "efforts to target chronic violators of workplace safety laws."

In a piece last week, I referred to a Cato Institute graph of workplace fatalities that indicates that the Occupational Safety and Health Administration (OSHA) has had no effect *at all* during its forty years of existence. Anyone who points to OSHA as a success story is either ignorant, not serious, or being deceptive (the reactions to Tucson caution against stronger language for a time).

Mr. Obama says he wants "disclosure as a tool to inform consumers of their choices, rather than restricting those choices." What is *that* all about? One thing consumers are capable of doing is demanding information—when they want it. If companies discover consumers want information, they'll provide it. That's one way companies compete. What we have now is TMI—too much information—required by: guess who.

"[F]inally," Mr. Obama writes, "I am directing federal agencies to do more to account for—and reduce—the burdens regulations may place on small businesses."

Certainly the cost of regulations to small businesses is a lot greater proportionally than it is to big businesses. According to

Nicole V. Crain and W. Mark Crain, businesses "with fewer than 20 employees incur regulatory costs 42 percent greater than firms with between 20 and 499 employees, and 36 percent greater than firms with more than 500 employees." In addition, some of the legislation, e.g., the Americans with Disabilities Act, hurts precisely the people it is intended to help. (Surprise!)

Toward the end of his piece, Mr. Obama writes, "Despite a lot of heated rhetoric, our efforts over the past two years to modernize our regulations have led to smarter—and in some cases tougher—rules. . . . Yet according to current estimates of their economic impact, the benefits of these regulations exceed their costs by billions of dollars."

You have to smile.

Here are three actions the president could have taken if he were serious:

1. Propose the elimination of one major regulatory agency. OSHA would be a good place to begin. Meddling by OSHA is estimated to cost around $65 billion a year, and has been completely useless. Small businesses would applaud.

2. Propose that all regulations that impose their requirements on businesses with fifteen or more employees be amended wholesale to affect only businesses with fifty or more employees—the threshold, not incidentally, for Obamacare. If fifty is good enough for socialized medicine (sorry, Tucson, time's up) it ought to be good enough for all other regulations. A hundred would be better. But Rome wasn't burned in a day.

3. Appoint a panel of experts, all skeptics of regulation, to estimate the *real* cost of regulations. The government's estimates are just what you'd expect from . . . government. Nicole V. Crain and W. Mark Crain estimate the cost to be at least $1.75 trillion, or 14 percent of US national income. By comparison, the income-tax burden is about $2.3 trillion. If people could wave the real figures at their congressional representatives, we might get real reform.

A good post-Tea-Party-election guess is that all three of these things will happen in the next ten years. A better guess is that they won't happen on this president's watch.

The New America Firsters
February 7, 2011

As we mused a few days ago—in a piece pointing out that deregulation had to begin somewhere—Rome wasn't burned in a day. (According to the Roman historian Tacitus, the fire in AD 64, actually burned for five and a half days.)

The Republican Study Committee, the caucus of the conservative members of the House of Representatives, has lighted a small fire by drawing up a list of proposed cuts that are described by an incensed Left (the crowd that always puts government first) as deep, dramatic, and radical. Veronique de Rugy of the Mercatus Center, however, points out, complete with graph, that the cuts will hardly make a dent in the federal deficit. (See www.nationalreview.com/corner/257701/spending-reduction-act-perspective-veronique-de-rugy.)

That may be true, but the collection of proposals is, nevertheless, the most breathtaking Washington had ever seen—until Senator Rand Paul came along with a list of bigger cuts. Not since Ronald Reagan campaigned on abolishing the Department of Education—you've seen the hole on Independence Avenue, haven't you?—had anyone seriously proposed cutting the federal government.

It may be true that eliminating the subsidy for mohair will save, annually, only $1 million, and the USDA Sugar Program, only $14 million, and the International Fund for Ireland, only $17 million.

But those cuts are important for three reasons. They can lead to a change in the culture. They can introduce, if not complete, a lesson of shared sacrifice. And they may remind us that, for a while, we will have to go back to basics.

Central to America's financial good health is a change in Washington's culture. Many years ago, the libertarian economist Murray Rothbard proposed denationalizing the lighthouses, partially on the theory that a people debating the merits of denationalizing lighthouses would be less likely to nationalize the steel industry.

Changing America's culture, so that it will put its financial house in order, will be, distressingly, more challenging than winning World War II. At the height of that second Great War, America had twelve million men and woman in uniform, of whom seven million were overseas, in harm's way.

But before America's entry into that war, it was not apparent to everyone, certainly not to the 800,000 America Firsters, that America had a stake in the struggle being waged in Europe. Then early one December morning a man named Yamamoto made that thinking outmoded.

After Pearl Harbor, the nation knew it had a problem. And knew it would have to make sacrifices to solve it. And, for a time, it would have to go back to basics: America's superfluities would have to give way to support for its soldiers. In a moment, Admiral Yamamoto had changed America's culture.

No real progress toward averting the nation's coming fiscal disaster can be made without changing the culture of entitlements. And no real progress in cutting entitlements can be made without changing the culture of spending.

If we cannot eliminate the $167-million subsidy for the National Endowment for the Humanities, we cannot make changes in Social Security. If we cannot eliminate the Department of Energy's $530-million program of Weatherization Grants to states, we cannot make changes in Medicare.

And if we cannot make changes in Social Security and Medicare, we will go broke.

Unfortunately, the Republican Study Committee's culture-changing proposal, which also would eliminate the National Organic Certification Cost-Share Program, the Ready-to-Learn Television Program, and the death gratuity for members of Congress—stop smiling this instant!—can hardly be described as a "shared sacrifice" or "back to basics" proposal. Getting Americans to understand sacrificing and going back to basics may require leadership from the president. But as we saw in the State of the Union speech, it will not come from this president, tethered by youthful ideology untempered by experience, and that means we may have to wait six more years.

Even as the conservatives in the House of Representatives are listing cuts that will hardly make a dent in the federal deficit, the president, with the support of his Government Firsters, is planning additional spending that will hasten the day of financial reckoning. The inevitable day.

Inevitable because, as the economist Herbert Stein once famously said, "If something cannot go on forever, it will stop." Sooner or later our financial house will have to be put in order. If we don't do it ourselves, the Chinese may do it for us. Then will we learn what deep, dramatic, and radical really mean.

The Republican Study Committee has tried to start a fire. We cannot know now if it will succeed—succeed in burning away the old ways and making way for new.

If it does not, then when the fire goes out, as it did in Rome after five and a half days, it will be cold. Cold enough, perhaps, finally— but is this what we must hope for?—to be, for the Government Firsters, a modern Yamamoto moment.

Mitch Daniels and the CPAC Moment
February 14, 2011

Is Indiana governor Mitch Daniels running for president? That was one question on the minds of some of the eleven thousand people who attended the American Conservative Union's Conservative Political Action Conference last weekend.

Daniels went to the CPAC and gave a terrific one-legged stool presidential campaign address. The minimum number of legs for a stool, however, as many people from the state of Indiana know— Indiana has 154,000 milking cows—is three.

Daniels gave a sober, but not somber, thirty-one minute speech which was interrupted by applause forty-two times. Flown in from Indiana on a friend's plane, Daniels was relaxed, poised, teleprompted, and, yes, presidential, in part because a teleprompter prompts people to think of presidents.

Daniels summed up his economic philosophy early on: "We [Hoosiers] believe in paying our bills. We have kept our state in the black throughout the recent unpleasantness, while cutting rather than raising taxes, by practicing an old tribal ritual—we spend less money than we take in."

The lefties, if they had been listening, would have been scandalized to hear the governor say, echoing Milton Friedman: "When business leaders ask me what they can do for Indiana, I always reply: 'Make money. Go make money. That's the first act of corporate citizenship. If you do that, you'll have to hire someone else, and you'll have enough profit to help one of those non-profits we're so proud of."

Friedman also pointed out that you can only make money (which the Left thinks is greed) by serving people (which the Left thinks is the exclusive preserve of government).

Daniels said Indiana had cut property taxes to the lowest level in America, and designed the health plans for both the state employees and for low-income Hoosiers as Health Savings Accounts. And he spoke of Indiana's intention to create a voucher program for every low- and middle-income family in the state.

Having presented his bona fides, Daniels then addressed the nation's most pressing problem, what he called a new Red Menace: the sea of red ink drowning the US economy.

As the elections of last November indicated, that is now the central concern of Americans: an economy incarnadined by the hand of Barack Obama, the one we had been waiting for. Yet who would have thought the one we had been waiting for would have had so much red ink in him?

Daniels said we need to cut government spending, redesign the tax code so it will promote private growth (flatter is better, flat is best), deregulate, and stop denying ourselves the energy—oil and gas—that is under our own land.

He spoke about Americans "still on the first rung of life's ladder." He urged the audience to "distinguish carefully skepticism about Big Government from contempt for all government."

Then he asked for "thoughtfulness about the rhetoric we deploy in the great debate ahead." And, having thought for just a moment himself, decided time was up: whereupon he announced that "our opponents are better at nastiness than we will ever be. It comes naturally. Power to them is everything, so there's nothing they won't say to get it." How do you speak truth when truth is unpleasant?

Daniels also urged "great care not to drift into a loss of faith in the American people" saying "Americans are still a people born to liberty."

So far, so good, and very good indeed. Thirty-one minutes. Forty-two applause lines. That's a great speech. George Will, introducing Gov. Daniels, said, "Our speaker has twice been the right choice for Indiana. Some people think that the other forty-nine states deserve the chance to make the same choice."

But other people aren't so sure. Two legs of the stool were missing: social policy and national security policy.

Daniels said last year, as reported by Andrew Ferguson in the *Weekly Standard* that to solve the economic problems, "the next president would have to call a truce on the so-called social issues."

That may make sense, at first: if the country goes broke, a lot of things will have to change. Perhaps the country will have to economize by laying off the Supreme Court.

But even assuming solving the economic problem must come first, how are we going to avoid rafting on Barack Obama's great rolling river of red ink all the way to bankruptcy on the rocks of entitlement programs?

Daniels said that Americans "are still a people born for self-governance. They are ready to summon the discipline to . . . put the future before the present, their children's interest before their own." Fine, but putting children's interest before their own—even getting married and having children—takes character. And the kind of people who have that kind of character tend to be social conservatives.

The governor's gamble may be that social conservatives know he is one of them; and they may understand that he doesn't want to scare off those people who are concerned about the economy but are not social conservatives. Perhaps.

The other missing stool was national security—foreign policy and defense. The governor's only reference to national security was to say that even national defense, which he called "the first and most important mission of government," could not get a free pass when it came to cutting the budget.

The same day the governor spoke, the Egyptian government, our ally for decades, had fallen, casting the whole Middle East into confusion at best, chaos at worst.

Now the cons and the neocons, and the realists and the idealists, and the State Department long-timers and the Freedom Agenda proponents are all arguing about what we should have done, and what we should do.

A reasonable position for Daniels would have been to cut through that fog of argument and call for *increasing* the defense budget. Another position would have been to call for *not* cutting it, and notwithstanding that the Pentagon's balance sheet is as unyielding of useful data as a black hole.

Daniels understands that we cannot balance the budget by eliminating fraud, waste, and abuse. But neither can we wait around for the Defense Department to produce a clean balance sheet before buying the defense we need.

Hoosiers are not much affected by illegal immigration, nor is Indiana involved in national security. Hoosiers also know their state government can't determine national abortion policy. Nor can Indiana do much to affect today's culture, which drives so many of the social issues. It may be possible therefore to avoid discussing social issues when running for governor of Indiana. But not for president of the United States.

Because Daniels avoided both the social issues and the national security issue at CPAC, many observers thought it fair to conclude from his speech—a very good speech indeed—that he is not running for president. Or, at least, not running for president yet.

Dracon for President?

February 21, 2011

"Draconian" was the way one Democrat described, surprisingly accurately, the budget cuts the Republicans in the House of Representatives passed before the dawn's early light last Saturday. Dracon, who gave his name to the Democrat's adjective, was a seventh-century BC Athenian legislator who replaced the rule of lawgivers with the rule of law, an act that to this day rankles believers in a living constitution. Some of Dracon's laws were harsh. Some of the Republicans' cuts are also being described as harsh.

The new Republican members of the House did what they had promised to do when they got to Washington (behavior sometimes referred to as operational consonance): they cut the budget and with it bennies for bureaucrats.

When the Republicans had finished their handiwork, Democrats described the results as drastic, double meat ax, death-spiral, and, yes, draconian. Republicans called it democratic.

The Republicans voted to cut $61 billion out of the federal budget over the next seven months, taking non-security discretionary spending down to where it was way back in . . . 2008, a time, for the historically minded, when flowers bloomed, children played, dead people in Chicago voted, and life was, on the whole (if you weren't a progressive frustrated that you had not yet managed to control . . . everything) quite good.

The cut in the budget is being called "the largest cut of its kind since WWII." But the cuts are being measured from President Obama's Brobdingnagian 2010 spending level and his über-Brobdingnagian Jonathan Swiftian 2011 budget request, both examples of the progressives' ratchet theory of history: spending that goes up must never, ever, be allowed to come down.

More than a hundred programs will be eliminated. Hundreds more will have their funding reduced. Some of the highest-octane proposals were elimination of funding for the pro-abortion organization Planned Parenthood, cutting off funding for implementing Obamacare, and cutting the Environmental Protection Agency by a third.

Federal bureaucrats, unable to adapt to the spirit of the times, were not amused by the Republicans' keeping their promises. Nevertheless, the Internal Revenue Service's announcement that the cuts would adversely affect its operations must have brought a wry smile to a face or two, perhaps even to the face of Treasury Secretary, and chief IRS tax collector, Tim Geithner.

The National Labor Relations Board also said the cuts would have adverse effects. Given the Obama administration's pro-union activities in Wisconsin, where public employees are protesting like Greeks—but not the Greeks of Dracon's day—the NLRB's announcement must have been particularly welcomed by that state's governor.

Funding for some of President Obama's White House regulatory "czars" was also cut, but not, unfortunately, funding for Czarbanes–Oxley.

Maya MacGuineas, president of the Committee for a Responsible Federal Budget (an organization whose logo might feature a unicorn), described the Republicans' efforts as "not a thoughtful exercise." But it is the exercises, thoughtful or otherwise, of the budgeteers of the last several years that have created the current crisis. Perhaps what Americans want now is less thought and more excising?

Those who think the country will not easily survive, or survive at all, the cuts made by the Republicans should remember this: on the morning after the Republicans passed welfare reform in 1996, the sun . . . rose. The reform is now generally agreed to have been a great success. President Clinton had vetoed the reform bill twice, before bowing to public pressure to sign it. Democrats had predicted death, literally, in the streets. All that died was one more piece of the liberal dream: that the people cannot manage their own lives.

Republicans need to make it clear that they understand that some of the programs they have cut or killed may well be important, at least to some people, but that nothing, *nothing* is as important as the financial health of the United States, which it is their solemn duty to protect. If they fail in their duty, they will deserve the blame that historians of democracy in the future will heap upon them, always assuming that in that future there will be historians of democracy.

Dracon, according to the historian Plutarch, was asked why most of the offenses he had listed were punishable by death. Well (to paraphrase), he said, "the lesser crimes deserve death. And for the greater ones, there is, alas, nothing more draconian."

The Democrat who called the Republicans' cuts "draconian" was more accurate then he probably realized. The Republicans have condemned to death hundreds of minor programs. Many greater programs still await their sentencing.

Social Security and the Ghost of Ephram Nestor
April 1, 2011

Very few senior citizens have heard of Ephram Nestor. And not many junior citizens, either. Nestor was a Bulgarian who came to America in 1913 and lived here continuously for forty-three years. Then, in July 1956, he was deported for having been a Communist from 1933 to 1939, a period of time during which membership in the Communist Party as such was not illegal and wasn't even a statutory ground for deportation.

For nineteen years, Nestor and his employers had made regular payments into the Social Security system. In 1955, he became eligible for payments from Social Security. When he was deported, the government cut off his payments. Nestor sued.

Nestor lost. The case, *Flemming v. Nestor* (Flemming was the secretary of Health, Education, and Welfare), established the principle that entitlement to Social Security benefits is not a contractual right.

Seniors today worry about that principle even though they have never heard of Ephram Nestor. They are right to worry, and all the more so when they read statements like the following one from *Washington Post* columnist Robert J. Samuelson. (See https://tinyurl.com/rnqdgf6.)

He described as "highly misinformed" Americans, including the elderly, who believe that the elderly have "earned" their Social Security through their lifelong payroll taxes. Both Social Security and Medicare, Samuelson writes, "are pay-as-you-go. Today's taxes pay today's benefits; little is 'saved.' Even if all were saved, most retirees receive benefits that far exceed their payroll taxes."

Of course they do! What should they expect? Only to get the same number of dollars back, without any return on the funds and without any compensation for inflation?

Proponents of changes to the Social Security program will not win the support of seniors, or juniors, by making that argument.

People who have paid, for decades, into a retirement system are entitled to think they are entitled to get their money back with decades' worth of interest.

The point Samuelson ignores is that if people had not been required to pay into the Social Security system, they could have put that money in the stock market instead. In which case, their retirement payments would not only be more secure but also larger than the payments they will get from the current Social Security system.

Reformers—in the nature of things, that means Republicans— must make a different proposal, one that addresses the concerns of future recipients, who believe, correctly, that their benefits under the current system are no more secure than Ephram Nestor's were.

The only sensible proposal will include allowing workers to save some of their retirement funds in personal accounts that they can invest, in some sort of fund, in the stock market. That obvious concept has been demonized by liberals with the word "privatization," privatization being to liberals what garlic is to Dracula.

Rep. Anthony Weiner (D–NY) mocks the concept of allowing workers to invest in the stock market: "Boy, that seems smart, huh? Investing Social Security in the stock market." "Boy, talk about lessons unlearned."

President Obama also dissed the stock market in his State of the Union speech: "We must [solve the Social Security problem] . . . without subjecting Americans' guaranteed retirement income to the whims of the stock market."

Democrats love to dump demagogically on the stock market when it takes a tumble. Today, however, the market is making a magnificent comeback. But the key point is that one year—one decade even—does not a retirement fund make.

A few years ago, the Congressional Research Service studied thirty-five different forty-one-year time periods and determined that there was not a single period in which a worker would not have been better off investing his payroll taxes in stocks than remaining in the Social Security system. Boy, doesn't that make investing your retirement fund in the market sound like a good idea, huh? Who's unlearnèd now?

The president said in his State of the Union speech that "the state of our union is strong." Though not strong enough, apparently, for Americans to invest in.

But Chile is strong enough for Chileans to invest in. Chile privatized its retirement system in 1981. Workers are required to invest at least 10 percent of their salary in a personal retirement account, but they can invest more, and they can determine when they retire—whether it be age 45, age 65, or age 85. The poor and people unable to work can still be covered by a government plan.

If Chileans can have private plans, why can't Americans?

Because the liberals won't let them. And unless the Republicans can learn how to teach Americans about personal retirement accounts, Americans will be doomed to the clunky Model T retirement system designed by Franklin Roosevelt and preserved by generations of big-government liberals.

Small-government Republicans will have a receptive audience. A Pew Research poll taken last September found that 58 percent of the public favors allowing workers younger than age fifty-five to invest part of their Social Security taxes in personal retirement accounts. *Seventy* percent of those younger than age thirty favor personal accounts, while—pay close attention, please—66 percent of those under age thirty voted for Barack Obama. Wow! That's called an opportunity.

If Republicans lack the imagination to seize that opportunity, they deserve to be haunted for life by the ghost of an ex–Social Security recipient, a poor, unfortunate, ex-Communist Bulgarian immigrant named Ephram Nestor.

Conscripts in a Ponzi Scheme
June 13, 2011

The spit turns slowly over the Social Security roasting fire but there is no whimpering from the children being cooked. Yet.

Jonathan Swift's *Modest Proposal* (one of English literature's great satires) for preventing the children of poor people in Ireland from being a burden to their parents or their country, and for making them beneficial to the public was: to eat them.

Our problem is almost precisely the reverse. We have too much food, as Mrs. Obama reminds us, and we have too few children: too few to guard the gates of Western Civilization, too few to pay the bills coming due for the welfare state, primarily for Social Security and Medicare.

What to do? Two facts deserve our preliminary attention.

One. In the 2004 presidential election (a more typical election than the 2008 election) only 17 percent of the eighteen to twenty-nine-year-olds voted, meaning 83 percent didn't bother to vote. That's called potential.

Two: The youngest voters haven't, recently, seemed to care much about even issues that directly affect them. When was the last time you heard about a student movement? Why is it, for example, that young people don't lobby and vote to make the drinking age eighteen, which it was in many places until 1984? Perhaps buying alcohol with a fake ID out the back door stimulates sophistication, but it tends to stultify the exercise of civic responsibility.

Grownups may think that presidential elections are about

important issues, but it's not obvious that the kids care about policies at all. Oh, yes, they get caught up in the hoopla of a presidential campaign. But do they think that the policies a president will pursue will actually affect them?

If young people really cared about public policy, they would be frantic about the financial state of the country. Debts are piling up higher than the Washington Monument, and *they* are being set up to pay them off. Yet not a single college student that we know of has let out a whimper.

But can the older folks count on the continuing civic lassitude of the young? We don't know. But we do know that the current fiscally absurd Social Security scheme might not survive the kids' discovery of democracy's power. The fact is, the kids in America are being had, even as the poor citizens of the Arab states, whom we have been watching on television in recent months, have for so many years—decades even—been had.

One thing is clear: in order to "fix" Social Security, we will have to recruit the young and assign to them the following tasks: pay more and retire later. But what's in that fix for them?

Not a lot. At least, not a lot compared to the alternative, a privatized Social Security system. Both skeptics and progressives (aka liberals) will vehemently oppose privatization of Social Security, the skeptics because they fear it won't work, the progressives because they fear it will.

But of course it *will* work. It *is* working, in Chile. Workers there have been getting rich on their social security accounts since 1981.

Why don't we privatize our Social Security system? Because if today's young people were released from the bondage of Social Security, who would pay into the system the funds necessary to provide the benefits promised to today's retirees? As everyone is finally discovering, Social Security is not a lock box. The money flows out in benefits as fast as . . . actually, starting last year . . . faster than it is paid in in taxes. Legislators call that a pay-as-you-go scheme.

Prosecutors call it a Ponzi scheme. The young are like Bernie Madoff's clients. Or like pigeons, a term given to investors duped into supporting a theatrical enterprise that the insiders have come to realize will flop financially. Like, say, Springtime for Obama in Balanced Budget Land.

The dirty big secret of Social Security reform is that it depends on keeping the young as conscripts in a Ponzi scheme. Where's the morality in that in an enlightened Western democracy?

The answer to that question may be that the government promised—well, sort of: see the story of Ephram Nestor (page)—the older folks (whom *Time* magazine in 1988 dubbed the "Greedy Geezers") that they would receive Social Security benefits when they retired, and it would be immoral not to honor that promise.

But that is a moral claim that may have to give way to a new democratic imperative in the coming years if the young decide that being roasted on the Social Security spit like pigeons no longer appeals.

Intelligent Design
A Review of *If Not Us, Who?: William Rusher,* National Review, *and the Conservative Movement* by David B. Frisk

August 2, 2012

If William F. Buckley Jr. was the light shining from the lighthouse of the conservative movement, William A. Rusher was the lighthouse. If Buckley designed the lighthouse, Rusher built it. If Buckley was the "conservative," Rusher was the "movement." And move he did. As political scientist David Frisk shows in his biography, *If Not Us, Who?*, Rusher moved as much as Buckley, and *that's* moving. Rusher was less frenetic, but more focused. He was the long-time publisher of *National Review*, even as Buckley was its long-time, and founding, editor.

Unlike Buckley, with whom Rusher will always and inevitably be compared, Rusher was an only child. His parents divorced when he was still a teenager, he never married, and he had few close relatives. But like Buckley, who, although one of ten children had only one child himself, Rusher never lay awake worrying about children and so was able to devote almost all his energy to his primary passion: the politics of saving America. And it is a fair judgment that save it he did, at least for the time being.

He knew he was saving it. His innumerable memos make it clear that he had a sense of mission and that the cost of failure was doom. To various people Rusher predicted catastrophe if his approach to whatever was the issue of the day wasn't followed. Those of us who lived through this period of American history, and who knew Rusher and Buckley well, may tend to forget how epochal it was. And those who didn't experience it probably haven't a clue. But American history changed course between 1955 and 1980, as it had during the New Deal era.

★ ★ ★

In 1950, American politics was a vast cruel sea of liberalism. In *The Liberal Imagination*, literary critic Lionel Trilling wrote that

> in the United States at this time liberalism is not only the dominant but even the sole intellectual tradition. For it is the plain fact that nowadays there are no conservative or reactionary ideas in general circulation. This does not mean, of course, that there is no impulse to conservatism or to reaction. Such impulses are certainly very strong, perhaps even stronger than most of us know. But the conservative impulse and the reactionary impulse do not, with some isolated and some ecclesiastical exceptions, express themselves in ideas but only in action or in irritable mental gestures which seek to resemble ideas.

Trilling died on November 5, 1975, and almost exactly five years later, on November 4, 1980, Ronald Reagan was elected president. The impulse to conservatism was indeed much stronger than Trilling knew in 1950, but he must have known how strong it was by the time he died. Buckley had started *National Review* in 1955 to express in ideas the conservative impulses. Barry Goldwater had been nominated by the Republicans in 1964. Buckley had run for mayor of New York City in 1965.

Ronald Reagan had been elected governor of California in 1966. And James Buckley had won a US Senate seat from New York on the *Conservative* Party ticket in 1970. Events like those don't happen by chance. They happen by intelligent design, and one of the most significant intelligent designers was William A. Rusher.

★ ★ ★

In his early years, Rusher had been a regular Republican and worked for regular-Republican candidates. In 1954, he discovered that he was also, and primarily, a conservative. In 1955, he learned that *National Review* was about to be launched and he signed up as a charter subscriber. In 1955, a piece that he had written for the *Harvard Times-Republican* (yes, Virginia, but that was a long time ago) was brought to Buckley's attention. In that piece, Rusher warned: "The one sin for which nature exacts the supreme penalty of national extinction is a failure on the part of the members of a society to believe [in] its inherent worth." Rusher said that the struggle for survival must not be led by "some doubt-ridden egghead exquisitely poised between Yea and Nay. The world will go—and perhaps rightly—to those who want it most." Five decades later, the poise of the doubt-ridden eggheads is still exquisite.

Buckley quoted extensively from Rusher's piece in his column in *National Review*. He sent Rusher a pre-publication copy and asked for an opportunity to talk. They met, and Buckley tried to get Rusher to write articles on legal subjects for the magazine. Rusher, a Harvard Law School graduate who was practicing at a major white-shoe law firm in New York City, had to decline, though he was not at liberty to say why: he was on his way to Washington to serve as counsel for the Senate Internal Security Subcommittee. In the spring of 1957, they met again, and Buckley asked him to join *National Review* as publisher.

It was, undoubtedly, the perfect position for Rusher, even though as time went on friction developed—inevitably perhaps—between Rusher and Buckley. Not debilitating friction, but intermittent sparring between two unusually capable, and verbal, people with different skills, if common goals. Rusher's position as publisher allowed him to become the conservative movement's driving *political* force. He was the prime mover of the 1964 Goldwater presidential campaign: he started it and marshaled the forces to make it happen. Without Rusher's persistence, Goldwater never would have run. In fact, Goldwater never really did want to run. Can you blame him? After he was nominated, California governor Pat Brown (father of the present governor) said "the stench of fascism is in the air." Senator William Fulbright said Goldwater was "the closest thing in American politics to an equivalent of Russian Stalinism." And Democrats get upset today when people call Barack Obama a socialist?

But Rusher and his gang dragged Goldwater along until he saw he had no choice. It was no easy task. Goldwater could be . . . difficult. After the founding of the American Conservative Union, Goldwater said that he had tried to stop it and that it wouldn't go far. "That's the *National Review* crowd—you know: Frank Meyer, Bill Rusher. When I listen to those guys I start looking under the bed." He mellowed, a bit, in his later years.

The theory behind the Goldwater run for the White House was expounded by Rusher in a piece for *National Review* in 1963 titled, "Crossroads for the GOP." He said the Republican Party had "a rendezvous with a brand new idea"—the "Southern Strategy." "Flipping the south," as M. Stanton Evans, another central figure in the conservative movement, commented later, was "the key to the presidency, the key to the Congress. You had to have those votes, and when we got 'em, we won—and Bill saw that." Rusher was not just an activist. He was a strategist—*the* strategist.

* * *

Not all of his plans worked out, of course. The early 1970s were not good years for conservative Republicans. The Nixon administration was lurching left with the Philadelphia Plan (which Rusher called "black quotas on Federal construction projects"), the creation of the Environmental Protection Agency, flirtation with the Family Assistance Plan, Nixon's announcement that "I am a Keynesian now," his visit to Red China, détente with the Soviet Union, Strategic Arms Limitation Talks, and his New Economic Policy, which included wage and price controls.

By 1971, conservatives had lost their patience with Nixon, and by 1974 Rusher had lost his patience with the Republican Party, and set out to form a third party in time for the 1976 election. *National Review* was skeptical about the new party, as was Ronald Reagan, whom Rusher tried to enlist in the project but who instead challenged President Gerald Ford in the GOP primaries and lost narrowly. On Election Day, Rusher's two years of effort exploded into a huge political black hole as the American Independent Party, headed by a candidate Rusher and his allies hadn't wanted—the notorious racist Lester Maddox—got one-fifth of 1 percent of the vote. But Rusher moved right on . . . and later that year was visiting the Reagans, preparing for the future.

If Goldwater hadn't run for president, would Reagan ever have been discovered? Who knows? Goldwater *did* run, because Rusher made it impossible for him not to, and Reagan *was* discovered. If Buckley hadn't started *National Review*, would Rusher have become the powerhouse he was? Who knows? My guess is both would have happened. But they were not inevitable.

David Frisk shows that Buckley was cooler to both Goldwater and Reagan than one would suppose, or remembers, looking back from the height of the post-Reagan years. Not only was *National Review* cautious on Goldwater, but in 1967 Buckley backed Nixon over Reagan, whom Rusher was imploring people not to underestimate. Buckley said it was "preposterous even to consider Reagan as an alternative . . . an ex-actor, who has been in office now for a month." Even Nixon disagreed with Buckley, because the office Reagan occupied was that of governor of California. The point Frisk makes clear throughout this book is: Rusher was the driving political force that made the Right a major power in American politics.

★ ★ ★

In a biography—in real life—there isn't always the conflict, crisis, and resolution that is required in fiction. Although there was certainly conflict (though low key) between the two heroes, Rusher and Buckley, there never was a crisis. Early on, Buckley knew, as did his sister, managing editor Priscilla Buckley, that Rusher didn't quite fit in at *NR*. His lonely childhood had made him temperamentally different from the fun-loving, high-spirited, prank-playing Buckleys. Rusher thought that the magazine should be more focused on politics, and that Buckley should pay more attention to it. Neither man would change in those respects, though Rusher changed in one crucial respect, becoming a practicing Christian of the Anglo-Catholic variety in 1978. And there was really no resolution, until (perhaps)

Rusher moved to San Francisco when he retired, San Francisco being about as far away as you can get from New York City and still be in the United States without wearing a lei and still be able to find a good restaurant with the indispensable bottle of first-class wine, perhaps already listed in the little black notebook Rusher always, always carried with him.

Frisk has told an important story about a major figure in American history and told it well. *If Not Us, Who?* is essential reading for people interested in twentieth-century American politics.

A Valentine's Day Shooting in the Other Washington

February 20, 2014

Last Friday afternoon, Makayla Darden, an eight-year-old girl, was hit by a stray bullet in Southeast Washington DC. Unlike Trayvon Martin, she was not instantly adopted by President Obama. Two men, Karie Brown, 19, and Nathaniel Patten, 21, also of Southeast Washington DC, have been arrested and charged with assault with intent to kill while armed.

Last Friday was St. Valentine's Day.

There were ninety-one murders in the District of Columbia last year (not counting the twelve people gunned down at the Navy Yard). The figure is up from 2012 (when Washington ranked eighth in murders per capita among American cities), but down from previous years, which may dampen the public's interest in crime news from Washington's more crime-ridden neighborhoods. Crime, whether it's up or down, takes place primarily "somewhere else," in the . . . lower-class neighborhoods of Washington: not the part where President Obama sends his children to school.

Government in Washington DC, known as "self-government," would be a late-night television joke to someone with no feelings for what can accurately be described as the underclass. The government's corruption and incompetence are as obvious and permanent as the two large warts on your grandmother's nose—and it's just not terribly polite to talk about them either.

But the dysfunction is real. And the *Washington Post* (give it at least one star) even has a feature: "DC corruption scandals: A primer." Click on any button and learn how the city fathers steal from the people.

But of course that's not street crime. It's only thievery, and does thievery, even high-level thievery, really affect ordinary people? Can't we spin the facts, the way former mayor Marion Barry did years ago, when he said Washington would have one of the lowest crime rates in the country—if it weren't for the murders.

Let thieves be thieves: we adults care—with Hillary—about the children.

So how are the children doing? According to the US Department of Education, in 2011 Washington DC had the worst high-school graduation rate in the country.

Fortunately for President Obama's children, their school's graduation rate is 100 percent. He can afford the tuition of $35,288 (which includes a hot lunch). He can also afford to be relentlessly ideologically opposed to school choice. As is, you will not be surprised to learn, the National Education Association (the teachers' union), for which school choice is a cross fashioned from garlic.

As the figures show, violent crime is trending down in the District. But probably not illegitimacy, now so rampant as to be normal—70 percent among blacks, almost three times the level of the 1960s. Today, it's not illegitimacy that's déclassé. It's the word "illegitimacy" itself. "Out-of-wedlock" is the quaint mot du jour. Liberal progressives (President Obama's forebears), who in the 1960s promoted a reinterpretation of the Aid to Families with Dependent Children law, may not have caused the increase in illegitimacy, but they made having illegitimate children financially viable, even profitable.

A search of the news accounts of Makayla Darden's shooting turns up no mention of a father. Only a mother, a grandmother, and an aunt. The statistics tell us that even if her father and mother are together, it's not likely that her friends live in two-parent homes.

Fortunately for President Obama's children, their parents are married.

A few years ago, a middle-class white person asked a middle-class black person in the adjacent bus seat whether he had any thoughts on why the black community they had just visited was so dysfunctional.

The black person looked back in astonishment: "My mother is a lawyer. My father is a doctor. I have absolutely nothing in common with these people."

One has the sense that President Obama might have been the person occupying that seat.

Meanwhile, Makayla Darden fights for her life in a Southeast Washington hospital, in critical but stable condition. And if she recovers, she will return to a community President Obama seems to have absolutely nothing in common with.

By the way, how did you spend St. Valentine's Day?

Republican Social Justice?
March 11, 2014

The soul of the Republican Party, always assuming it has a soul, is back in play. Arthur Brooks has written a piece in *Commentary* decrying conservatives' reluctance to articulate a social justice agenda. Peter Wehner lauded the piece in his column in *Commentary*. Power Line's Paul Mirengoff dissented from Wehner's defense of the term "social justice," and Wehner responded.

Inside baseball? Perhaps. But it's spring training for the big game in 2016, and that game will decide, in the short term at least, the fate of the nation.

Brooks lays out his view of the problem. Under Obama's policies, the rich have been getting richer—they're all Goldman Saxons now. Meanwhile, the poor are suffering—indeed, have become desperate. A smaller percentage of Americans are employed than at any time since the Jimmy Carter daze, and a higher percentage are on food stamps than in 2009—almost 50 percent more, Brooks says, although he doesn't mention that food stamp eligibility requirements have been reduced in recent years. Clearly the president has failed to achieve his goals, but that won't stop the Democrats from campaigning on issues like income inequality. What conservatives need, Brooks says, is a social agenda of their own.

Some of what Brooks says may be true, though it is simply not clear how many people are really, really poor. Nevertheless, as we have witnessed for years, conservatives are portrayed (by the left-wing media, to be sure) as hard-hearted. Then they lose elections. Then the left-wing (or kind and gentle compassionate Republican) victors promote more bad policies, and the cycle repeats.

With a few exceptions, that is what's been happening for the last, oh, sixty years. Since the launching of *National Review* in 1955, government has grown relentlessly, with, perhaps, three exceptions: Reagan's reduction of the top income-tax rates, welfare reform in the 1990s, and victory in the Cold War, which allowed us to reduce military spending (but did taxes go down?). Other than those victories, conservatives have been losing ground under both Republican and Democratic administrations.

Whatever conservatives have been doing, it hasn't been translating into votes for their presidential candidates recently, or into policies (with those three exceptions) for decades. In sports, when you're losing, the proper strategy is to change your game. That, expressed differently, may be what Arthur Brooks is saying.

Brooks's game-changing solution is for conservatives to "articulate" a social justice agenda of their own. Based on his interviews with actual poor and vulnerable citizens, he says that what the poor truly need is: transformation, relief, and opportunity.

By "transformation" he means "personal, moral transformation," the constituent parts of which are faith, family, community, and work. "Relief" refers to programs that provide cash, some with incentives attached (e.g., the Earned Income Tax Credit), some without. "Opportunity" means, essentially, better education.

But it isn't immediately clear whether Brooks's argument relates to a need for new programs or only for new packaging.

There isn't a goal that Brooks suggests that hasn't been part of the conservatives' agenda for years, though they may not have been calling it social justice. As for specific programs, Brooks doesn't propose a single one in his 5,500-word piece. Looking at welfare reform, he says only that "the beginning of an answer . . . lies in the welfare reform movement of the 1990s." Yes, and remember how that was vilified—until it was successful; and even then, under Obama, some of the reforms were undone because it didn't seem, to some people, "socially just" to impose work requirements on the poor.

Social justice turns out to be a double-edged sword.

Even so, Peter Wehner supports social justice, although he

concedes that Friedrich Hayek believed the term was a "hollow incantation," an "empty formula." Wehner quotes Irving Kristol: "Can men live in a free society if they have no reason to believe it is also a just society? I do not think so." Kristol said that man "cannot for long accept a society in which power, privilege, and property are not distributed according to some morally meaningful criteria." But distributed by what agency? There are only three possibilities: the market, individuals, or the state. In most of the world the state distributes. In most of the world people are miserable. In looking around at most of the world it is not obvious that a reasonable man would prefer to live in a "just" society over one in which he was free.

And what, on Earth, are "morally meaningful criteria"? Wehner refers us to Psalm 33:5, which in his preferred translation says, "The Lord loves social justice." But unless the Lord has decided to concern himself with groups instead of individuals (will He—finally, after their twelve-year losing streak!—be pulling for Army next year?) "social justice" refers to the actions of individuals—which, yes, would include individuals acting as a group, but only as uncoerced members of a group.

Paul Mirengoff would seem to agree. He says the concept of social justice just doesn't make sense. Justice is "individual-centric." "When a person goes to court," Mirengoff says, ". . . our system strives to provide him with a result that is fair given what he has done or failed to do." Yes and no.

Mirengoff may be right about the concept of social justice not making sense, but his example sounds more like social justice than he probably intends. A person's day in court is supposed to provide him with justice, which may or may not be fair. What we hope is that at least the justice system is fair. For example: Suppose a plaintiff is clearly in the right, but he has waited too long to file his claim, and so it is denied. Is that fair? Perhaps not to the plaintiff, but it is to the defendant, who would otherwise be liable indefinitely. That's why we have statutes of limitation.

Still, Mirengoff's instincts are good. He says, "The pursuit of social justice may also lead to action that is inconsistent with justice, such as granting racial preferences or expropriating someone's property for 'the greater good.'" Correct. But then he says he agrees with Wehner that "any society that fails to dispense some measure of sympathy and solicitude to others, particularly those living in the shadows and who are most vulnerable to injustice, cannot really be a good society."

But the issue is not dispensing sympathy and solicitude, which Peter can scatter luxuriantly without diminishing Paul's supply. The issue is taking a portion of the finite number of dollars Mr. and Mrs. America have so they can be redistributed to Ms. Welfare Mother and her third illegitimate child, whose father was last seen starring in a security-camera video. Mirengoff doesn't say, specifically, whether he approves of that redistributionist policy. He does say that "vulnerability to injustice can be countered by the rigorous pursuit of simple justice." But what does that mean? Being poor is a form of injustice? The question is: Does Mirengoff favor, say, food stamps, or does he not?

Perhaps Mirengoff's point is that if a society is going to claim that it is just for the state to help the poor, it must also claim that it is just for the state to tax the non-poor in order to redistribute their wealth—and therefore we have no need to call that taxing and redistributing "social justice." But he doesn't say that, and so we are left wondering which if any welfare programs Mirengoff would have society support in order to be the good society that Wehner describes.

Wehner does not describe the individual programs a society should adopt in order to be socially just, but we can make some guesses by looking at his record as a member of the compassionate conservative Bush administration, which gave us No Child Left Behind, the Medicare prescription drug program, and nation-building in Iraq.

Wehner concludes the debate by saying that his differences with Mirengoff are more about semantics than about ends. But that isn't clear, because Mirengoff doesn't say what programs or policies his non-social justice polity would sanction. If none, then Mirengoff and Wehner are poles apart.

Where does that take us?

Back to Arthur Brooks. Conservatives may fret over Brooks's piece because they may think he has a whole packet of social justice reforms up his sleeve.

That, I think, would be to misread Brooks. He is talking about semantics: how conservatives should sell the policy goals, and policies, they have supported, if inarticulately, for years. He must be talking about semantics, because if he's suggesting that conservatives haven't been in favor of the policy goals he recommends, he . . . hasn't been paying attention.

Brooks says that for too long conservatives have been against things instead of "for people." Perhaps, but they may have taken their cue from the Ten Commandments, eight of which are negative, or from the Bill of Rights, which is a negation of government power. Our founding documents were crafted specifically to protect us from people like Barack Obama.

Conservatives know the value of faith, community, and work. Heaven knows they know the value of family and of education—look at the efforts they have made to promote various non-governmental solutions to the problems in these areas. And their proposal for Social Security is not to abolish it but to privatize it. Brooks may think that conservatives have been insufficiently articulate, and given their presidential and policy track record, he has a point. But is his point augmented or diminished by Gallup's finding that 72 percent of Americans describe themselves as either conservatives or moderates? Have conservatives done well, and would they have done better flying a social justice banner? Or worse?

Mirengoff says there are dangers in marching under a social justice banner, and he's right. One danger is that liberals always have bigger banners. Home ownership for the poor, achieved by requiring Fannie Mae and Freddie Mac to lower their underwriting standards, was the social justice cause of the last decade. Describe and discuss (use only one blue book).

In addition, many people won't understand what the social justice banner means. Just explaining how much conservative programs would benefit the poor is not likely to sway voters who neither trust conservatives nor understand why government is, or should be, limited.

Finally, one gets the sense that Arthur Brooks thinks a conservative social justice agenda might play well in the liberal press. If so, Houston, we have a problem.

Maybe, just maybe, the way to capture the public's attention is to fly a freedom banner and propose something truly new: a massive— 20 percent? Wow!—reduction in welfare programs and regulations. Scrap agricultural supports. Abolish the Department of Commerce. Eliminate OSHA. That may be too libertarian for most Republicans, but those kinds of ideas seem to have traction on the campuses. And couldn't such a program be described as justice, maybe even social justice? If a time limit on filing a claim in court is justice for potential defendants, why isn't not having to pay taxes to support a thousand wasteful social programs justice for working people?

Well, maybe Brooks is right: Perhaps it's just semantics after all. Conservatives can continue to care about the nation as they have since, let's say, 1955, but in public they must emphasize their "sympathy and solicitude" for the poor. Maybe. Maybe not.

What if the Republican Party renamed itself the Sympathy and Solicitude Party. That would shake up 2016, which, conservatives should remember, is an away game. They're all away games. The sportscasters are the *New York Times* and the *Washington Post* and their affiliates, and all the ads will be for liberal candidates.

Brooks is saying, I think, that conservatives have the products. They just need to create better ads. That's one way of looking at it.

Play ball.

After Ukraine, What Should US Strategy Be in Europe?

April 7, 2014

As Russia amasses troops on Ukraine's borders, Americans—and especially Europeans—should be asking two questions: What country in Europe is America willing to fight for, and for what country in Europe has America committed itself to fight? These questions may have different answers.

The first question leads to the subsidiary question: How should we fight? With guns or barter—military hardware or trade and currency? Different measures bring hardships to different sectors of society.

Will the Americans fight for Notre Dame? We have before, but really it would be considerate if the French would stop selling arms to the Russians.

Will the United States fight for Ukraine? Certainly not militarily, and probably only in limited way economically. Even then, it may be difficult to get the European countries—we used to call them nations—to go along. Moreover, how can sanctions work without Europe's enthusiastic cooperation?

Then the important question is: Why should we do anything?

The answer to that question may be: If we don't keep order in the world, who will? However, that may not yet be a good enough answer to convince the American people that it is only they who can, and therefore must, step into the breach.

Define "breach."

One definition: An attack on the Cathedral of St. Stanislav and St. Vladisla.

Come again?

An attack on the Cathedral of St. Stanislav and St. Vladisla.

Which cathedral?

That is the problem. The Cathedral of St. Stanislav and St. Vladisla is not Notre Dame. It's located in Vilnius, which is located in Lithuania, which is located about forty minutes from the border with Russia, "in current traffic," according to Google.

Forty minutes is less time than President Obama spends each morning looking in the mirror and rereading his speeches. If the Russians want the Cathedral of St. Stanislav and St. Vladisla, they're going to get it.

You say no? You say: What about NATO?

When was the last time you read the NATO treaty? The part that barks is Article 5, in which the parties agree "to assist the Party or Parties so attacked by taking forthwith, individually and in concert with the other Parties, such action as it deems necessary, including the use of armed force, to restore and maintain the security of the North Atlantic area.

The words "such action as it deems necessary, including the use of armed force" clearly contemplate action that does not include the use of armed force, and at most only such action as each party deems necessary.

You were probably thinking of the 1948 Brussels treaty, the predecessor to the NATO treaty. Its key phrase obligated the parties to "afford the party so attacked all the military and other aid and assistance in their power." That is not what the NATO treaty provides, and the change in the wording would probably support the argument that that is not what the NATO treaty intended.

It is not beyond imagining that Mr. Obama, whose foreign policy accomplishments in his first two years, in his own words, "stack up against any president in modern history (with the possible exceptions of Johnson, FDR, and Lincoln)" could decide that the loss of the Cathedral of St. Stanislav and St. Vladisla and the twenty-five thousand square miles of the country in which it is located (about the size of West Virginia) would not so damage the security of the North Atlantic area as to require military intervention.

The seven hundred thousand Americans of Lithuanian extraction might disagree, but Mr. Obama doesn't need their support for his next job. Any president who has unilaterally amended a national health insurance law thirty-eight times won't be stopped by a few words in an old international agreement. Lithuanians would be right to worry.

As would Estonians. And Latvians. And Romanians and Bulgarians.

What about NATO member Poland? Ah, Poland's different—and, er, incidentally, did you know that there are more Polish Americans living in Chicago than there are Romanians or Bulgarians living in all the United States?

An attack on Poland may be a primary definition of "breach."

How else "breach" can be defined is a problem the United States and NATO should start thinking about now, as Russian troops amass on the Ukraine border.

Hey, Hey, Ho, Ho, Student Debt Has Got to Go!
May 8, 2014

Student debt is a public-policy issue that will keep on giving—giving problems to the Democrats, who created it, and the opportunity of a lifetime to Republicans, if they have the wit to seize it.

The total student-loan debt is huge, an estimated $1 trillion. Average debt per borrower in 2012 was $24,800. Of the trillion dollars, about $758.5 billion is owed to the federal government. The rest is owed to private lenders.

There are three problems with the student loans, two of which receive some coverage, but one of which is never mentioned by the left-wing press—and that's where the opportunity for Republicans lies.

The first problem is that the loans encourage students to spend years at an institution from which many of them will derive no benefit, for three reasons.

The first reason is the nature of the curriculum at too many modern universities, where there is likely to be a department of Feminist, Gender & Sexuality Studies, offering courses like "Kings, Queens & Queers," or "Cross-Dressing in Nineteenth Century Literature" (the latter, obviously, is a graduate course).

The second reason is that the nature of work is changing. In a recent column in the *Wall Street Journal*, William Galston referred to three Canadian economists whose research calls into question the proposition that a college education is the key to a young person's future. The theory is that information technology tends to make whatever is learned in college, if not the graduates themselves, less valuable. As any parent of a twelve-year-old knows, you don't need a college education to do complex tasks on a computer.

The third reason is that some people simply cannot profit from any college experience. We have to remember that, even in the fifth year of the reign of Obama, half of all students are below average. If they go to college, they will spend their time, except during Sex Week, studying subjects and reading authors they have no particular interest in and insufficient training or sophistication to understand. Many of them would profit from learning a useful trade far more than from spending years at a college.

Only a few days ago, Josh Mandel, the treasurer of Ohio, wrote about a company that was paying sixty of its welders more than $150,000 a year, a salary that puts them in the top 10 percent of earners. He cited a 2012 Bureau of Labor Statistics report that found that 48 percent of college graduates are working at jobs that don't require a four-year college degree. About one-third of the Millennials (people between the ages of twenty-two and thirty-two) say they should have gotten a job instead of going to college. Flipping hamburgers at McDonald's may be a great training job for a teenager, but not for a college graduate with $30,000 in student loans and a degree in Women's Studies. Skilled blue-collar labor has to be more rewarding, financially and emotionally—even if tony liberals look down their long noses at it.

The second problem is that student loans allowed colleges to raise their costs—to feather their nests at students' expense. College costs have risen much faster than inflation. To take just one example, in 1966, tuition at the University of Southern California was $1,200 a year, which in today's dollars would be $8,751.59. So how much does a year's tuition cost today? $42,162! No wonder students have become indentured servants, in hock to the federal government and other lenders till they reach their forties, at which point the lucky ones may have to co-sign their children's student-loan papers.

From a *Huffington Post* survey comes this sobering comment: "During college I made an enormous mistake: I accumulated $83,786 in student loan debt, getting a Master of Music in opera performance. . . . In my current circumstances, I cannot pay $1,000 or more per month. I know that I got myself into this situation, but it distresses me that my horrible judgment during one period of my life is likely to impact my life negatively forever."

What a great society! As banks were said to have lured unsuspecting borrowers into unaffordable housing mortgages before the 2008 crash, so the federal government, and others, have for years lured unwary students into taking out loans that don't advance their careers. Someone ought to find out where the inventor of federally guaranteed student loans for all, Lyndon Johnson, is hiding and drag him out so he can be horsewhipped.

But it's the third problem that Republicans ought to pay special attention to. Student loans, and all the other federal aid-to-education programs, are the irrigation for the fever swamps of the Left. The colleges and universities in this country are shills for all the leftist nostrums that afflict us—and it's the federal government (which means taxpayers) that pays the bills and makes it possible.

The University of California at Los Angeles Higher Education Research Institute surveyed faculty members nationwide and concluded that in 2010–2011 the political breakdown of faculties was: far left—12 percent; liberal—50 percent; middle-of-the-road—25 percent; conservative—11 percent; and "far right"—0.4 percent. But we really didn't need a survey to tell us that.

The Center for Responsive Politics reported in September 22, 2010, that employees at Harvard, Stanford, and Columbia Universities gave at least 75 percent of their collective political contributions to Democrats. And they should be allowed to go on contributing to Democrats and being as far left as they want—just not on the taxpayers' dime.

What all this means is that firing an Exocet missile into the heart of the American higher-education establishment should qualify the trigger man for a place on Mount Rushmore.

Here's the missile: Republicans commit, as part of their 2016 platform, to (1) canceling all student loans owed to the federal government and paying off all loans owed to private institutions and (2) eliminating all federal aid, grants, support, etc., to postsecondary educational institutions. It's a package deal: no elimination of aid, no cancellation of debts.

Hmm. I wonder how the 38 million people with student-loan debt would vote on that issue. In 2012, 60 percent of Millennials voted for Obama. It doesn't have to be that way.

You ask, how can the country possibly afford to cancel ("forgive" sounds too religious, doesn't it?—might cause it to be overruled by the Supreme Court) a trillion dollars in debt? And how can we afford to do that now, in this time of financial distress? Isn't that irresponsible?

Actually, it's not—I wouldn't have suggested it if it were.

Total federal aid to higher education (if you call courses in human sexuality and women's studies higher education) is about $99 billion—$34 billion in grants to the students themselves, and an additional $65 billion in "Direct Loans" subsidy allowances. In addition, the federal government pumps about $40 billion into the system for research, at least $10 billion of which, and perhaps more, could be eliminated without serious consequences. (Approximately $600 million goes to Harvard University, which has an endowment now of $30 billion. About $46 million goes to Brandeis University, which reversed its decision to grant an honorary degree to Ayaan Hirsi Ali, for which behavior alone its grants should be cancelled.)

So: if total student debt is a trillion dollars, and annual federal support to higher education that can be eliminated is $109 billion, cancelling both would allow the Treasury to break even in only nine years—and that assumes that if the trillion-dollar debt were not canceled, all of it would eventually be repaid, which it obviously wouldn't be. The default rate is about 10 percent.

If federal grants are eliminated, some institutions will collapse, of course, but most of them will be institutions that really aren't providing any value to their students.

And some of the research, which has exploded in recent decades, is probably worthless. Do we really need one book a week on Shakespeare? Do we need to spend $2.19 billion a year for environmental sciences research, and another billion or two or three for research on political science, psychology, economics, sociology, business management, library science, humanities, law, and social work? The list goes on. Research that is essential will be supported by the market—corporations and rich individuals—as it has been for years.

Students for whom college makes sense will still be able to get loans—from friends, banks, perhaps companies, and the colleges themselves—as long as they can persuade the lenders (e.g., by having decent SAT scores) that they can truly profit from college.

According to the Pew Research Center, Millennials continue to view the Democratic Party more favorably than the Republican Party. But that's changing. They're getting older, and they are facing the reality of huge student-debt payments (as well as "membership"—compulsory, of course—in the Social Security Ponzi scheme, which will run out of money before they retire). They are waking up to what liberals have done to them.

This is the moment Republicans have been waiting for. They have a historic opportunity to free the current indentured former students from their debts and open up a brighter future for them, and to prevent another generation of young people—or two generations, or five, or seven—from wasting years at college and going into debt to do it, and then living a life of agony trying to pay off that debt.

Hey, hey, ho, ho, Aid to Ed has got to go!

D-Day 2014: A Remembrance

June 8, 2014

Normandy, France—June 6, 2014. At dawn on D-Day 2014, the breeze was soft, the weather warming. The temperature would reach the high eighties. This was not the Longest Day's weather.

All highways and major roads near the Normandy beaches were closed to general traffic in order to facilitate travel by buses (scores of them) and cars and limousines carrying more than three thousand people, many of them Americans, to the ceremonies marking the seventieth anniversary of the landing of Allied troops on the Normandy beaches. June 6, 1944, was, after all, finally, the beginning of the end of World War II in Europe.

World War what?

On one bus going to the American Cemetery in Colleville-sur-Mer, a young girl and her younger first cousin, a college student in Pennsylvania, were looking after their grandfather. He had been a nineteen-year-old engineer in 1944, and had landed on June 9, to build anything and everything that the engineers built, but especially landing strips. He had not been back to the beaches since his first visit. His wife of sixty-six years had died two years ago, and so it fell to his granddaughter to look after him. She was justly proud of her grandfather, and admitted, lovingly, that his stories did change a bit each time he told them. And he kept worrying that the ceremony might start without him. It would not have.

She was less proud of her friends and her cousin's classmates, who, she said, had little or no interest in where they were going or why. "Oh, you're going to France," they said. "What are you going to do there?" She explained. They didn't seem to understand.

According to the American Council of Trustees and Alumni, only 40 percent of Americans know that June 6 is the anniversary of D-Day. And 25 percent don't know that D-Day occurred during World War II. College graduates aren't much better: almost 10 percent of them say that if you visit the beach where D-Day took place, you'll be at Pearl Harbor.

We are tempted to laugh, in that nervous way we laugh at other people's ignorance. Or perhaps we remember instead, especially if we have been to the Visitors' Center at the American Cemetery in Colleville-sur-Mer, that many of the young soldiers who came from all over America to those Normandy beaches also had no idea, before they got there, of where those beaches were, no idea of where they were going—going, many of them, to die.

But that was then, before the greatest amphibious landing the world had ever seen—or ever will see. You might think that, today, the battle that changed the course of Western Civilization would have a bit more resonance.

The course of what?

What was World War II all about, anyway?

President Obama, in his address at the American Cemetery, indicated that it was about liberty, equality, freedom, and the inherent dignity of every human being. Just how liberty and freedom differed was not explicated—perhaps tighter editing would have eliminated the issue. Equality is a big campaign issue for the president, so it may not be surprising he would include it. And we certainly believe in the inherent dignity of every human being. But was that all there was to a war in which millions died?

Obama's list seems weak, desiccated, especially in comparison to President Franklin Roosevelt's understanding of World War II, and of D-Day in particular. Early on the morning of June 6, 1944, President Roosevelt asked the nation to "join with me in prayer," a portion of which had been read two days before Obama's speech by a different speaker at a ceremony at the French–American Memorial Hospital in Saint-Lô—a town so destroyed it was nicknamed "The Capital of Ruins."

Almighty God: Our sons, pride of our nation, this day have set upon a mighty endeavor, a struggle to preserve our Republic, our religion, and our civilization, and to set free a suffering humanity.

Today, our religion and our civilization are controversial subjects, subjects to be fought over in debates, not for in battles.

Roosevelt ended his D-Day prayer with the words "Thy will be done, Almighty God. Amen."

There has been a movement in recent years to add FDR's prayer to the World War II memorial in Washington DC. Not surprisingly, perhaps, the Obama administration has opposed the move. Robert Abbey, the Obama-appointed director of the Bureau of Land Management, has resisted adding FDR's prayer, saying that any plaque or inscription of the prayer would "dilute" the memorial's central message, and therefore that the memorial "should not be altered."

The day before D-Day this year, a bill sponsored by Senators Rob Portman (R–OH) and Mary L. Landrieu (D–LA) to add the prayer to the World War II memorial passed the Senate unanimously. Approval by the House is expected, which will force President Obama to confront the issue. And perhaps force Americans in general to confront the issue of what America is all about, and why over four thousand American soldiers died on a stretch of beach most of them had never heard of only a few months before they got there.

By "our civilization," Roosevelt meant Western Civilization—the mores, habits, and culture that define us, Americans and Europeans, and that over centuries have made us who we are today. Those mores include the freedom and "the inherent dignity of every human being" that President Obama mentioned. But Roosevelt seems a lot closer to the grandeur of the common experience of America and Europe, and without a common understanding of that heritage in America, and how it links us to Europe, it seems entirely possible that D-Day never would have happened.

It is primarily a religious heritage, and you can see it glistening like mica in President Reagan's D-Day speech in 1984 at the US Ranger Monument at Pointe du Hoc in Normandy.

That heritage is fading now, along with the memories of what it was that happened that day in Normandy. But there are still, and will be for a few more years, granddaughters looking after their grandfather-heroes, and we will look to them to help us keep warm the memories of the glorious exploits of June 6, 1944. They will help us remember what happened there, then. But it will be up to us to engage in the longer and more difficult struggle to remember why.

A Birthday Wish for John Dingell

July 7, 2014

After 127 years in Washington, Rep. John D. Dingell, who turns eighty-eight today, has decided to call it quits. Actually, it's only been fifty-nine years. It just seems longer.

"I don't want people to say I stayed too long," Mr. Dingell said, displaying a now greatly impaired sense of timing.

He claims the current climate on Capitol Hill is "obnoxious." It will soon improve.

The Michigan Democrat was infamous for his dirty tactics: Put the prey on the stand, grill him mercilessly, make him suffer, leak to the media. You can find the details of two sordid cases on the internet—look under Ann Gorsuch Burford, President Reagan's EPA head, or Nobel laureate David Baltimore.

The pre-1995 Dingell was a rabid dog, an egotistical, power-crazed subpoena-issuing committee chairman—and then the Republicans took control of the House of Representatives and he lost his chairmanship, and with it the ability to issue subpoenas.

I was a Dingell target once, but I was lucky.

In 1988, when I was chairman of the Federal Trade Commission, I gave a speech in which, probably injudiciously, I described Congress as the "realm of the sugar plum fairies doing business as Candy Land USA."

A few weeks later (after more than a quarter of a century some—but not all—of the details have faded), Dingell sent word demanding my presence. I complied, as was customary when a congressman asks for a meeting. I and my aide went to his office, having no idea what he was up to—but it was a safe bet he wasn't serving the cause of good government. The two of us and his aide were seated in a room in his office. Mr. Dingell came in and remained standing. He was agitated and irritated.

He asked who had written the speech I had given. I, probably injudiciously, shot up my hand and said, "I did."

Mr. Dingell paused, fumed, and shook. "You little pipsqueak!" he shouted, and continued in that extraordinary manner for a few minutes. It was a stunningly rude performance by a stunningly rude man.

I got out of my chair. I went up to him and stood in front of his face as close as a drill sergeant stands to a scared recruit. I stared at him and said, "Don't you ever speak to me that way again." Shaking, he said (remarkably egotistically, when you think of it), "You will never gain my respect." To which I replied, "I didn't come to Washington to gain your respect."

I turned and walked out, and as we left, my aide heard him say to his aide, "Get Oliver."

A few months later, someone at the Federal Trade Commission did something that was not improper, but was probably injudicious. Dingell announced he was going to have a hearing, and demanded my presence.

I was lucky. I'd seen him operate and knew his tactics. Dingell would question the victim for a whole day—six hours or more at the microphone—then have his henchmen scrutinize the testimony searching for inconsistencies. When they found some, Dingell would attack.

I hired counsel (at my expense). We reviewed the files for a whole week and prepared my testimony.

The day came. The hearing began. Mr. Dingell started asking questions. A few minutes into the hearing, my two attorneys walked in and sat down in the back of the room. Mr. Dingell paused, turned to his aide and, undoubtedly, asked him who the heavies were. His aide knew. They were known quantities. A short while later, Mr. Dingell gaveled the hearing to a close.

It was over. I walked out. We'd beaten him. It still makes me smile.

I hope he remembers it. And in case he's forgotten, this reminder is my birthday present to him.

Go, Mr. Dingell. Go, and do not come back. Washington will be a less obnoxious place when you are gone.

John Kerry: "Some of My Best Friends are Jews"
November 6, 2014

That's not exactly what Secretary of State John Kerry said, but neither is it as ridiculous as what he actually did say.

He was quoted in a *Washington Post* article reporting that the State Department, "which has been on the leading edge of policies affecting lesbian, gay, bisexual and transgender federal employees," has decided finally—we shared your impatience—to eliminate the "transgender exclusion" from the department's largest health-insurance plan. What the *Washington Post* piece says is that although policies generally exclude services "related to sex reassignment," in fact, "insurance companies often view this exclusion in the broadest possible terms, excluding care that clearly has no relationship to gender status such as cancer treatment and routine preventive care."

It's impossible to know that without investigating insurance companies' practices, but somehow it seems unlikely. It might be that once a person gets hired by the State Department he or (. . . hmm) should have the same coverage as others have, with restrictions no more onerous. So, for example, if an employee regularly engaged in dangerous limb-threatening sports—bull riding, street luging, or mixed martial arts—it might be appropriate for his health-insurance company to refuse to insure him or at least to demand a higher premium. After all, life-insurance companies regularly charge higher premiums to smokers.

Which, if you think about it, may not be fair after all: people are, irremediably, the products of their environment, so if someone's parents smoked or ate too much, he is likely to do the same—and so we can't blame him, can we? Who in his right mind would suggest today that obese people should pay more for health insurance even though they may cost the insurers more? And isn't it the same, mutatis mutandis, with gender identification? Aren't we all in this together?

Anyway, an exclusion for sex-change operations really seems odd—hardly worth the paperwork. No doubt such procedures can be expensive—see below—but how many State Department employees would you expect to change their gender in any given year? But of course that's not the right question, which is, rather, how many State Department transgender people would you expect to have that operation in a given year?

(Not so long ago, people who had had sex-change operations were denoted "transsexual," and the newer term "transgender" referred to dressing and behaving like the "target gender," with perhaps a bit of hormone therapy. No longer. Now, as one "transgender rights activist" explains, any definition "that pit[s] biology against psychology or the body against the mind . . . denigrates transgender peoples [sic] self-identified genders.")

To figure out how many transgender operations there might be each year, we first have to estimate how many transgender people there are at State. Who knows? The State Department website says there are 13,000 people in the Foreign Service corps, 11,000 in the Civil Service, and more than 45,000 "locally employed Foreign Service staff overseas," for a total of 69,000.

But, how many of those 69,000 are trans? Again, who knows? A 2003 survey taken in California found that 0.1 percent of adults there identified as "transgender," which would put the number of trans-genders at State at 69. We're getting closer. How many of those 69 would you, or the insurance company, expect to have the operation each year? And how much would it cost?

For computing the cost, we're in luck. The Philadelphia Center for Transgender Surgery has an online price list. Picking from the "Male to Female" list, we see that an abdominoplasty (tummy tuck) is $8,500, although a mini is only $5,300. A buttock augmentation (implants) goes for $9,500. And an unmentionable procedure—the queen of the lot—is really expensive: $19,750. If you do everything on the list (and you probably wouldn't), the cost would be $120,700.

If ten people opted for surgery in any given year, the total bill would be $1,207,000—but that would be spread out among the premiums of the 69,000 employees, which comes to only $17.50 a person. That is not a big deal. At least not a big financial deal.

So why all the fuss? What's really going on here?

Identity politics.

Listen to Kerry, as quoted in the same *Washington Post* piece: "I've met transgendered [sic] colleagues at the Department and in addition to being brave and strong, they're just good officers." Really? How many brave transgender officers are there at State, anyway? And just where has Kerry met them? Not, presumably, in the private elevator to his eighth-floor office, and probably not in the ground-floor cafeteria.

We note first that he's talking about "officers," so that must exclude non-officers. The State Department doesn't have ready figures (or won't release them) on how many of its 69,000 employees are officers, but presumably not all of them are. If a third are, that would mean there are 23,000 officers. But Secretary Kerry cited those who were "brave," which further reduces the number, because not all officers would serve in positions that offer the opportunity to be brave. In fact, probably no more than 10 percent of the 23,000 officers, or 2,300, could be described as "brave."

And of those 2,300, how many are transgender (not "transgendered," please, as Kerry calls them)? Well, 0.1 percent, or 2.3 people. And Kerry hasn't just met them. He knows all 2.3 of them well enough to have formed an opinion of them, that they are brave and strong, and good officers.

Spinach!

What we are seeing, of course, is a frantic Democratic Party. The Obama administration is in disarray, its policies—to the extent it has formed them—failing, its popularity plummeting, its corporate-funding buddies switching sides. Frantically, frenetically, the Obama people play the gender card, or cards, and the race card.

It was that old card, racist Democrat Hugo Black—under attack, when he was nominated to the Supreme Court, for having been a Ku Klux Klansman—who made "Some of my best friends are Jews" famous. Shelley Berman, a 1950s stand-up comedian, had a better line: "So-and-so," he would intone confidently, "isn't a Jew. He's just Jewish." Berman could get away with it.

Kerry should have stuck with Hugo Black's line. At least it's probably true. And we can say about John Kerry, though perhaps without Shelley Berman's confidence, that the secretary's not a fool. He's just foolish.

The Federal Trade Commission's Unwelcome Birthday

November 6, 2014

Happy Birthday, Federal Trade Commission—I guess. This Friday the FTC is holding a jamboree in Washington DC to celebrate one hundred years of nonstatutory lawmaking, commonly referred to as regulating.

The FTC was midwifed into this world on September 26, 1914, by President Woodrow Wilson—not an auspicious beginning. Wilson thought separation of powers belonged in the dustbin of history. The FTC is now the oldest surviving so-called "independent regulatory agency," the Interstate Commerce Commission having departed this life in 1995.

Since its beginning, the FTC's record has been checkered at best. It's not difficult to find an economist who thinks the FTC's net effect has been negative.

The Federal Trade Commission Act bans "unfair methods of competition." Exactly what is unfair is left to the FTC commissioners' discretion, as modified from time to time by courts. That kind of power was Wilson's sweet dream.

The trouble is, the most unfair method of competition, and the most demonstrably harmful to consumers, is getting government to rig the market in your favor. Many anticompetitive practices are not just sanctioned, but are required, at both the federal and state levels, making the FTC really only a fig leaf of anticompetitive respectability.

The financial damage of government-mandated anticompetitive behavior is difficult to estimate. This is very complex stuff. But then so are any benefits from FTC actions difficult to estimate.

In a document titled "Performance Plan," listing "objectives and measures," the FTC estimates that in fiscal 2012 it produced consumer benefits of somewhere around $1 billion. That may sound like a lot, but it's mouse droppings compared with the consumer loss from anticompetitive restrictions at the federal and state levels.

Wayne Crews at the Competitive Enterprise Institute estimates that the US sugar program costs consumers $4 billion a year. Chris Edwards at the Cato Institute estimated in 2009 that the US dairy program costs consumers between zero to $2.5 billion a year, depending on the market price of milk. Let's assume it's 50 percent each year, or $1.25 billion.

Adam Summers of the Reason Foundation estimated in 2007 that state licensing laws cost consumers between $35 billion and $42 billion a year. Occupational licensing laws require workers who want to enter certain fields to meet specific requirements—usually a minimum amount of course work, exams, and other prerequisites. The rationale is that the requirements guarantee quality of service and protect the public health. The requirements may make sense in some highly specialized fields (medicine), but their benefits are speculative at best for hair braiders or interior designers.

Just those three kinds of regulations add up to about $40 billion a year, compared with the FTC's own estimate of its benefit to consumers of only $1 billion.

It is true that the FTC has opposed some state-level anticompetitive behavior. It currently has a case before the Supreme Court challenging the practice of the North Carolina Dental Board of Examiners for restricting competition.

That's not as good as it looks, though. The Supreme Court has held that if such restrictions are truly imposed by a state government, rather than just by the members of a profession, they are immune from attack (under the "State Action doctrine"). For example, if a particular profession has been able to persuade the state government to rig the market in its favor, the FTC will be powerless to act to benefit consumers.

What should FTC commissioners do? Take to the road and explain to the American people that government is the primary cause of anticompetitive activity. In almost any media market other than the top ten—and sometimes there, too—a speech by an FTC commissioner will be carried by the evening news. Yes, the result of such activity is speculative, but then, as numerous economists agree, so is the benefit of most antitrust cases.

Five FTC commissioners—crusaders for competition—crisscrossing the country telling the truth about governments' anticompetitive practices would be news in itself.

State and federal government officials undoubtedly would howl that the FTC commissioners were out of bounds. Perhaps. Out of bounds is where the work needs to be done, though.

Teaching the American people the true facts about competition policy might take a hundred years. Which means they should begin at once.

Marriage: Obama's Last Chance
December 2, 2014

It's over for Barack Obama. But it doesn't have to be.

It's true the economy languishes. Obamacare remains hugely unpopular. People hate the tone of Washington politics, which Obama said he would change, and which he has changed—for the worse. Obama's foreign policy embarrasses the professionals and scares the amateurs. Only a quarter of Americans think the country is on the right track. And public confidence in the presidency is at a six-year low. This guy can't hit.

It's true also that he got his most important bills passed, but only through deception, subterfuge, obfuscation, and dubious parliamentary maneuvers, which—serves him right—increases the chances that his signature piece of legislation will be repealed. He can't field either.

People who can't hit or field shouldn't play baseball.

The president should try a different game. Fortunately, there's one waiting for him. If he played it well—or even if he just showed up in uniform—he could go down as one of the country's great presidents. Sadly, it's more likely he'll just go down, with Jimmy Carter.

At this stage in Barack Obama's presidency it is no longer scandalous to say he is an affirmative-action president. We know that, not just because he received, twice, a huge majority of the votes of black Americans (95 percent in 2008, 93 percent in 2012), but also because almost every member of the VRC (vast right-wing conspiracy) has a friend who voted for Obama, because he was black.

Barack Obama needs to face the plain truth, no matter how unpleasant it may be to his post-racial self-conception: he is black. But by being black he has special resonance with black Americans and with "the black community." The terms may not be coterminous, but they're close enough for government work, which is what Obama does.

One of America's least tractable problems is the growth of the underclass (read Charles Murray for details). The collapse of marriage and the rampant growth of illegitimacy condemn millions of Americans, first as children, then as adults, to lives of poverty and despair.

According to the Heritage Foundation, "Over a third of single-parent families . . . are poor, compared to only 7 percent of married families. Overall, children in married families are 82 percent less likely to be poor than are children of single parents."

The only hope for young children is parents. Not a village, pace Mrs. Clinton. Parents. Two of them.

The illegitimacy rate among blacks is 72 percent, higher than among any other group. It's true, of course, that there are more illegitimate whites than illegitimate blacks (blacks are only 13 percent of the population), and true also that we can't blame all of society's ills on the black underclass.

Nevertheless, illegitimacy is a disaster for the people in the underclass who are black, and someone who has standing and credibility should try to do something about it. Who might that someone be? Why not our president?

The president should spend every Saturday from now until he leaves office going to a black wedding, a wedding—need it be said?—of a man and a woman. The president needs to make getting married the coolest act in town.

And he might even enjoy it. Just the other day he said, "I love just being with the American people. . . . You know how passionate I am about trying to help them." How better to help them than by spending the remaining hundred Saturdays of his presidency going to weddings? (And people can get married on other days of the week too.)

You can already hear the objections, one of which will relate to security. There are two solutions to the security problem. The first is to have less of it; the presidency is already far too imperial. Who would be surprised if it were only the professionals who think it's all necessary?

The other solution is to have the weddings at the White House, or perhaps just the receptions. Are there better uses for the building? Name three.

The president doesn't have time, you say? He's too busy keeping America safe and prosperous? Golf balls! Look, and laugh, at a list of Obama's 203 presidential golf outings.

Marriage is the linchpin of Western Civilization, which, unfortunately, the crowd Obama runs with dismisses as a cultural affliction imposed by, primarily, dead white males. They're wrong. Western Civ gave us, preeminently, equality, respect for women, and freedom from state oppression.

President Obama should be bounteous with his attendance. No couple getting married is without merit. Rich man, poor man, beggar man, thief: marriage can redeem them all. The president could become known as the Marriage President—perhaps in time even, in history books, the Dearly Beloved President. Seriously.

More likely, alas, the president won't change. Few people over forty do. He'll continue to be aloof, spiteful, polarizing, shunned, even by his own party.

In which case: it's over for Barack Obama.

Too Late Now to Sell Obama Short
December 10, 2014

Senator Mary Landrieu's defeat in the Louisiana run-off election last Saturday spells curtains for holders of Barack Obama stock.

Back in February of 2009, I asked readers whether, if Barack Obama were a stock, they would be buying or selling. I recommended selling. At the time, Obama Inc. (stock symbol BHO) was already down on the Rasmussen Approval Index History exchange from its January 2009 price of 27 pct to 11 pct. The stock recently went down another 20 percent!

People who followed my advice, especially those who sold short, made millions—or have recently been elected to office.

No one's buying BHO now because Obama Inc.'s only asset—being president—is a wasting asset, known in the profession as a "lame duck."

BHO has two product lines, domestic policy and foreign policy. Both have been spectacularly, all but unprecedentedly, unsuccessful.

What looked initially like a success—getting the Patient Protection and Affordable Care Act, known on the street as Obamacare, passed by Congress—turned into a tremendous liability. The CEO of the company knew the product's success in the marketplace was a long shot, which is why, arrogantly, it was written in incomprehensible terms and enacted in a patently sneaky way: by attaching it to a reconciliation act, which, because reconciliation acts are not subject to filibusters, required only fifty-one votes in the Senate instead of the sixty that would have been needed to break a filibuster if it had been an ordinary bill.

And then, adding incompetence to arrogance, his management team produced the most spectacularly and embarrassingly botched rollout imaginable—a rollout that will live for decades in textbooks as the prime example of progressive government's hubris.

More than half of Americans disapprove of the law, which allowed a BHO rival to compete successfully in early November for the public's business.

Other domestic products have fared no better. The economy remains sluggish, after six years. Job growth has remained sluggish, after six years. Workforce participation is at the lowest rate in thirty-six years. Median income is 8 percentage points lower than it was in 2007, before the recession began. And a record number of people are on food stamps.

Stockholders may be asking, "What ever happened to the American Dream?"

Even the CEO's wife raised that issue. She said, in public, that achieving the American Dream is "no longer possible" for many middle-class Americans—a comment that had the street asking if she was a highly placed agent provocateur for a rival company.

In addition to the failures of the economic products, the company's administrative abilities have been breathtakingly deficient. The Veterans Administration has been exposed as being staggeringly incompetent. And the CEO's personal handling of the Ebola threat was, again, both arrogant and embarrassing.

The company's other product line, foreign policy, has been no more successful.

In the last year alone, the company suffered the advance of Islamist forces in Libya and a Russian invasion of Crimea, with the consequent destabilization of Ukraine and the potential destabilization of parts of Europe and perhaps even the collapse of NATO.

In a previous year, there was the Red Line Catastrophe: the company's CEO drew a red line which he dared Syria's strongman to cross—and which said strongman crossed without suffering the slightest consequence, the line existing apparently only in the CEO's highly refined imagination. The disdain of foreign-policy establishments around the world, as well as BHO's potential customers, was palpable.

The product news has been bad, but the public's evaluation of all suppliers has been worse.

According to the Gallup organization, public confidence in all three branches of the US government has reached record lows—weighed down undoubtedly by BHO's performance: for the Supreme Court, 30 percent; for Congress, 7 percent (2 points above used-car salesmen but 9 points below lawyers!); and for the presidency a six-year low of 29 percent, down 7 percentage points from just last year. Only a quarter of Americans think the country is on the right track.

Actions, it turns out, not just ideas, have consequences. The result of the company's performance with both its domestic and foreign products has been the forced or voluntary retirement of a significant number of its dealers.

When the company went national in 2009 (it had started out as a local enterprise in 1997, and then become a statewide organization in 2005) it had 58 dealers in the Senate, now down to 44, and 256 dealers in the House, now down to 186. In the same period, the company's state-house dealers have been reduced from 28 to 18.

The CEO brought his company to Washington in 2009 vowing to make history and be a transformational CEO. He has kept his word: famed corporate strategist Michael Barone has said that it looks as if Obama Inc.'s CEO has left his brand in worse shape than any CEO since Woodrow Wilson almost a hundred years ago.

In 2009, I asked, "Could Obama Inc., long on rhetorical smooth talk and media hype, get lucky?" My answer was, "Of course. But savvy investors don't bet on luck and hype. That's why the smart money is selling Obama short."

People who didn't, have only themselves to blame.

(The material contained herein is for discussion purposes only and is not an offer to buy or sell securities, Hillary futures, aka Enron bonds, or anything else. Performance data presented is no more reliable than government statistics and represents only past performance—duh!—and does not guarantee future performance. And please remember to floss after every meal.)

Merry Christmas, Kim Jong-Un
December 25, 2014

What I want to know is, where were the North Koreans when we needed them?

They've been getting terrible ink recently, even though most Americans have precious little interplay with them. In fact, most Americans have never even seen a North Korean in the flesh, not even at Walmart. We've seen pictures of some of them, though, and they don't have a warm and fuzzy look; in fact, they look quite cold and grizzly. They don't seem to be the kind of people we aspire to be. In the old days of radio, there was never a game show called "Who

Wants to be a North Korean?" And their founding fathers, or at least their uncles, tend to vanish into history.

Still, they do seem to be onto something with this movie business.

I haven't seen *The Interview*, and you probably haven't either, because although Sony Pictures Entertainment reversed its decision not to release the movie, few theaters signed on to show it on its release date, Christmas Day. That seems to me an unlikely time to release a movie, given that most people are tired, having, late the night before in church and then during the day itself, been busy celebrating one of the two central events of Western Civilization: the birth of Him who came to offer hope to all men and salvation to sinners. Who could need hope more than North Koreans? And the latter seems like an appropriate description of the rulers of North Korea, unless you're one of those nonjudgmental New-Age diversity types who think all beliefs and feelings are equal and shouldn't be repressed or discouraged by socially prejudiced, culturally imperialistic people.

For most people—or at least most of the people I know—people who aren't in sync with popular culture, Christmas is just not the most appropriate time to hustle the family into the SUV and, with bells jingling, dash through the snow to see a movie in which a nasty dictator gets blown up in his helicopter on a silent, holy night.

I suppose it's mathematically possible, however unlikely, that the North Koreans were just trying to preserve the spirit of Christmas against the assault of America's popular-culture barbarians. Even if that's not what they intended, does lack of intent (in the law it's called scienter) really matter? Not according to Attorney General Eric Holder, who claims that in certain civil rights cases, statistical disparity of race alone should be sufficient to convict. If Holder is right and if intent is not necessary to convict, then perhaps we can find the North Korean rulers guilty of . . . aiding and abetting the cause of Western Civilization by standing athwart Sunset Boulevard yelling "Stop!"

But back to the original question: Where have the North Koreans been when we needed them?

Say, back in 1995, when the movie *Kids* was released. The film (I crib from the AMC website, shamelessly editing and altering for effect) is shocking. It "follows a few characters through one day in New

York City. Telly . . . and his buddy Casper . . . skateboard, do a little petty thievery, drink malt liquor, hustle drugs, beat up a black man, throw some dice, and if a virgin or two happen to cross their path, Telly is only too happy to perform a little 'virgin surgery.' When the boys aren't wandering, they're talking. And when they're talking, it is always about sex. . . . [T]he dialogue is totally disgusting."

For this, God gave us light?

Midnight Cowboy (1969) is the only X-rated Best Picture winner. This gritty movie discomfited some viewers with its frank, nonjudgmental depiction of homosexuality.

Brokeback Mountain (2005), the first mainstream gay/bisexual romance, was deplored by political and religious conservatives, but (or is it "and"?) garnered both critical and popular acclaim. As the AMC website puts it, "The love story depicted in *Brokeback Mountain* is as traditional as that depicted in *Casablanca, Romeo and Juliet,* or *Gone with the Wind,* but instead of war, family rivalry, or the general bitchiness of one of the characters getting in the way, societal prejudice is the culprit." Produced by Hey, Hey, Ho, Ho, Western Civ Has Got to Go Studios.

Then there is *Avatar* (2009), about which Nile Gardiner, writing in *The Telegraph* (London), said: "Washington is one of the most liberal cities in America and you come to expect almost anything here—but still the roars of approval which greeted the on-screen killing of US military personnel were a shock to the system. . . . [*Avatar* is] one of the most left-wing films in the history of modern American cinema."

For this, Thomas Edison gave us the light bulb?

But there's more, much, much more, enough to fill a North Korean gulag. There are genres—single-mom movies, single-dad movies, and chatty, funny little movies and television sitcoms that normalize promiscuity and illegitimacy, and make fun of traditional behavior and morality. Great fun for the upper classes.

According to the Heritage Foundation, "Over a third of single-parent families . . . are poor, compared to only 7 percent of married families. Overall, children in married families are 82 percent less likely to be poor than are children of single parents."

But, hey, it's just entertainment—except when it isn't, which is when the people who populate Charles Murray's Fishtowns and the poverty statistics take the characters as role models and their behavior as imitable. Then we get a tangle of pathologies that fifty years and $20 trillion of Great Society programs have been unable to untangle.

Ask not who wants to be a North Korean. Ask who wants to be the illegitimate son of a single mother who is the illegitimate daughter of a drug addict.

Our hearts go out this Christmas to the wretched people of North Korea, whose best hope is the United States, whose best hope may be to return to the mores of yesteryear, when mothers and fathers and their children could gather in the public square and, unhindered by popular-culture honchos and their allies in big government, wish each other, shamelessly, a Merry Christmas.

Let's Make A Deal with the Middle Class
January 5, 2015

Happy New Year, middle class. Now let's have a serious discussion.

After the electoral shellacking the Democrats took in November, Senator Chuck Schumer (D–Govt.) said the Democrats should propose more middle-class-oriented programs to try to win back the core: white, working-class voters.

Middle-class income is said to be down, and the middle class is said to be upset. But it's not clear that the first statement is true, or that the second statement is important—except electorally.

Meanwhile poverty persists, after fifty years of poverty programs. There are two kinds of poor people: the really poor, people described as the "underclass" (perhaps the bottom 4 to 10 percent of all people classified as poor), who live terrible lives, lives without family, skills, incentives, or hope. They are in desperate need, and far more so than people who might be called the "statistically poor," people who have TVs, air conditioning, PlayStations, one car or maybe two, a counterful of kitchen gadgets, too much food—and a fistful of enervating government handouts that ensure they will never have the satisfaction of being self-supporting adults.

There is, of course, only so much government can do about serious poverty: it is a conservative tenet that not all problems can be solved, by government or anyone else. Even so, that is not a justification for ignoring the plight of the poor, notwithstanding the admonition that they will always be with us. Nor does our inability to cure poverty mean it is impossible to alleviate it: we have witnessed a breathtaking decline in poverty around the world because of the spread of free-market ideas—that is, by structural means, not by charitable works.

If government has any function at all, beyond protecting us from enemies foreign and domestic (preeminently Rush, Fox News, and the Vast Right-Wing Conspiracy), surely constructing a welfare system that does more for the poor than special-interest legislation does for the sugar growers—and a thousand other groups that have learned how to farm the Congress—should be the top priority.

The much-pitied, and too much caterwauling, or caterwauled over, middle class is in fact not so badly off after all. Their income may be down a few percentage points, though that is not clear. Mark J. Perry points out that one reason they may have less income than they used to is that they work less than they used to. They may work less because government programs like Obamacare discourage employers from paying workers for more than twenty-nine hours a week. And they may work less because they are older. In addition, "households" have less income these days because many of them have only one wage earner instead of two—partly because so many women have been liberated from the oppression of marriage and economic dependence on men.

Some of the articles commenting on stagnant or decreased income emphasize that the rich are getting a larger slice of the "national income," which means those articles are really just excuses for banging the fairness drum.

But life will never be fair, as St. John of Hyannisport (taking a much needed break from the exertions of the flesh) pointed out years ago, and liberals and everyone else will simply have to get used to it. Wise middle-class parents tell their children that life isn't fair—and they should be glad of it.

More interesting than the slightly lower income of the middle class, or the disparity between their income and the income of Obama's friends, is the style of life that most of the middle class enjoys today.

Income may be important. But wealth, broadly defined, is more important. Middle-class people, like almost everyone else in this country, today live far better, far richer lives than most rich people lived only a few decades ago. They live longer, and in bigger spaces, and have better and more abundant food than our parents had, and they have more graphic pornography; they live in air-conditioned homes, drive safer automobiles, enjoy limitless online gambling and dating; fly in safer and cheaper airplanes; watch more amazing television; enjoy texting, sexting, and Mexican food; and experience far, far better medical care, as evidenced by a cornucopia of pharmaceutical discoveries, including antibiotics, Viagra, the smallpox vaccine, statins, Cialis, and treatments for venereal diseases that themselves didn't even exist a generation ago; as well as an abundance of surgical procedures such as heart transplants and computer-assisted robotic laparoscopy—not to mention m2fgrs (male-to-female gender reassignment surgery).

Put differently, what's the problem—other than that Obama's friends have much, much more money than middle-class people have, and probably more wives too?

Meanwhile, the really poor (and a sizeable segment of the statistically poor) languish, for a number of reasons, but primarily because of rampant illegitimacy, which, like homosexuality, can no longer be objected to in polite, sophisticated (read "liberal") society. The poor also accept welfare with a sense of entitlement instead of shame. And they tend not to work. Is this news? Who would dispute that welfare is a narcotic, a subtle destroyer of the human spirit?

So, to alleviate poverty, we have to stigmatize illegitimacy, welfare, and laziness. That is not going to happen in Washington.

But it can happen in the states, which means we need to make a structural change in the delivery of welfare if we are going to alleviate the plight of the poor. Feeling their pain won't do. Poverty programs must be run by the states, or, preferably, at the local community level.

Only then will the underclass poor have a chance at a better life. Welfare promoted by individuals and families, community charities, service organizations, and churches—priests too? Oh, the horror!—could support the deserving poor, and not the others, not, e.g., men who knock up a girl a week. At least St. John was . . . prudent. Word would get around in an afternoon. Hunger is a great teacher.

The states could also surely do a better job of assisting the rest of the poor, who are now supported by eighty programs run by Washington at a cost that amounts to more than $700 billion a year. It takes an army of bureaucrats to dispense that much money, an army that predictably and regularly votes for its employer, Chuck Schumer's party of government.

But effecting a monumental change in the country's welfare system requires votes. Where will they come from?

From the middle class, out of their charity for the poor, and in return for eliminating bank bailouts and big-business bennies like the Ex-Im Bank, as well as several decades of regulations. The deal (raise and double, Chuck) is that the regulations that afflict middle-class businesses, as well as the businesses that hire middle-class workers, would be cut so extensively the *Washington Post* would have a Kool-Aid party. Decimating Washington's bureaucratic domains could make the middle class richer than Croesus—and think what he would have given for just a handful of middle-class staples: say, ten rolls of Cottonelle, a tall skinny soy vanilla doublecaf latte, and a bottle of Levitra.

As President Reagan said, we waged a war on poverty, and poverty won. The numbers show no net decrease in poverty since the sixties. Lyndon Johnson's goal was to cure poverty and make the poor self-sufficient. That goal has not only not been achieved, it has been abandoned by modern liberals, whose continuing devotion to their post-LBJ war on poverty is one of the seven scandals of the modern world.

The liberals have had their way of dealing with poverty for fifty years. But still, the numbers remain unchanged, and, still, the underclass poor live terrible lives, without family, skills, incentives, or hope of even dreaming about the American Dream. It's time to try something new.

Jeb Bush's Toaster Problem

January 12, 2015

There are many conservatives who say that neither of the two Bush presidents ever disappointed them—they got just what they expected.

That being the case, why would they risk a third?

A useful rule in life is, if an item you bought breaks immediately, don't get another one just like it. If you buy a toaster and it doesn't work, don't buy the same model again hoping it will be better. The rule also holds for a bottle of 1945 Château Mouton-Rothschild (considered by some to be the greatest claret of the twentieth century, to be served only in the finest crystal): If the first bottle has gone off, probably the whole case was left in the sun.

Jeb Bush has spent his whole life in the sun: the acronymically nicknamed John Ellis Bush, second son of President George H. W. Bush, grew up in Texas, went to college in Texas, and then at the age of twenty-seven moved to Florida. Fortunately, by then, air conditioning in Florida was more prevalent even than octogenarians, and there is no reason to assume that Florida sunshine did to Jeb Bush what it would do to a case of '45 Mouton-Rothschild.

Sun or no sun, however, it is true that birds of a feather flock together and, if they are frugivorous, eat apples, which don't fall far from the tree. That, in a nutshell, is at the root of conservatives' problem with Jeb Bush. But it's also true that not all birds fly together, and that some apples roll their merry way down hills, coming to rest far from the tree that bore them. And true too that God, as conservatives especially should understand, made each of us distinct.

It simply won't do to say that because Jeb Bush's father and brother were dreadful (i.e., anti-conservative) presidents, he would be a dreadful president too. That is a form of discrimination—that taxi driver cheated me: I hate taxi drivers; the policeman gave me a ticket: I hate cops—that believers in individuality should neither practice nor condone.

The rejection of Jeb Bush for purely dynastic reasons, however, is more solidly grounded. After electing Franklin Roosevelt four times, the people of this country decided in their wisdom that four terms were too many. Two too many.

To have another four or eight years of a Bush presidency suggests the poverty of the electorate's collective imagination, of a kind nicely illustrated by the story of the Glaswegian who proclaimed at the end of his speech, "I was born a Scot; I've lived a Scot; and I'll die a Scot!"—to which a booming brogue from the back of the hall replied, "Faith and begorrah, man, have ye no imagination?"

Conservatives look at the country and see a continuing decrease in freedom, caused by ever-growing concentration of authority in Washington, dating from FDR. They know imagination will be required to stop the slide into darkness and start the steep ascent back toward the sunlight. That is why they cotton to candidates who propose structural changes and, inevitably, confrontation with special interests, including public employees.

Senator Rand Paul (R–KY) says he would eliminate the Departments of Education, Energy, Commerce, and Housing and Urban Development—though probably not by executive order.

Senator Ted Cruz (R–TX) wants to abolish the IRS after instituting a flat tax. That position and his visceral anti-Washington bias, displayed in his attempts to shut down the government, will arouse enthusiasm among conservative Republicans.

Governor Rick Perry (R–TX) would also eliminate several cabinet-level departments—as we remember from his . . . memorable performance in the 2012 debates.

Governor Scott Walker (R–WI) sheared the public employees' union in Wisconsin, won a recall vote, and then won reelection. Walker, Perry, Cruz, and Paul understand that making changes requires confrontation. But confrontation will attract supporters, convincing them that the candidate indeed intends to make changes.

What does Jeb Bush offer that will attract conservatives? The *Miami Herald* said his foreign policy closely mirrors that of his brother, former President George W. Bush. His signature domestic issue is education, and it is true that he supports vouchers; but he also supports the Common Core curriculum, which suggests he doesn't understand the problem of accumulated power in Washington. His position on immigration might be perfect, but it is likely to be misinterpreted (deliberately or otherwise) and is in any event not the central issue.

We have not, so far, heard from him a single bold, freedom-promoting idea, without which Jeb Bush (whose salary as a senior adviser to Barclays, the British bank, has been reported as being a million dollars a year) is just Mitt Romney—without the dog on the car roof.

What ails this country is, simply: Too. Much. Government. Unless Jeb Bush can make it crystal clear that he understands that reducing the size and scope of government is the central issue of our time, he will be seen by conservatives as just another, same-model toaster.

Jafar for President: Forgive Student Loans
January 20, 2015

In his State of the Union message on January 20, President Obama will propose that the federal government pay for two years of community college for every student who wants to go. The estimated cost ($3,800 a year each for nine million possible students) is $35 billion a year. The idea is to jack up the number of people who will vote for the Party of Bigger Government.

A few months ago, Sen. Elizabeth Warren (PBG, MA), also interested in jacking up the number of Democratic voters, introduced a bill to allow former students to refinance their loans at the current federal rate (about 4 percent), which in some cases would be half of what they are currently paying.

Obama's proposal has no merit whatever: it makes more sense for most of the people who might go to a community college to take a route more calculated to achieving employment and mobility.

Warren's proposal has some merit: mortgages can be refinanced; why not student loans? Millions of Americans would benefit from her proposal—40 million former students collectively owe $1.2 trillion. That's upwards of 40 million people (more recent borrowers have loans with post-QE interest rates) who would be more inclined to vote for the Party of Bigger Government.

Both Obama's and Warren's populist proposals are meant to make Republicans look like anti-learning skinflints. Two parties can play the game of giveaway. The Democrats always play it. The Republicans should play it, because if they adopt the right measures, they can drive a stake partway through the heart of liberalism—militant, secular, statist, collectivist, politically correct, (all aboard!) liberalism. What's not to like? And if Republicans don't play it? The Party of Bigger Government wins.

Last May, a proposal was made on this site to have the federal government forgive all student loans owed to it and pay off all student loans owed to private lenders—in return for cancelling basically all federal support to higher educational institutions. It's a crack-a-jack idea.

There are essentially three problems with student loans. Easy-to-get loans encourage many young people (some of whom can't possibly profit from college) to waste crucial years of their lives at an institution from which they will derive no benefit, partly because the curriculums are useless today and partly because the nature of work is changing. As many people now realize, the primary effect of student loans has been to enable colleges to raise costs, to feed their largely left-wing professoriat.

If federal grants were eliminated, some institutions would collapse, of course, but most of those would be institutions that really don't provide any value to their students.

Students for whom college makes sense would still be able to get loans from friends, banks, perhaps companies, and the colleges themselves, as long as they could persuade the lenders (e.g., by having decent SAT scores and a marketable major) that they could truly profit from college.

Despite the proposal's obvious appeal, a number of people expressed concerns.

First, many critics said, correctly, that it seems unfair to forgive all student loans. Perhaps. But fairness isn't the only goal, as some critics recognized when they said that it was unjust or immoral to have pushed these loans on unsuspecting young people in the first place. They were seduced by society into borrowing money to prepare for their future, and then given little or no guidance on how to make that preparation worthwhile. It's not only youth that is wasted on the young.

Some critics even raised the question whether people who make such unwise decisions—incurring massive debt with little thought of how it can be paid off—should be allowed to vote. Interesting question, but not for today.

Second, some critics suggested that forgiving current student loans wouldn't be fair to those people who had paid off their loans. But that's not clear. Would we refuse to free a slave simply because his brother had bought his own freedom the week before? The parable in the Bible about the laborers in the vineyard suggests that those students who have paid off their loans got what they bargained for and that their real complaint is that someone else is getting a better deal.

But that's also true when you pay full price before a sale begins. A good lesson to learn, and the earlier the better, is that life isn't fair—and most of us should be glad it isn't.

Some critics suggested that former students should be able discharge their student-loan debts in bankruptcy proceedings. (Before 1978, student loans were dischargeable in bankruptcy just like other consumer loans.) The implication is that student loans are the only kind of debt you can't get free of.

That's only partly correct. Anyone who has had his debts discharged in a Chapter 7 bankruptcy proceeding needs to wait eight years before he can file again for the relief bankruptcy affords.

If student loans were dischargeable in bankruptcy, at what point should a debtor be allowed to file? Marie Brunner poisoned that well when, in the 1980s, having just completed her master's program, she filed for a discharge in bankruptcy within a month of the date the first payment on her loans came due. The court was not sympathetic, and the decision stands—in the way of borrowers who legitimately make hardship claims.

Perhaps a former student could file for bankruptcy only after, say, ten years, by which time he might have acquired some assets. But, assuming his debts exceeded his assets (otherwise bankruptcy wouldn't be necessary), at that point he would have to liquidate all those acquired assets and pay the proceeds to the lender to get his debt discharged. That would certainly discourage many graduates from acquiring assets, especially if they were not to begin acquiring them until they got near the ten-year mark. Who would start saving $5,000 a year with only three years to go before the date at which he could file to discharge $20,000 in debt? Better to stay judgment-proof until after getting all debts discharged.

One suggestion is to make the colleges and universities the

ultimate guarantors of the loans. That's in line with the thinking—correct—that in time the private sector would produce alternatives to the current government system. Use the market force, Luke.

The key is stopping this business in the future, "this business" being both giving seductive loans to students and making grants to institutions. Given the size of total student debt ($1.2 trillion) and the amount of aid going to institutions of higher learning ($109 billion a year) the country would break even in a decade or so. Of course, we taxpayers are going to pay off some of those loans anyway—the default rate is about 11 percent.

Education is changing, More than one graduate has concluded that he could have learned all he knows without going to college. We can hope that in the coming decades more and more high-school graduates, especially bright, aggressive, self-motivated ones, will skip expensive colleges and grad schools and go to professional or training schools instead, or take courses online.

But hope is not a strategy. Massive federal grants to brick-and-mortar institutions slow down the process of change, at the same time feathering the nests of aging 1960s radical students-turned-professors.

So: we need to stop funding the universities. But how are we going to get the votes in Congress to do that? The answer is, by enlisting the graduates who've been had by the current system: by appealing both to their financial interest and to their eleemosynary concern for the students, potential snookerees, who will follow them.

That may not seem very conservative. But Republicans shouldn't be so squeamish. They're already in the business of paying off groups—farmers, bankers, insurance companies—but without getting the complementary benefit of defunding liberalism.

Reluctant Republicans should channel their inner devious royal adviser Jafar, and realize that desperate times call for desperate measures.

What is Jeb Bush Hiding? And Why?

February 24, 2015

Over a nine-day period, my research assistant sent six emails to Ms. Kristy Campbell at the Jeb Bush organization requesting copies of the speeches Gov. Bush had given in 2014.

The first two emails went unanswered. After the third email Ms. Campbell replied: "What is this for?"

Gov. Bush wants to be president of the United States, and he has an aide who asks why someone wants to see copies of his speeches?

Ah, Ms. Campbell, Mr. Oliver has run clean out of kitty litter. . . .

My research assistant (whose name in the copies of the emails below I have changed to that of Raymond Chandler's famous private eye—they share capabilities) told her I was the former chairman of the board of *National Review*. He also said that I didn't want to rely on what the media reported about the governor's speeches, but wanted to be able to read what the governor had actually said. Wouldn't you think . . . ? You would be wrong.

What difference does it make who asks for copies of the governor's speeches? Or why?

Perhaps Ms. Campbell is just a doe-eyed college sophomore doing her mid-winter intern program at the Bush headquarters. Actually, she's not. She has been, according to her website profile, deputy communications director for Romney for President, communications director for Foundation for Florida's Future (Jeb Bush's think tank), and even press secretary in the Executive Office of Governor Bush for a year.

It is true that I wrote a piece recently entitled "Jeb Bush's Toaster Problem" in which I said that if the governor couldn't articulate some truly conservative proposals he risked being regarded as just another Mitt Romney—without the dog on the car roof. Given that Ms. Campbell has worked for both Mitt Romney and Jeb Bush, that might have offended her. But are we to believe that only friendly reporters get copies of the governor's speeches? That is not presidential behavior.

Read the emails and marvel.

And remember that a few days ago, Gov. Bush accepted the resignation of a young assistant who had been hired as chief technology officer, but who had made what the same Kristy Campbell called "regrettable and insensitive comments." Perhaps he and Ms. Campbell should start their own firm together.

The Emails

From: Philip Marlowe <PhilipMarlowe@yahoo.com>
To: "kristy@jeb.org" <kristy@jeb.org>
Sent: Monday, February 2, 2015 4:52 PM
Subject: Jeb Bush speeches 2014 transcript/texts request

Hello, Miss Campbell ~

My name is Philip Marlowe. I am a researcher for Daniel Oliver, the former Chairman of the Board of *National Review*. We are trying to get the transcripts for Jeb Bush's 10 latest speeches. Here are the ones I have found for 2014 (it appears, indeed, he only gave 10 speeches in 2014). Out of these, I have found three videos (pasted below). But, for the other ones, there are no transcripts or texts available.

I am imagining that perhaps you would have them available? We are operating on deadline and I would really like to get this information as soon as possible.

If you can't proffer the texts, please let me know. Also, if I am missing any speeches listed below, please by all means don't hesitate to inform me of which ones I have left out. Thank you very much for any help/assistance here!

Best,

Philip

P.S. Feel more than free to ring me on my mobile @ 415-359-2868 anytime!

===========================

From: Philip Marlowe <PhilipMarlowe@yahoo.com>
To: "kristy@jeb.org" <kristy@jeb.org>
Sent: Thursday, February 5, 2015 1:22 PM
Subject: Fw: Jeb Bush speeches 2014 transcript/texts request

Hello, Kristy,
Did you get this message?

I have noticed that sometimes my emails—because it is a Yahoo
account—go straight into the Spam box.

Philip

===========================

From: Philip Marlowe <PhilipMarlowe@yahoo.com>
To: "kristy@jeb.org" <kristy@jeb.org>
Sent: Friday, February 6, 2015 12:47 PM
Subject: Fw: Jeb Bush speeches 2014 transcript/texts request

Hello, Kristy,

Did you get my message??

Philip

===========================

From: Kristy Campbell <kristy@jeb.org>
To: Philip Marlowe <PhilipMarlowe@yahoo.com>
Sent: Friday, February 6, 2015 1:07 PM
Subject: Re: Jeb Bush speeches 2014 transcript/texts request

Philip, what is this for?
Kristy
Kristy Campbell 571-287-1269

===========================

From: Philip Marlowe <PhilipMarlowe@yahoo.com>
To: Kristy Campbell <kristy@jeb.org>
Sent: Friday, February 6, 2015 3:28 PM
Subject: Re: Jeb Bush speeches 2014 transcript/texts request

As I understand it, it is for an article on Jeb Bush's outlook, and is
to be based off of these 2014 speeches. He does not want to go off
of what the media reports said about each speech, but what the
speeches actually do say.

===========================

From: PhilipMarlowe@yahoo.com
To: kristy@jeb.org
Sent: Tue, Feb 10, 2015 11:01 AM EST
Subject: Fw: Jeb Bush speeches 2014 transcript/texts request

Hello, Kristy,
Just called/txt'd. Any word on this?
Thanks for any assistance!
Philip

===========================

From: Philip Marlowe <PhilipMarlowe@yahoo.com>
To: kristy@jeb.org
Sent: Wednesday, February 11, 2015 3:46 PM
Subject: Fw: Jeb Bush speeches 2014 transcript/texts request

Hello, Kristy,

So it's nearly been two weeks now. . . . I know you are busy, but
eventually we have to go to print. I take it you are not going to
proffer the transcripts of the speeches? That's what I am going to
mark down, unless I hear otherwise. I don't know how difficult

this task is but I am sympathetic, but this is a total blackout on your end.

Again, these speeches are important so we can see what was actually said and not the media's interpretation.

It is very important I get these speeches/transcripts but I understand you cannot help.

Best wishes,
Philip

Bare Ruined Choirs
February 25, 2015

There are 1.6 billion Muslims. Even if 99 percent of them don't believe in blowing up infidels (i.e., us), we still have a problem.

Is Islam a religion of peace or of war? The debate rages on. Were the Paris terrorists, and all the rest of them, representatives of a militant Islam or apostates from a religion of peace? Experts (whoever they are) differ. Bernard-Henri Lévy, writing in the *Wall Street Journal* claims that "the *Charlie Hebdo* killers are not 'the Muslims,' but rather the small fraction of Muslims who confuse the Koran with a death warrant." But in her book *Infidel*, Ayaan Hirsi Ali writes, "I wanted secular, non-Muslim people to stop kidding themselves that 'Islam is peace and tolerance.'"

Do we, or our political representatives, know enough about Islam to come to a valid conclusion? Can we possibly learn enough? How can we laymen learn enough to make informed decisions if people who have studied Islam for decades, or lived it, disagree?

The answer is, we can't. We can't know what the true essence of Islam is. We can't know for sure what Allah wants. And it may be that no one can, perhaps because there is a variety of Islams, some peaceful, some not. Allah may not be fickle, but he may be inscrutable. Or Mohammed (AD 570–632), to whom the Koran was said to have been revealed by the Angel Gabriel over a period of twenty-three years (longer than *Downton Abbey*), may just not have been good at backing up his work.

But the real question is, does it matter? How does the answer to the question "Is Islam a religion of peace or not?" affect what we do? How does the nature of Islam affect how we respond to a particular attack, and how we respond generally to terrorism?

There are 1.6 billion Muslims in the world, approximately 23 percent of the world's population—which means we should hope, and, yes, pray, that Islam is a religion of peace.

There are estimated to be on the order of four thousand al Qaeda adherents and another, let's say, twenty thousand "practicing" ISIS militants currently in the Middle East, primarily in Iraq and Syria.

Since the first modern terrorist attack on the United States, the 1993 bombing of the World Trade Center, there have been only a few major attacks throughout the world, but innumerable minor ones (e.g., roadside bombings). Nevertheless, the total number of attackers is probably only a few thousand at most. If there are, or have been, a total of, let's say, five thousand terrorist attackers, that would be 0.0003 percent of the Muslim population of the world. You say ten thousand? Fine. That's still only 0.0006 percent of the Muslim population. Even 0.125 percent is a small fraction of the Muslim population—but it's the number of Episcopalians in the United States.

The point is, even if Islam is a religion of peace, and if only a fraction of a fraction of the Muslim population are apostates, that's still more than enough to create havoc amongst us. That is why it really doesn't matter, for security purposes, what the true nature of Islam is.

What we need is not a scholarly answer to a fundamental and essentially academic (and certainly politically charged) question. We need only to develop a public policy that will keep our citizens safe—or as safe as we can make them.

In the course of developing this policy we should try to enlist any Muslims who say they are peaceful, making it reasonably clear that we think it would be a terrible shame to have to recall Gen. Curtis LeMay in order to dial them all back to AD 569.

Meanwhile, there are other questions, perhaps more fundamental, like: Is Western Civilization up to the task of surviving alongside a religion that, whether it is peaceful or not, is in many respects incompatible with our most cherished beliefs?

Western Civilization is our heritage. And Western Civ was created by, and is defined by, Christianity.

You say no? Listen to President Roosevelt. Early on the morning of June 6, 1944 (for the history-impaired, that was D-Day), President Roosevelt asked the nation to "join with me in prayer." Imagine that. "Almighty God: Our sons, pride of our nation, this day have set upon a mighty endeavor, a struggle to preserve our Republic, our religion, and our civilization, and to set free a suffering humanity." Roosevelt ended his D-Day prayer with the words "Thy will be done, Almighty God. Amen."

Now Christianity, in Europe anyway, is certainly in decline, and probably in retreat. The *Wall Street Journal* reports that "the Church of England closes about 20 churches a year. Roughly 200 Danish churches have been deemed nonviable or underused. The Roman Catholic Church in Germany has shut about 515 churches in the past decade. . . . [I]n the Netherlands Roman Catholic leaders estimate that two-thirds of their 1,600 churches will be out of commission in a decade, and 700 of Holland's Protestant churches are expected to close within four years." In Arnhem, Netherlands, the Church of St. Joseph has been turned into a skateboarding hall.

Christianity, and religion in general, is under attack here too. The First Amendment is being converted, by über-secularist liberals, into a guarantee of freedom *from* religion.

One suspects that if the radical Islamists (assuming there is another kind) were bright, they would not direct their fire at America and Europe but simply wait while Christianity collapses. Of course, that does require taking the long view, and taking the long view may not earn as many black-eyed virgins.

Meanwhile, Christianity grows furiously in China and Africa, where the ground may not seem to us to be hospitable, but where it is also inhospitable to strangers wearing keffiyahs. It is estimated that there are 65 million Christians in China and 516 million in Sub-Saharan Africa.

God moves in a mysterious way. By the time our bare ruined choirs are occupied by Muslims, or skateboarders, the church may be alive and well, and flourishing, in far-off lands.

Join the Army, See the World, Change Your Sex
March 9, 2015

> *Transie Mansie, pudding and pie,*
> *Spilled the beans, the nasty guy;*
> *Into prison he was hurled,*
> *Now we must pay to have him girled.*

Bradley Manning, convicted of leaking national security secrets and sentenced to thirty-five years in prison (though he'll probably be out in seven), has been granted the right to receive, at taxpayers' expense, hormone treatment to transition from his current gender to one more compatible with his recently chosen new first name, Chelsea.

The cost of the treatment has not been disclosed by the army, but we can get some idea by visiting the website of the Philadelphia Center for Transgender Surgery. The opening paragraph tells us, "If you're considering Male-To-Female (M2F) gender reassignment surgery (GRS), no doubt you have many questions and concerns." Questions, maybe, but even if you'll be out in only seven years, you may not have that many concerns. M2FGRS has to beat serving time in a men's prison.

Of course, Manning won't get to experience the "supportive, caring environment dedicated to handling your every care and need . . . and one of the world's most experienced in every aspect of transitioning and well-being" that the Philadelphia Center for Transgender Surgery offers. But it's not wholly unfair that there are some costs for having leaked the largest cache of classified documents in US history.

Now, please understand that the Philadelphia Center for Transgender Surgery is no fly-by-night operation. It has standards and "Mandatory Prerequisites for Gender Reassignment Surgery." Let's see if she meets them.

What about the cost of the whole hebang? Well, M2FGRS is surprisingly affordable because, like other free-market medical procedures (e.g., laser eye surgery), it's not mandated by Obamacare. The cost for all the itemized procedures, everything, is $108,000, but you probably wouldn't opt for all of them. And—Philadelphia really is the City of Brotherly Love—you get, as it says in capital letters at the bottom of the price list: discounts on surgical fees for multiple procedures. That means you can discard every trace of the sex God gave you for only $100,000.

Only in America.

Still, someone has to come up with the $100,000. But who? Why not the Chinese?

[White House telephone transcript, made available per FOIA Request #47cfr0461.]

Barack Obama: Who's there?
Xi Jinping: Hu long gone.
Barack Obama: Oh hang!
Xi Jinping: Jiang gone too.
Barack Obama: Who's he?
Xi Jinping: I'm Xi.
Barack Obama: Well, I thought so, but I'm not known for jumping to conclusions.
Xi Jinping: <Chuckling sounds> What can I do for you, Bo?
Barack Obama: C'mon, Xi. Please don't call me "Bo."
Xi Jinping: Hee, hee. What can I do for you, Bo?
Barack Obama: I need 100,000 fortune cookies.
Xi Jinping: Ooh. Big party. What for?
Barack Obama: M2FGRS.
Xi Jinping: <Pause> Must double funds to guarantee Republican subservience?
Barack Obama: No. Gender reassignment surgery.
Xi Jinping: Ah. Sorry to hear. We like Michelle.
Barack Obama: No, not for me.
Xi Jinping: Ahhh. You have found solution to Ted Cruz problem?
Barack Obama: No. It's for Bradley Manning.
Xi Jinping: Ahhhhh! Honorable Bradley E. Manning, PFC, United States Army, RA 12 523 650, date of birth: December 17, 1987. Pasty face. Weak chin. Will cause you trouble, skinny little bastard.
Barack Obama: He'll be a bitch.

Xi Jinping: We eat dogs.

Barack Obama: We have strict moral rules against animal cruelty.

Xi Jinping: Of course you do.

Barack Obama: Can you help, Xi?

Xi Jinping: What precisely is in it for the people of China?

Barack Obama: Afterwards I may have more flexibility.

Xi Jinping: Ah, reset, of course. Yes, I'll help. You remember old Chinese saying?

Barack Obama: Refresh my recollection.

Xi Jinping: Give a man sex, own him for night. Change a man's sex: own her for life.

Barack Obama: Thanks, Xi. Sayonara.

Xi Jinping: You Americans all look alike too. Hasta la vista.

Actually, only (!) 8 percent of US debt is owed to China. The rest we owe to a variety of lenders, including—ourselves! Which, in progressive liberal thinking, means we'll never have to pay it off. If only.

It is We the People who will get to pay for Manning's hormone therapy. And Manning will probably be out of prison in only seven years, which means that if he goes on to have a sex-change operation (also courtesy of us the people?), he will probably be free before his scars have healed. What a country.

You can't make this stuff up.

Will the *Washington Post* Investigate How a Woman with a Drinking Problem and a Steady Male Companion Got to be an Episcopal Bishop?

March 19, 2015

In a quite unbelievably awful piece that has to be read not to be believed, *Washington Post* reporter Michelle Boorstein wrote about Heather Cook, the suffragan bishop of the Episcopal Diocese of Maryland, a woman who, while driving drunk last December, hit and killed a bicyclist then fled from the scene of the crime. Cook has now been indicted on thirteen counts, including vehicular manslaughter. Clearly, she should not have been a cleric of any kind.

The basic facts, or at least some of them, were covered when the homicide occurred, and Boorstein's piece is what might be called, loosely—as loose as an intensely grungy nomad big-pockets trench coat or a quirky slouchy oversized baggy Parisian boho chiffon sack dress—a "think piece." She begins: "With a history of sherries at church coffee hour and wine during Holy Communion, Episcopalians have long endured—and shared—jokes about their drinking. (For example: 'Wherever two or three are gathered, there's a fifth.')"

After you stop laughing, or crying, you can break that sentence down into some of its constituent parts, and get: "With a history of [drinking] wine during Holy Communion, Episcopalians have long shared jokes about their drinking." Wow, Nellie!

The clear implication of Boorstein's piece is that many Episcopalians drink lots of wine when they receive Holy Communion, and that they drink even to excess. Then at the coffee hour following they joke about it—always assuming they are not too drunk to stand up. That is a truly breathtaking implication, which anyone who has ever been to a Mass and seen one chalice administered to fifty people would know.

Clearly Boorstein is not a Catholic, not even of any kind. But surely there must be one person at the *Washington Post* who knows something about the sacraments of the Episcopal Church—or of the Roman Catholic Church (whose US branch is about thirty-eight times as big as the Episcopal Church): someone who knows that the amount of wine consumed by communicants is only a sip.

Boorstein goes on to quote, uncritically, "a top [but unnamed] church leader" who said "the case of Heather Cook . . . revealed Episcopalians' 'systemic denial about alcohol and other drug abuse.'"

Systemic? I.e., pertaining to or affecting the body as a whole? Which is to say, all Episcopalians? As in: All Episcopalians deny there is such a condition as alcohol and other drug abuse?

What kind of person would say that? And what kind of person would report the quote uncritically?

The answer to the first question is, sadly, a "top" leader of the Episcopal Church, though we have only Boorstein's word for his altitude—and, don't we have to assume, his sobriety. The answer to the second question is: a top reporter at the *Washington Post*.

The real story is probably one Boorstein approaches but doesn't recognize, or isn't willing to address: Why was Cook allowed to become a bishop?

Boorstein paraphrases Byron Rushing, the vice president of the House of Deputies of the Episcopal Church:

> The church needs to dig more deeply into how church leaders and culture may have contributed to the Cook case, he said, and that may include both insufficient attention to drinking as well as other factors—namely the transparency of the bishop-picking process.

Heather Cook—who in her bio states, "Supporting me in my vocation is my steady companion, Mark"—was elected the first female bishop of Maryland last May. It's a good guess that the powers that be in the Episcopal Church were willing to move Heaven and Hell (assuming they believe Heaven and Hell exist) to get this woman installed, even though—you can't make this stuff up—all the other nominees were women, too (perhaps they didn't have steady companions). This is part of the feminist, culture-bashing agenda of the power players in the Episcopal Church.

The real questions are: What did the powers in the Episcopal Church know about Cook's drinking, and when did they know it? Apparently, that Cook had been convicted of drunk driving four years prior to the fatal hit-and-run accident—and therefore prior to her election and installation as bishop—was known. But was the extent of her drinking problem not known? And if not, why not?

And what was done with whatever knowledge the "authorities" did have? That remains to be determined, and reported. The true scandal here may be a cover-up. But for that story we'll have to await, with sherried breath, Boorstein's next installment.

Stan Evans: Everyman's Bill Buckley
March 26, 2015

Stanton Evans, who died on March 3, was Everyman's William F. Buckley Jr.

Buckley, who died in 2008, was eight years older than Evans, but their early training was similar, and they were both precocious, productive, and busy. Very busy.

Both went to Yale. (Stan graduated magna cum laude, Phi Beta Kappa.) Both were editors of the *Yale Daily News*. After Yale, both wrote for *The Freeman*, a conservative magazine edited by Frank Chodorov, and both wrote for *Human Events*. And both were writing for *National Review* by 1956. Buckley had founded the magazine the previous November, at the age of twenty-nine; Evans was named editor of the *Indianapolis News* at the age of twenty-six, making him the country's youngest editor of a metropolitan daily newspaper.

Both helped create the conservative movement. Buckley played a founding role in Young Americans for Freedom, the New York State Conservative Party, the Philadelphia Society, and the Fund for American Studies. Evans, at the age of twenty-six, wrote the Sharon Statement and Young Americans for Freedom's guiding principles, the latter still the Declaration of Independence of the conservative movement. Evans also founded the National Journalism Center and the Education and Research Institute.

Both wrote columns, both appeared on television, and both gave speeches.

But they were very different people. Buckley was a suave, patrician, boarding-school, secret-society (Skull and Bones) Yalie, with an international upbringing (his first language was Spanish; his family lived for a time in France and England when he was a boy), a cosmopolitan demeanor, and an accent so famous it made a cameo appearance, with the help of Robin Williams, in the movie *Aladdin*. Evans was born in Texas but grew up in Maryland, going to public schools—except for his final year of high school, when he went to a private school because he was too young to go to Yale. Evans spoke with a drawl that seemed to unwind itself all the way from Texas to Maryland.

Buckley had smart dogs—mostly Cavalier King Charles spaniels. Sometimes two of them at a time. Very smart. Evans had one dog, Zip. With three legs. Nothing unusual, he would say, just your average three-legged dog.

Buckley traveled in a 60-foot schooner, a 44-foot yawl, a 36-foot sloop, and a stretch limousine, often with a gourmet meal packed by his wife, Pat, and Julian, the cook. Evans drove old Mustangs, T-Birds, and hatchbacks, and ate at Roy Rogers.

Buckley played the harpsichord. Evans played the guitar. Buckley liked Bach. Evans liked rock 'n' roll. Buckley had a staff of Spanish-speaking servants. Evans lived alone.

Buckley skied fanatically (he once raced my eleven-year-old son down a mountain in Switzerland, launching him over a mogul; my son landed, did a yard sale, and broke both skis). And for a decade or two he exercised regularly at a gym (he called it "my mortification of the flesh"). There is no record extant, on Earth or in Heaven, of Stan Evans's ever having exercised. He said he didn't like sports that required you to put something special on your feet.

Buckley worshiped regularly, and preferably in Latin. Evans was born a Methodist—at least, he was born of a Methodist. And he liked Calvin. But he said, in his last years, that if he ever joined a church, it would be a serious church (he meant the Roman Catholic Church), and he was baptized on his deathbed. Even so, he was temperamentally Methodist–Calvinist.

But the real difference between the two men was their public, and their style. Both wrote and spoke extensively. But Buckley's public was vast. His column, "On the Right," appeared in hundreds of papers; his television program, "Firing Line," was widely seen and ran for thirty-three years. He was famous the world over. Evans never came close to matching that.

But Evans taught. His primary audience was his students. He started the National Journalism Center in 1977 and taught (for about twelve weeks each year) over a thousand students. And for more than twenty years, he was an adjunct professor at Troy State University's school of journalism, where he taught thousands more. And he mingled with young conservatives at their gatherings for decades. He was their mentor. He was their colleague. He was their friend.

Buckley lectured, and far more often than Evans (or almost anybody else), but always from on high. He met hundreds of students, but most of them only briefly. Each year he took a student or a recent graduate to Switzerland to help him research that year's book. But only one a year. In the early days of the conservative movement, Buckley had, probably, physically touched—laid his hands on—almost everyone who would become a conservative leader or activist. But only briefly.

Buckley was a superstar. Evans, like Whittaker Chambers, wore rumpled clothes (except when he spoke in public), and had a rumpled look, which matched his drawl.

Buckley made a point of befriending liberals or, perhaps more accurately, of not not befriending liberals, and of entertaining them at his maisonette in New York City and his house on Long Island Sound, which meant he had lots of friends among high society, limousine liberals, many of them media stars. Buckley was able, probably, if not certainly, to influence his liberal friends, at least to expose them to strange conservative ideas. Evans got at liberals through his analysis and humor, but not at the dinner table. He never gave or went to parties.

Buckley was a very stylish writer, which may have made him seem less accessible to the general public, although in fact he was every bit as personable as Evans. Evans used to revel in a remark made by William A. Rusher, the long-serving publisher of *National Review*: "If Karl Marx had been a stylist, Buckley would have been a Communist." Funny, perhaps. Unfair, of course. Rusher didn't do style. And neither did Evans.

Remarkably, given Evans's ability to produce politically savvy and hilarious one-liners—he retired the cup—he refused to put his humor into his writing. (*National Review*'s junior editors were astonished one day when Evans made a joke in his "At Home" column for the *NR Bulletin*. What's going on? they asked one another.) Buckley remarked on the lack of humor in Evans's writing more than once. Perhaps Stan saved his jokes for his friends. Not a bad rule.

All those friends have a favorite Stan Evans one-liner, but it's hard to beat this one, reported by Steve Hayward: "What do you get when you cross Chronic Fatigue Syndrome and Attention Deficit Disorder? A college student." That was not the kind of wit Buckley had.

The four pillars of conservatism in our time have been Barry Goldwater and Ronald Reagan, political practitioners; and Bill Buckley and Stan Evans, intellectuals and teachers, who made Goldwater and Reagan possible. Could there have been a conservative movement without Buckley (or a United States without Washington)? Perhaps. But look at the influence of *National Review*'s founder. Could there have been a conservative movement without Evans (or a United States without Madison)? Perhaps. But read the Sharon Statement, and reflect on the life of its author.

Stan kept his wit, and his wits, almost to the very end. He said to me not long before he died, "Dan, I'm not dying, but I don't want anyone to know it." If only. If only we could have one more Stan Evans joke.

What do you get when you cross Bill Buckley and Stan Evans?

The conservative movement.

Now their busy world is hushed. Conservatives grieve over their deaths, but give thanks for their long, busy, productive, patriotic lives. Requiescat in pace, Bill. Rest in peace, Stan.

Tell a Joke: Save a Civilization
March 26, 2015

A recent piece in *The Daily Caller* (https://tinyurl.com/normwd9) prompted the comment that the piece was in poor taste. That is good news, of a sort: it implies that there is still good taste. But the poor grade offered was for the article only, not for the behavior the article described. That raises the question: Is there any *behavior* that is in poor taste? If there is, can we talk about it—without being accused of poor taste?

The behavior described in the article was Bradley Manning's sex-change hormone treatment. Manning is the soldier who leaked more national-security secrets than anyone else in US history. He was sentenced to thirty-five years in prison, but because he was given credit for the time served before trial and because of the way the system works, he will be eligible for parole in a few years, which means that, in reality, he is facing only about seven years in prison—and hormone treatment preliminary to a sex-change operation. Manning will *not* be facing free facials, free manicures, or, you may be relieved to hear, free pedicures.

One question raised by the comment on *The Daily Caller* piece is: How robustly can we discuss Manning and his treatment? How technical do we have to be? Can we make snide jokes at his expense? Can we call him "Transie Mansie"? If we can't make snide jokes at the expense of a traitor, at whose expense can we make snide jokes?

The politically correct answer is: No, we can't do any of those things, because the most important thing in life is being nice. Being snide is not being nice.

That, of course, is one of the central problems of our time: *not* being *not* nice. We have been cowed by the PC police into not opposing, even in language that is in good taste, the assault on Western Civilization's culture.

Major aspects of that culture have vanished as if swept away by a tsunami.

But they were not swept away by a tsunami. They were swept away by liberal progressives who sought to make a new society, free of the guiding constraints of a culture that had taken centuries to develop.

The result has been a disaster, and that disaster is progressive liberalism's greatest triumph—and one of the seven scandals of the modern world. But above all it is the scourge of the "lower classes," those people who live in Charles Murray's Fishtowns, who lead the lives that liberals love to promote (but wouldn't dream of living themselves), and whose resulting plight produces floods of liberal crocodile tears. And legislation that makes their plight worse.

The most obvious public-policy failure for those who believe in the Western code involves sex and marriage. According to one source (http://uvamagazine.org/articles/the_marriage_crisis)— you can find plenty of others—fifteen times the number of couples today live together outside of marriage than did in 1960. For other statistics, read reports on the fiftieth anniversary of the Moynihan Report, which described the then-nascent and now-endemic collapse of the black family in the inner city.

But traditionalists, the guardians of Western morality, may be more to blame. Liberals may not have realized the consequences of the revolution they midwifed (though they probably did). But traditionalists, perhaps equally ignorant of the consequences, nevertheless knew the behavior the liberal revolution sought to regularize was wrong.

What they failed to do was speak out forcefully enough against the liberals' new morality. They were cowed by the PC police. They abandoned their posts as guardians of the culture.

Not that opposing the culture vandals is easy. We have seen harassment of people who have made the attempt. An Oregon bakery that refused to bake a wedding cake for a couple of lesbians was fined $150,000 by the state's Bureau of Labor and Industries.

The question facing those who still think the culture is worth fighting for is, What to do? One answer is to stop being nice to the vandals.

If vandals came to your town and busted up the war memorial, cut down the flagpole, defaced the doors of the church, and then started destroying the furniture in your house and smashing the crockery—and unplugging the TV—how un-nice would you be inclined to be?

So much more un-nice should you be—should we all be—when what the vandals are destroying is the culture that has sustained our civilization for centuries.

One method of opposing the culture vandals is to make fun of them. We need to tell jokes about them, including, most especially, those who would debase—who have debased—our sexual culture and the related family culture. Once upon a time, many years ago, we coexisted with homosexuals. They let us alone, and we let them alone, for the most part. But then some of them became vandals, and sought to wreck our culture of marriage and family.

We should have been, and should now be, ferociously opposed to them and their allies, and should tell jokes about them—sometimes ribald, bawdy, nasty jokes. Did you hear the one about the two queers who . . .? Three lesbians walked into a bar, and. . . . Sing along with me: "Transie Mansie, pudding and pie. . . ." Scholarly disquisitions on cultural degradation may do for toney intellectual journals and high-IQ, super-zipcode Ivy League graduates. But a more robust vernacular will be needed to galvanize the masses into taking up their pitchforks and sticking it to the vandals.

Telling anti-gay/lesbian/transie jokes is as anti-PC as you can get today. But anti-PC jokes are the weed killer we put in the garden of our culture. Weed killer should be handled with care, of course, but without it the precious plants and flowers, tended lovingly by generations of our forebears, will die.

Telling jokes about people may not be very nice, but it may teach the children that there is a difference between right and wrong. And that the liberal creed on sex—if it feels good, do it—and the homosexual-inspired agenda should be rejected.

Did you hear the one about the three agendas—homo, lesbian, and transie—adrift in a lifeboat in the middle of the Pacific without food or water? It has a delicious ending—especially if you're a shark.

Indiana Burning
April 8, 2015

Liberal fire and brimstone rained down on Indiana after the legislature passed its new Religious Freedom Restoration Act. Riding a wave that has grown, since the Civil Rights Act of 1964 was passed, into a force against any right to be selective (always derogatorily described as "discriminating"), progressive liberals now seek to eliminate the basic right of Americans to choose to deal, or not deal, with homosexuals.

Indiana has just become the *twentieth* state to pass a Religious Freedom Restoration Act, the purpose of which is to allow individuals not to enter into commercial transactions of a sort that would substantially burden their ability to exercise their religion. (The United States has a law similar to Indiana's, which was signed by President Clinton in 1993, having been passed unanimously in the House, and in the Senate by a vote of 97 to 3.)

In effect, Indiana's law contemplates that a bakery could choose *not* to bake a cake for a homosexual couple, so long as the proprietor had a religious reason not to. The impetus behind this is clear: The Sweet Cakes by Melissa bakery in Oregon was fined $150,000 by the Oregon Bureau of Labor and Industries (and has since gone out of business) for refusing to bake a wedding cake for a lesbian couple. The absurdity of the decision is plain—unless you are a crazed progressive liberal. The next time such a scenario arises, perhaps the bakery should simply comply with the request, but, par erreur, forget to put the sugar in. We all make mistakes; in which case, as they ask in law school, What crime, if any?

Shortly after the Indiana bill was enacted, Governor Mike Pence was asked repeatedly if the law would allow people to discriminate on the basis of gender "preference" (as in "God chose maleness for me but, hey, I prefer femaleness, or perhaps, you know, something else, and what does God know anyway?"). Pence refused each time to answer the question on the reporter's terms, each time saying the bill was designed to protect the religious freedom of individuals in Indiana: "This bill is not about discrimination."

Maybe. But the real question is, Why *shouldn't* people be allowed to discriminate on the basis of what is known as sexual orientation? In a country where the right to associate is guaranteed, and the right not to associate is protected, why should people be required to associate with people they don't want to associate with?

The answer is: They shouldn't be (unless their refusal puts someone in danger of bodily harm—they run the only inn for fifty miles and a tornado is coming).

But the concept of being free to choose with whom to deal was, understandably, drowned out during the tumultuous debate over the Civil Rights Act of 1964. The injustices meted out to blacks for two centuries militated against reasoned analysis of the rights and freedom of anyone except, and now perhaps including, blacks—causing William F. Buckley Jr. in 1961 to hope that "when the Negroes have finally realized their long dream of attaining to the status of the white man, the white man will still be free. . . ."

However free the white man may be today, he is not free enough, at least not in Oregon, to refuse to bake a wedding cake for homosexuals.

Promoting "civil rights" for blacks has now become an industry, a huckster's dream. Barack Obama, Eric Holder, and . . . and. . . .

I digress—to report that I couldn't think of the name of Obama's black rabble-rousing friend who was involved in the Tawana Brawley scandal, has a few tax problems, and has visited the White House seventy-two known times in the last six years. So I entered into the Google search box: "black reverend tax cheat friend of Obama's." In 0.79 seconds Google found "about 7,560,000 results" and reminded me of the name of Barack Obama's best friend, Al Sharpton.

But equal rights for blacks has expanded into equal rights for homosexuals, a cause trumpeted by the *New York Times* and other liberal organs. (You can hardly blame them for wanting to deflect attention from their other, often absurd, and always failed, public-policy prescriptions.)

What is remarkable, and hugely disappointing, is that there are apparently no blacks sufficiently prominent to object effectively to the hijacking of the noble civil rights crusade in order to pander to homosexuals—who, after all, constitute only 2 percent of the population.

The "religious freedom" test of the various Religious Freedom Restoration Acts is insufficient to protect all people who choose not to associate with homosexuals, though it may serve as a beginning. How religious do you have to be to invoke it? Do you have to be a Roman Catholic? Do you have to be a *good* Roman Catholic? Who decides? Can you be a Protestant and invoke the exemption? What if you're *really* Protestant—the transcendentalist Walden Pond kind? What if you're a Scientologist? (Or are only movie stars Scientologists?) What about—minor change of subject—discriminating against women who've had an abortion, of whom there are millions?

Suppose you just have a cultural aversion to homosexuals, homosexuality, and abortion? Where did that aversion come from—except from the culture that is Western Civilization, which itself, of course, is a product of Christianity? Does osmotic absorption of Western values qualify you for the religious-freedom exemption?

Aren't these precisely the sort of questions we do *not* want courts deciding?

The problem with the Religious Freedom Restoration Acts is that they focus on only the religious reasons for exercising freedom of choice (i.e., for discriminating). That permits the argument for freedom to be characterized as an effort of the crazy Republican religious right, thereby demeaning and marginalizing it. We should instead use Indiana's burning to light the way to a far wider freedom of choice, for all Americans.

Closing Time for the So-Called Independent Regulatory Agencies

April 19, 2015

Unlike Jacob Marley, Scrooge's partner, who was dead to begin with, William E. Humphrey was not dead to begin with: not in 1925, when he was appointed to the Federal Trade Commission by President Calvin Coolidge; not in 1931 when he was reappointed by President Herbert Hoover; not in October of 1933, when President Franklin Roosevelt sent him a letter saying, "you are hereby removed from the office of Commissioner of the Federal Trade Commission"; and not when he refused to leave office. But he was dead four months after his dismissal, and so it fell to his executor to sue for the salary he was owed from the time Roosevelt fired him until his death. In 1935, the executor won the suit for Humphrey's back salary in a case the US Supreme Court got terribly wrong, known as *Humphrey's Executor v. United States*.

Which takes us to President Obama's interference with the decision-making process of the Federal Communications Commission and, possibly, of the Federal Trade Commission as well.

Humphrey's Executor v. United States stands for the proposition that the so-called independent regulatory agencies, which is to say, their commissioners, are independent of the president. The court held that the Federal Trade Commission's duties "are neither political nor executive, but predominantly quasi-judicial and quasi-legislative."

Eighty enlightened years after *Humphrey's Executor v. United States*, we should be asking, Where on earth—or more precisely, where in the US Constitution—did the Court find justification for the existence of a body truly independent of the executive, the legislative, and the judicial branches? The right answer, of course, is: nowhere. The Constitution makes no provision for such a government entity. Articles I, II, and III (and specifically their "Vesting Clauses") vest the legislative powers in the Congress, the executive powers in the president, and the judicial powers in the courts. There is no provision for a body that is "neither political nor executive, but predominantly quasi-judicial and quasi-legislative."

Nevertheless, for decades the so-called independent regulatory agencies have operated independently (more or less), relying primarily on the Supreme Court's decision in *Humphrey's Executor v. United States*.

From time to time, though not always, the various commissioners of the so-called independent regulatory agencies have been reluctant to seem to be taking directions from the White House.

The agencies' relations with Congress have been more problematical. Congress has oversight responsibilities over the agencies, but is supposed to avoid bringing undue pressure, or even giving the appearance of bringing undue pressure, on the agencies to make decisions.

Sometimes a congressman will step, or fall flat on his face, over the line. In 1987, a congressman called the chairman of the Federal Trade Commission while the commission was investigating a merger of two corporations in his state and threatened to take away his dining room if the FTC's decision went against the congressman's wishes. The congressman was politely told that the chairman of the FTC didn't have a dining room.

In *Humphrey's Executor v. United States* the Supreme Court said, "The debates [over the creation of the Federal Trade Commission] in both houses demonstrate that the prevailing view was that the commission was not to be 'subject to anybody in the government, but . . . only to the people of the United States'; free from 'political domination or control' or the 'probability or possibility of such a thing'; to be 'separate and apart from any existing department of the government—not subject to the orders of the President.' "

But that, on its face, upends the whole constitutional scheme. By attempting to make the commission subject "only to the people," Congress made it subject to no one. Being "free from 'political domination or control' " means being free from democratic accountability.

Until, perhaps, now. Last fall, President Obama announced his position that the internet should be regulated like any other public utility. His announcement is said to have blind-sided officials at the Federal Communications Commission, who had been planning far more modest regulations. However, the chairman of the FCC, Tom

Wheeler, fell into line, and in February the FCC voted to impose the "net neutrality" policy. So much for independence from political control. Now Rep. Jason Chaffetz (R–Utah), chairman of the House Oversight and Government Reform Committee, is planning to investigate the decision-making process.

Chaffetz may profess to be shocked to find executive-branch "interference" going on at the FCC. But in fact, President Obama's "interference" is good news for constitutional government. Decisions like Chairman Wheeler's should not be made by people who were not elected and are not accountable to anyone.

But wait: there's more. Google officials had a plethora of meetings with White House officials while the Federal Trade Commission was contemplating bringing an action against the company (an average of one meeting a week, totaling 230, constitutes a plethora). The FTC finally decided not to take action.

There's an old New York State case that holds that when a man and a woman, not his wife, register at a hotel under assumed names and spend the night together, it is presumed they did not spend their time discussing the weather.

The same presumption, *mutatis mutandis*, holds for the Google officials and the people they met at the White House. But there's no venality on Google's part. They had the access, and if they hadn't used it, the stockholders would have been right to complain.

We don't know if President Obama put pressure on the FTC commissioners, but why should we be surprised if he did? The FTC commissioners may profess to be shocked, shocked, that anyone could even think such a thing. But our experience with the Federal Communications Commission's decision makes that thinking entirely plausible.

Here's the point: President Obama—indeed, any president—*should* seek, not just to influence the decisions of the so-called independent regulatory agencies, but to command them. Then, if the people don't like the decisions, they can vote for a different kind of president in the next election.

And the next president, if he's a Republican, should fire all the Democratic commissioners (and also any "misbehaving" Republican commissioners) of all the so-called independent regulatory agencies, starting with Tom Wheeler at the FCC. They would sue, allowing the Supreme Court to overturn *Humphrey's Executor v. United States* and establish, once and for all, that the independence of the so-called independent regulatory agencies is dead. Really dead. Every bit as dead as Marley was to begin with.

Would the US Go to War for Lithuania?
May 5, 2015

You have to feel sorry for Lithuania and its three million inhabitants. Lithuania may be the largest of the three Baltic countries, but it is still only as big as West Virginia. It may be a member of the European Union, the Council of Europe, the Schengen Agreement, and the North Atlantic Treaty Organization, but it still has a 422-mile border with Belarus, a Russian lackey state.

Lithuania and the other Baltic states were part of the Russian empire for centuries and suffered under Russian Communist domination for fifty years. Being a part of historic Russia is not an experience the Lithuanians want to repeat.

The Lithuanians, 150,000 of whom are Russian-speakers, have provided moral support to the Ukrainians in their struggle with Russia, but only limited tangible support: "elements of armaments," according to Linas Linkevicius, the foreign minister of Lithuania, and mittens for freezing Ukrainian hands, knitted to mark the occasion of Lithuania's presidency of the European Union.

Now, as the Lithuanians watch the European Union's quarter-hearted resistance to Russian war-making in Ukraine—against the backdrop of NATO's decades-long history of being underfunded, and the Obamic "strategic patience" of the United States—their future looks as cold and bleak as the Ukrainians' bare hands if Vladimir Putin decides to move to "protect" the Russian-speaking population in Lithuania and reintegrate the country into historic Russia.

Meanwhile, Greece toys with abandoning, or being abandoned by, a failing experiment known as the euro (which Lithuania adopted only this January 1), and Britain contemplates leaving another failing experiment known as the European Union. And coming soon: an adult discussion of what exactly the North Atlantic Treaty requires its signatories to do. Feeling sorry for people may not be seen as an adequate reason to go to war, at least not with a country that has 1,600 deployed nuclear warheads. Sixty-six years after its founding, NATO may be closer to failure than the euro and the EU.

At a small dinner in Washington recently, a knowledgeable Lithuanian made the case for Western support for Ukraine, including lethal but defensive weaponry. Inferentially, he was making a similar, prospective plea for Lithuania. He supported NATO maneuvers and said they should not be regarded as provocative. What was provocative, he said, was inaction—the failure to prepare.

Asked about the value of the NATO guarantee to Lithuania, he in turn asked what options Lithuania had.

There's a major problem with the NATO guarantee—a problem that must keep all the Baltic peoples awake during the long bleak Baltic winter nights. Article 5 of the North Atlantic Treaty states that the parties agree that "each of them . . . will assist the Party or Parties so attacked by taking forthwith, individually and in concert with the other Parties, such action as it deems necessary, including the use of armed force, to restore and maintain the security of the North Atlantic area."

But what kind of action so unequivocally constitutes an attack that the twenty-eight members of NATO will agree that it is an attack and therefore warrants action? We have seen, in Ukraine, a preview of Russian activity that has deniability—at least for those who want to find a reason not to act.

Greece, which joined NATO in 1952, has been cozying up to the Russians and will have no trouble finding such a reason.

But Greece may not be the only recalcitrant country. Other Europeans disagree on what, if anything, to do about Russia. People at the eastern edge of Western Europe tend, as you would expect, to be more nervous about Russia than are café sippers at the Deux Magots in Paris or Madeira drinkers at Boodle's in London. Many Europeans have more local concerns: unemployment is 10 percent in the EU overall, but higher in France, Italy, and Portugal, and much higher in Spain (24 percent). Some Europeans argue that Ukraine had an elected government that was overthrown in a coup, which makes the claim to legitimacy by the current crop of Ukrainian politicians tenuous. Our knowledgeable Lithuanian friend disputed that interpretation.

A senior European diplomat told me recently that many Europeans thought Putin was just being a "good Russian" and that the Ukrainians were a rum bunch. (Whether those Europeans, or their grandparents, thought Hitler was just being a "good German" we don't know.) I asked him if he thought the Russians would invade any more countries, e.g., Lithuania or other Baltic countries, expecting him to say no. He said he thought they might.

He said he thought the real, if longer-term, threat to Europe was China, but that a more immediate threat was immigrants—essentially an unlimited number of immigrants from North Africa. Not black Africans. Muslims. Americans, he said, have only Mexican immigrants to worry about, and they do not present the existential threat to America that North Africans (but not Russians) do to Europe, and to Western civilization.

That view may shock some Americans, especially those who are NATO-centric. They may be reviewing their pocket editions of the North Atlantic Treaty, brushing up on the argument for full-scale opposition to any new Russian "incursions," if not with boots on the ground, at least with bombs from the air. Or at the very least, with crippling economic sanctions.

But our Lithuanian friend was against the most crippling economic sanction, that of banning Russia from SWIFT (the international payment, clearing, and settlement system). He said that that was too radical a measure, that it would have negative consequences for everyone, and that there were other banking actions that should be tried first.

Given the reluctance of the European countries to invoke Article 5, what are the odds the United States would? Slim. What the treaty means to the United States is probably, for now, only what a strategically patient President Obama, channeling his inner Humpty Dumpty, chooses for it to mean—neither more nor less. After all, a man who has no qualms about changing the country's immigration law on his own should have no problem wiggling out of even an obvious NATO treaty obligation.

Wall Street too will be unenthusiastic, especially about economic sanctions. Like hippies who'd rather make love than war, the wolves—and crony capitalists—of Wall Street would rather make money than . . . anything. Lenin knew that.

But even Main Street Americans are likely to think that Lithuania is, after all, you know, well, kind of, a long . . . way . . . away.

In which case, it may turn out that the North Atlantic Treaty is a relic and type of our ancestors' worth, but not a good guide to their descendants' behavior.

A serious question, which will be raised again, and again, by disturbances and conflicts, actual and threatened, in the North Atlantic Treaty area and in other areas of the globe, is: Should the United States be guided by treaties or only by what is seen to be in its immediate national interest? Treaties are important. But their importance tends to be in inverse proportion to the power of the signatory. Of course, honoring the commitments of a treaty may be in the national interest even if, or perhaps sometimes especially if, the particular action required by the treaty seems not to be.

We are already up to our ankles in Ukraine. The question is, once we begin providing assistance, which means we've joined the fight, when do we stop? If we send mittens or Meals Ready to Eat, do we also have to send, eventually, tactical nuclear weapons? And if not, why not?

One answer to that question may be that we should provide some weapons to the Ukrainians in order to raise the cost to the Russians of their aggression, on the theory that if you make something more expensive, you get less of it—though maybe not in this case.

The North Atlantic Treaty Organization's top military commander, Gen. Philip Breedlove, said last week, "We see Mr. Putin is all-in, and they will proceed till their objectives are accomplished."

If we are prepared to be up to our knees in providing assistance, shouldn't we be prepared to be up to our keister? But according to Gen. Breedlove, even that may not be enough.

Which raises again the question: Is going part way, but not finishing the job, worse than doing nothing at all? Doesn't it give false hope, waste resources, and make us look fickle? If the United States is not prepared to take the last step, should it take the first step?

The answers to those questions may be numbing, but they should make us be more careful in the future about entering into treaties. If we husband our guarantees, they will be more believable—especially if they are seen as closely related to our national interests.

The United States has several strategic national interests, some more important than others. The three primary interests are protecting this country from the nefarious activities of China, Russia, and Muslim terrorists.

Securing the territorial integrity of Lithuania, or of Ukraine, against Russia is strategically necessary only if the Russian activity is understood as one more step in a long-term Russian strategy, which is likely to succeed, of destabilizing Europe (whatever that means). That is certainly contrary to US interests. But it is not clear yet that even a Baltic Dinner—a Russian three-course meal consisting of Lithuania, Latvia, and Estonia—would force the conclusion that Russia, an economically failing kleptocracy, presents such a threat to US security that intervention, even if only by the imposition of crippling economic sanctions, is required.

But that leaves open the question: Is US intervention required because of our expressed obligations under the North Atlantic Treaty even if Russia's actual activity does not (or does not yet) present a threat to our security?

The Russians, no doubt, are nasty people (by which of course we mean Putin and Co. are nasty people), and the Ukrainians may be a rum bunch too, as some Europeans say, and, for all I know, the Lithuanians are a bad lot, though our knowledgeable Lithuanian was an awfully pleasant fellow. But US policy cannot be based on who's naughty and who's nice, but only on what will produce peace and security, for us.

Our Lithuanian dinner companion described himself as an optimist. But I couldn't think why, given the options, and he didn't look optimistic as he left us. We felt sorry for him as he walked out into the cold, dark Washington night.

It's been cold in Washington for days. But it may be even colder in Lithuania, and in the other small countries on Russia's border, for many years to come.

Extra! Extra! Pope Denies Henry VIII
Late Checkout—Crisis Looms

June 11, 2015

Some of my best friends are Catholics. Actually, that's not quite right. Most of my best friends are Catholics. I use the term "Catholic" in the layman's sense meaning Roman Catholic, though I am a Catholic too, of the Anglican, not the Roman, stripe. I am an Episcopalian, but I consider my Roman brothers and sisters equal heirs to the Western Code.

Being an Episcopalian is challenging these days, many, perhaps most, of the clergy not having enough sense to come in out of the rain, and employing that diminished sense to gum up the doctrine, discipline, and worship of the Episcopal Church.

But I was recently chastised by an old friend of forty years or so for belonging to a church that was started by an English king who wanted a divorce, to wit, one Henry VIII. (My friend employed the same phrases that the founder of the conservative movement used to employ with me making the same point, suggesting that their claim was part of a standardized Sunday-school training.)

Henry VIII, as many will recall, had six wives, whose fates are remembered by the jingle: Divorced, beheaded, died, divorced, beheaded, survived.

But the description of the first fate is not accurate. What Henry actually wanted from Pope Clement VII was an annulment of his marriage to Catherine of Aragon, a request about as common then as asking for late checkout at a hotel is today.

The problem was that Pope Clement VII was at the time virtually a prisoner of Charles V, ruler of the Holy Roman Empire, whose troops were occupying Rome. And Charles V was a nephew of: Catherine of Aragon, and . . . well, you can see how it got complicated. In addition, there was a major political struggle going on. Rome's demands for money were bleeding England dry. Henry's leading the English church to independence from Rome was actually driven more by politics than by theology.

The motes my friend beholds in Henry's character may have blinded him to the beams in the papacy. For example, Pope Innocent X. Innocent may have been the brand name of his bath soap, but it didn't accurately describe the man, who spent most of his papacy satiating his grasping family's desires and piling up works of art.

And then there was Pope Benedict IX, described by Pope Victor III as vile, foul, and execrable, who sold the papacy in order to marry his sweetheart. And who, except perhaps my friend, could forget Pope Stephen VI? He exhumed the corpse of his predecessor, Pope Formosus, and put it on trial, and, following the surely inevitable conviction, amputated three of "his" fingers. And, not finally but we must move on, let us not overlook, let us not, Pope Alexander VI, born Rodrigo Borgia, who, and two of whose children, Lucrezia and Cesare, made their surname synonymous with ruthless corruption and sexual debauchery.

Compared to that crowd, Henry VIII was a saint.

But more to the point: St. Henry's break with Rome wasn't theological at all. Great care was taken by the English church to ensure that apostolic succession was maintained; and no beliefs were changed: the Anglican and Roman creeds to this day are identical.

It is true that Anglicans and Romans do not currently recognize each others' orders. St. Henry's daughter Queen Elizabeth I declared in 1570 that Roman orders were deficient from an Anglican perspective. Not to be outdone, Pope Leo XIII responded almost immediately (326 years later) that Anglican orders were invalid. And that's where the two denominations stand today.

Of course, the antics of the (so-called) Presiding Bishop of the Episcopal Church, Katharine Jefferts Schori, are enough to make anyone doubt the sanity of people who remain Episcopalians. Her denial that Jesus is the only way to salvation prompted the retired Bishop of South Carolina, The Rt. Rev. Dr. C. FitzSimons Allison, to say of her remarks: "It doesn't measure up to heresy. She is trying to reduce Christianity to the blank space in the creed between the Virgin Mary and Pontius Pilate."

But then the Roman Catholic Church has had its problems too: notably the recent, and well-publicized and rather expensive, pedophile scandal. Although it's true that the Romans' scandal involves only bad behavior, not basic belief, it is also true that bad behavior is the crux of my friends' brief against Henry VIII.

In the 1950s, Episcopalians and Roman Catholics kept each other at arm's length. It was not unusual for Episcopalians to avoid entering a Roman Catholic church. In boarding schools there were religious wars (fought with socks) between Roman Catholics and Protestants—though it was not always clear that the Protestants knew what they were fighting about. Jews were never involved—because there weren't any.

It was all quite wonderful, in a way, that way being that people took religion seriously. Now we're all—Catholics, Protestants, Jews—stuck nervously together in the same leaky boat, pulling hard for a shore that seems, always, to be receding. Some of us long for the day when we can start fighting each other again (if only with socks, and words), secure in the knowledge that the Western Code has prevailed.

Capture the Flag, B-word
July 28, 2015

Why is it that the further we get from slavery, segregation, and the civil rights battles of the Sixties, the more virulent the reminders seem to become? If the Confederate flag didn't have to go twenty, thirty, forty years ago, why now?

The easy answer is that pervasive racism has persisted longer than we thought. You can always count on a *New York Times* or *Washington Post* columnist to discourse on the prevalence of racism (is it perhaps increasing?) in the US. And after all, why should racism not have persisted, given the imprimatur it has received from the federal government's own program of affirmative action? But people who think racism is rampant in the US should pay more attention to the facts. A good place to start is Greg Jones's July 7 piece in *The Federalist*.

Is there racism left in the United States? Of course there is. We are imperfect beings. Some problems are simply not solvable, which means there will always be some racism, here and indeed elsewhere—even as there will always be conflict in the Middle East.

That may sound like bad news. But the news may actually be worse. What if the problem is not just vestigially racist whites but insufficiently attentive or motivated blacks? What if the fault lies not in the easy-to-blame stars of the Republican Party but in blacks themselves?

Blacks vote overwhelmingly for Democrats: 95 percent of the black vote went for Obama in 2008; 93 percent in 2012. (But be careful what you wish for, or vote for: Eugene Robinson says that a black family living in the White House has heightened racial anxieties and conflicts. [http://bitly.com/why-racism-still-flourishes] Who knew?) Blacks vote for Democrats and they get—surprise!—the policies that Democrats promote. See the recent speech by former Texas Governor Rick Perry for details. Perry pointed out that the prevalence of black poverty has increased under President Obama. Surprise!

Yet a recent survey found that most blacks wouldn't vote for a Republican even if the positions the candidate held were identical to those of a Democratic opponent. The survey respondents seem to lack any sense of political strategy. To the extent that they're typical of black voters, there wouldn't seem to be any political reason for the Republican Party to attempt to cater to whatever might in theory, but apparently not in practice, motivate blacks to vote Republican, including serious efforts to erase whatever vestiges of discrimination remain. Maybe black leaders lack political smarts, or gumption: how otherwise to explain their allowing homosexuals to hijack the civil rights analogy to promote their own weird cause?

An imaginative black community—in other words a community not led by the likes of Barack Obama's tax-cheating and slanderous friend, the "Rev." Al Sharpton—might long ago have appropriated Confederate symbols for its own purposes. As early Christians stole pagan symbols, blacks could have stolen the Confederate flag.

The National Association for the Advancement of Colored People (savor the quaintness of the unchanged name) is, if not the largest black rights organization in the country, certainly the most prominent. If the Confederate flag were such a poisonous reminder of Southern intransigence, why didn't the folks at the NAACP sanitize it by adopting it as their emblem?

News flash: "Today the NAACP adopts the Confederate flag as its symbol. The history of the South is, at best, mixed. Slavery was the economic linchpin, the dominating force. Even so, there was a style of life that all people, then and now, could aspire to. And even so, in that South, blacks led, where they could, lives of virtue among the suffering and indignity. Today we take that symbol of the South as our own, purge it of its history of racial subjugation and hatred, and fly it proudly as a reminder of the suffering, perseverance, and dignity of generations of black Americans, and of the hope for a better life that sustained them. The South shall rise again, as a living monument to the faith of Americans, black and white, who believed in the eventual triumph of equality under law."

Ha! First divest (with an assist by Abraham Lincoln) the Southerners of their "property" (slaves). Then capture their flag. Nice, yes?

But there's more. Why not neutralize the N-word too? (I will substitute the B-word here for the N-word. The B-word is "Bubba," for some, a derogatory term indicating a promiscuous, perjurious, and financially unscrupulous Southern male.)

Why don't the Harlem Globetrotters call themselves the Harlem Bubbas? Their skill at doing things with basketballs that defy both description and imagination suggests that Earth was not their native planet. They were, perhaps still are, hugely popular and predominantly black. The Harlem Bubbas are a hot property: they were sold two years ago for an undisclosed sum.

Why not the New York Bubbas instead of the New York Yankees or the New York Giants? (Press release plagiarizes shamelessly from the NAACP's.) Say it fifty times, quickly. All of a sudden, every kid who plays baseball or football wants to grow up and play for the Bubbas.

Why not? Ah, because then the whining might have to stop. And then what would the civil rights racketeers, the Rev. Al Sharptons, do for a living?

No, better to keep complaining and urging blacks to vote monolithically for Democrats. Tried and true. A comfort vote. Home, home on the plantation. Where the Dems and the liberals play. And where blacks suffer still.

And where year after year it will always appear that the skies remain cloudy all day.

Why Racial Discrimination Is Wrong

August 26, 2015

The Supreme Court's recent decision on homosexual marriage raises a troubling question: What is the moral case against discriminating on the basis of race?

Once upon a time the answer might have been that the Western code imposes moral obligations on us to act in certain ways toward our fellow man. Exactly what those obligations are, and how qualified they may be, is difficult to say. (For a discussion, particularly of the many qualifications posited by scholars, see the excellent piece by Donald Devine at www.libertylawsite.org/2015/07/02/elusive-discrimination.)

The moral obligation to treat people equally is now grounded, among other places, in Thomas Jefferson's line in the Declaration of Independence, "All men are created equal" (by which the slave-holding Jefferson, who was writing primarily for the French, may have meant, per Jeffrey Hart, only that Englishmen living in England were not superior to the colonists in respect of self-government). Manifestly, all men are not created equal, at least not with respect to brawn, brains, or bank accounts, or perhaps most importantly, both parents. Some other kind of equality, therefore, must be inferred from those words, which we have made talismanic, whatever Jefferson intended.

What kind of equality? Well, equality either in God's eyes (in which case, ahem, man should pay close attention) or perhaps only in the eyes of the state. But if only in the eyes of the state, how should we interpret the word "created," especially in light of the next clause in the Declaration, which says that all men are endowed "by their Creator" with certain unalienable rights?

Skipping the issue of whether the "endowment" came from God or government (will the real Creator please stand up?), we can say that there is something, even if we don't quite know what, fundamental about the obligation to treat people equally.

And that is where the problem lies.

Once you (or the state) start picking and choosing which moral commands are to be obeyed, which ignored, you (or the state) lose your moral authority. And that is true whether you think the commands are grounded in revealed truths or only in the acts of the state.

If we consider the Supreme Court to be the state (but only for argument's sake here because actually it's not, and a hearty resistance to it—hey! ho!—would be a good thing; vive the Second Amendment! And if you think the Second Amendment is only about hunting squirrels and other vermin you need to read "A Minority View" at http://humanevents.com/2015/07/01/a-minority-view-2, by Walter Williams and learn what kind of vermin the Founders thought guns would protect us from)—if we consider the Supreme Court to be the state, the state has now "repealed" a provision of the Western moral code (that marriage is a union between one man and one woman) that has been in effect for a couple of thousand years, and one that was common wisdom, and commonly accepted, until only a few years ago.

If one provision of the moral law (first we'll consider it to be God's law) can be repealed by five uber-law-school graduates, why shouldn't whatever God's law is on treating people equally, on not discriminating on the basis of race, be repealed by, well, any other group of five people, or by, say, the Confederate States, which consisted of rather more than five people?

Ah, you say, but it's not really God's law—it's not a natural law. It's just the law of man.

That really doesn't help, and is quite a dangerous argument. If the legislature, acting as moral arbiter, voted to do in the Jews (yes, I know: no legislature in the Western world would *ever* do that), what would be the principled objection? Suppose the legislature just decreed that Jews couldn't go to synagogues?

When the legislature says religious people no longer have the right not to associate with people they consider to be . . . immoral, where does true morality lie? The District of Columbia has passed a law making it illegal not to hire someone who has had an abortion. Could anyone except a crazy left-winger think there is morality lurking in there somewhere?

And wouldn't you think blacks would have been more solicitous of the good name of "civil rights" and not have allowed it to be hijacked by abortionists and homosexuals? The price for their negligence could be high.

We need to be very clear here. It is not conservatives, or Republicans, or Southerners (all broadly defined) who would be making the argument that the moral proscription on racial discrimination had been repealed. It would be the statist progressives, the intellectual heirs of the eugenicists of the early twentieth century. It is they who believe that morality is only whatever the editors of the *New York Times* and their ilk say it is and can get a legislature to enact, a regulator to impose, or a court to decide. And that kind of morality, morality du jour, can change from jour to jour.

Statist progressives lack the power of morality to guide behavior. In the end, their only power is the gun. In which case . . .

Vive the Second Amendment! And pray, brothers, while praying is still legal, that we won't have to rely on it.

Pulse and Breath Detected: Federalism Lives
November 12, 2015

> *"If the policy of the Government*
> *upon vital questions affecting the whole people*
> *is to be irrevocably fixed by decisions of the Supreme Court . . .*
> *the people will have ceased to be their own rulers."*
> —A. Lincoln

The Supreme Court having spoken its mind on the subject of homosexual marriage and the nation's marriage policy, the question now is: What happens next? One theory is that all states are now required to authorize homosexual marriages. But suppose they don't?

Following the Supreme Court's 1954 decision in *Brown vs. Board of Education*, which held that the states could no longer segregate schools by race, there were . . . recalcitrants. One of them, Orval Faubus, the governor of Arkansas, ordered the National Guard to prevent the integration of schools in Little Rock; whereupon President Eisenhower nationalized the Arkansas National Guard (removing it from the governor's control) and, for good measure, sent the 101st Airborne Division of the US Army into Little Rock to keep order.

Could that happen now if a state refused to issue marriage licenses to homosexuals? *En principe*, as the French say—when they mean "No." But does anyone think President Obama would send in the 101st Airborne to enforce homosexual marriage?

One difference between the two Supreme Court cases is especially significant. *Brown vs. Board of Education* was a unanimous decision by the Court, its unanimity reflecting the considered opinion of most of the country: that state-enforced discrimination had to go.

In the recent homosexual-marriage case, however, the Supreme Court was divided (5 to 4), and, again, that reflected opinion in the country: it is divided.

And because opinion is divided, the liberals are trying to hitch up the homosexual-marriage cart to the desegregation horse in order to shame people who don't accept the Court's marriage ruling: "Not so long ago, of course, government officials invoked religious beliefs to justify all manner of racial segregation and discrimination, including laws banning interracial marriage," wrote the *New York Times* (http://bitly.com/defiance-on-gay-marriage). (We should pause a moment to note the complete absence of any outrage from blacks at being thus analogized.)

For the most part today, the states have abandoned federalism: they're all on the federal dole. For highway money, for school money, for money to do 101 useless things which their citizens wouldn't vote for if they realized they were paying for them with their own tax money, but which they like because they appear to be freeeee.

State X doesn't want to follow the diktats of the Department of Education? Fine, but then the feds will withhold a $100 million or so in education funding. A $100 million here, a $100 million there—first thing you know, the governor won't be able to afford fuel for his airplane. You see the problem.

But what happens if a state doesn't issue marriage licenses to homosexuals? What on Earth—or what in Louisiana—would the 101st Airborne do if Obama sent it in?

The federal government's problem is that the 101st Airborne stick is too big to wield, and there aren't any relevant carrots to withhold.

This looks promising. Already six states (Alabama, Louisiana, Mississippi, North Dakota, South Dakota, and Texas) have expressed interest in resisting the Supreme Court's civilization-changing rule. They seem to understand what Lincoln was talking about: government by the people, not by the Supreme Court.

Meanwhile . . . last summer, five Republican governors said that they might refuse to put into effect President Obama's sweeping climate-change regulations. The governors' actions were instigated (that's likely to be the word President Obama will use—it makes the governors' actions sound so . . . criminal) by Senate Majority Leader Mitch McConnell (R–KY) who urged all governors to refuse to carry out the federal rules, promulgated by President Obama's Environmental Protection Agency. The regulations were finally published by the EPA on October 23, and now twenty-four states have filed lawsuits to have them overturned.

The rules are aimed, according to the enviro-mentally unstable turn-out-the-lights, take-cold-showers Obama administration, at reducing global warming. They will require states to shut down coal-powered electricity generating plants and replace them with plants powered by so-called "renewable sources"—solar and wind power (you just put your lips together and blow). President Obama sees this as a transformative policy.

So do the governors, who see their states being transformed back into the whale-oil era for the sake of the Left's only religious cause: stopping global warming, a dogma the governors and most other sensible people don't believe in.

"The EPA's latest attempt at imposing burdensome regulations represents an unprecedented meddling with Texas in order to push the Obama administration's liberal climate-change agenda," said Texas Governor Greg Abbott.

"The president's Clean Power Plan undermines the role of states in the federal Clean Air Act in an effort to realize a radical, liberal agenda that will lead to increased energy costs. While we believe the proposed rule should be immediately withdrawn, we are considering all options to mitigate the damage if it becomes final, including not submitting a plan," said a spokesman for Louisiana governor Bobby Jindal (http://bitly.com/republican-governors-intent-on-weather-rules).

Fighting words indeed. Federalism (of a sort). Finally.

And how can liberals object? For years they've been supporting the practices of "sanctuary cities" (almost two hundred of them!)—cities that have refused to follow the federal government's policy requiring that Immigration and Customs Enforcement officials be notified when an illegal immigrant is released from custody.

But surely the transformation of the culture from the traditional Western Civilization marriage and family culture to a hook-up, lesbian, gay, bisexual, transgender, queer (and disgusting, and Democratic party) culture is more consequential than having to turn out the light when you leave the bathroom. Gentlemen, please: Focus.

Still, we have to begin somewhere. The governors have to get the hang of protecting their citizens *from the federal government*, and the citizens may have to learn to enjoy being protected. Resisting the religious practices of federal voodoo climate-change believers may be a good beginning; a first, if small, step toward federalism—and freedom.

They say that after you've shot your first sweet, innocent, harmless, leaf-eating, doe-eyed little deer, the second one's easier.

And there's nothing sweet, innocent, or harmless about the US Supreme Court's marriage policy, which lovers of federalism and freedom should make sure is not irrevocably fixed.

Marco Rubio, If You Can
November 12, 2015

Because Marco Rubio got generally high marks in last Tuesday's debate, his positions should be closely scrutinized. There are two other real conservatives in the race, Ted Cruz and Rand Paul, and one of them might be a better choice. For conservatives.

In his answer to the first question, which was about the minimum wage, Senator Rubio said: "If I thought that raising the minimum wage was the best way to help people increase their pay, I would be all for it, but it isn't." Really?

At first hearing, that may seem like a good answer, but in fact it's like the first sip on a hot summer day of a cold, but third-rate, white wine. What Rubio needed was the fruit of a little more philosophical reflection, which he should have done before going on stage to debate, perhaps even before going to the Senate. Henry Kissinger said, famously, that you have to do your thinking before you go to Washington. When you get there, there isn't time to accumulate intellectual capital; you're too busy spending it. (Messrs. Trump and Carson, please note.)

Rubio's answer was correct: the minimum wage should not be raised. But his apparent reasoning was wrong. Even if requiring payment of a minimum wage would help a particular employee, why should an employer be required by government to spend his money helping, as distinguished from employing, a person? The point, and the correct answer, is: There shouldn't be a minimum wage.

Employers ought to be free to pay their employees whatever they want to pay them—and whatever they need to pay them in order to get them to work. They have no obligation to be welfare providers.

And that's a better answer structurally, too, because the same case can be made, *mutatis mutandis*, against probably thousands, or tens of thousands, of regulations imposed on businesses by the federal government. People ought to be free from all but the most necessary regulations.

The issue is freedom, not just, as Rubio puts it, "what works." What, after all, is America all about? The answer to that question is the title of a book by the late M. Stanton Evans, one of the founders of the conservative movement: *The Theme Is Freedom*.

The case against a minimum wage is the same case that can be made for school choice. Parents ought to be free to choose what schools their children attend, not because their children will necessarily get a better education, or even because Americans will then be able to beat the wily Japanese, whom God has put on earth for that purpose. Parents ought to be free to choose their children's school because: parents ought to be free to choose their children's school.

All this may seem to some like a quibble: C'mon, you know what Senator Rubio meant. The question was about the minimum wage, and he opposed it.

But his reasoning is important, because, as the philosopher Richard Weaver said, ideas have consequences.

Later the same evening, we should digress to note, Rubio took an oblique swipe at philosophers: "We need more welders and less [sic] philosophers." In fact, what we probably need is more philosophers. But not every student can or should study philosophy. Some will profit more by learning a trade. On that point the senator was certainly correct.

But the consequence of Senator Rubio's reasoning, if there was any, on the minimum wage also has led him to propose a trillion-dollar refundable tax credit for families with children—i.e., even people who haven't paid taxes receive cash from the government. We must assume he thinks that proposal "will work." Listen to the senator's utilitarianism: "It is expensive to raise children in the twenty-first century, and families that are raising children are raising the future taxpayers of the United States." Really?

If that's true, let's be even more utilitarian. Some of those children will be better taxpayers than others; and—this is important—WE KNOW WHICH ONES THEY ARE. They are the children who grow up in families with both a mother and a father in the house.

So here's a proposal that "will work" even better than the senator's: structure the refundable tax credit so that intact families get more than single-parent families (unless the single parent is a widow or widower). That would (in theory) encourage parents to stick together and raise better taxpayers.

But who's going to pay for that program? Whose freedom is going to be curtailed in order to fund the senator's centrally planned trillion-dollar program? And if a trillion-dollar program actually did work, how would we ever keep it from becoming a three-trillion-dollar program? Do I hear five trillion?

Better—more conservative, at least—to lower taxes and trust the people to use their freedom to make America great.

Better, Marco Rubio, to spend a little more time thinking about the philosophy of governing. If you can.

Minimum Wage as Affirmative Action
November 24, 2015

Minimum wage laws are the Midas temptation of the Democrats. Lay a hand on the wage rates of employees and—presto!—they become rich. It's malarkey, of course. As many a wit has said, if employees could be made better off by legislating higher wages, why be cheap and raise their wages by only a buck or two? Instead of legislating a minimum wage of $10.10, the current proposal of the Democrats, why not raise it to $15? Or $20? Or $25? I-have-$35-in-the-back-of-the-room-from-the-lady-in-the-big-hat-who'll-give-me-$45?

There is some dispute over the actual effects of minimum wage laws, with liberals extolling their virtues, conservatives decrying their effects. The liberal extolling is amplified by unions who may like to have the minimum wage increased because their contracts provide that union wages up the line be a multiple of the minimum wage.

A reasonable person might look at it this way: either a minimum wage law has an effect or it doesn't. If it has no effect, why enact it? If it does have an effect, that means it must do something for one set of people. (We could refer to them as an interest group, in fact.) But like any piece of legislation, if it does something for one person it must do something else to another person. Somebody must be on the losing side. Supporters say it is greedy corporations that will suffer. Puh-lese. Crony-capitalists suffer? What paper do these people read?

Economists generally agree that a minimum wage increase reduces employment for the least skilled workers. Those people tend to be younger and not heads of households, which means that households are not benefitted by a minimum wage, and younger people are disadvantaged by it, if it means they miss out on the experience of having a job and learning skills. It is estimated that half of minimum wage workers in the United States are under the age of twenty-five, and almost a third of them are sixteen to nineteen years old, i.e., part-time workers still in school.

Even though some may argue, and even if it's true, that the effects of a minimum wage are actually quite small, they are not small for the people not hired because of it. For them the minimum wage law is a disaster—a disaster that some supporters, and statist progressive techies, recognize but attempt to camouflage by callously calling the job losses "fallout"—as if unintended consequences didn't matter.

(Of course the real argument against the minimum wage is that it impresses employers into the welfare business. An employer's function is to pay a salary, not to provide welfare.)

It is probably also true that the first minimum wage law enacted was specifically designed to be anti-black: to discourage southern blacks from moving north to look for jobs. If you think Northerners during the post-Civil War period just loved blacks, read Gene Dattel's piece in *The New Criterion*.

But the sensible arguments against a minimum wage have never prevailed, with the result that those who oppose minimum wage legislation are portrayed as cheapskates, and sometimes even anti-black.

Minimum wage opponents need to change their game. They need to get the supporters of minimum wage legislation to become suspicious of the law. Some of those supporters may simply be feel-good artists: people who do things they don't understand because it makes them feel good about themselves. Other minimum wage supporters may really believe.

But how can they be made suspicious? Perhaps by goading them into inflicting a minimum wage on a small group of people, where the results will be readily visible and the politics disastrous. That would allow minimum wage opponents to claim the high ground when the results become apparent.

The idea needs to be floated—notice the passive voice—that minimum wage legislation should be made applicable to blacks only. That should make almost anyone suspicious—a good beginning.

The stated rationale for a blacks-only minimum wage would be either affirmative action, or reparations, or both.

Harold Meyerson, writing in the *Washington Post*, claims that the argument of the "die-hard" opponents of a minimum wage that it will lead to job losses is only a "flimsy veneer" of concern about the welfare of the working poor.

Okay, Mr. Meyerson, we confess (and without even having been water-boarded!) that the arguments against a minimum wage are specious. We now admit that a rise in the minimum wage will be effective in making working people better off. But we think that blacks deserve to be the special beneficiaries of this particular special interest legislation. Blacks have historically been discriminated against in the workplace, and this proposal will go part way towards redressing that injustice. Etc. Etc.

Bernie Sanders (Faux-Soc–VT) might agree. According to Sanders, "Today, more than half of all African American workers . . . make less than $15 an hour. . . . That is unacceptable."

The AFL-CIO says, "African Americans comprise 11 percent of the nation's workforce, but they are 14.8 percent of the workers who would be positively affected by raising the minimum wage."

And per the National Urban League, "Many African Americans

don't make enough money to save for retirement. As of 2010, only 43 percent of African American workers ages 26–61 were part of an employer-based retirement plan, compared to 50 percent of white workers. Raising the wage would allow more African Americans to save for retirement."

There you have it. Those quotes pretty much make the case.

Maybe.

Even so, a Brookings Institution report nags: "In a city like Washington, D.C., where unemployment among those with a high school education or less is at a worrisome 15%, jobless rates will almost certainly rise [if the minimum wage is increased]."

But we've heard that one before, haven't we, Mr. Meyerson—and what would you expect from the paleo-ultra-right Brookings Institution anyway? That's just the old "flimsy veneer" again. Given that the Brookings people are talking about Washington DC, probably many or most of the people who make up that 15 percent are blacks.

So this is the plan (don't tell anyone): inflict the minimum wage on blacks (or if you have a group more suitable for the didactic purpose in mind, that's fine), and then reap the kudos of feel-good liberals.

Will the feel-gooders enjoy their Midas touch? Midas became disillusioned when he laid a hand on his daughter. Years later, Midas ticked off Apollo, who then turned his ears into the ears of a donkey, which, somehow, makes Midas's bio seem like a cautionary tale for Democrats who support the minimum wage.

Does Donald Trump Think Black Voters Are Stupid?

December 15, 2015

> *"Democracy is the worst form of government, except for all the others."*
> —Winston Churchill

Donald Trump has been condemned for saying that 81 percent of whites who were killed last year were killed by blacks. There turns out to be no truth whatsoever in the statement, raising the question: Why did he say it?

Perhaps because the statement resonates with a significant number of non-blacks, raising Trump's poll numbers while not hurting him at all with African Americans, who, for some reason, simply do not vote for Republicans.

Why don't black people vote for Republicans? They used to. Before 1964, when Barry Goldwater ran for president, African Americans routinely voted for Republicans in significant numbers. From 1936 to 1956, the black vote for the Republican presidential candidate was between 28 and 39 percent. In 1960, Nixon got 33 percent of the black vote.

But Goldwater, whose reputation of not being a racist was well known, had voted against the Civil Rights Act of 1964, because he objected to the public-accommodations provision and the fair-employment provision, saying that he could find "no constitutional basis for the exercise of federal regulatory authority in either of these areas."

That didn't stop Democrats, who are still whining that Nixon's "Southern strategy" was immoral, from demonizing Goldwater for his principled stand. Lyndon Johnson, whose complete corruption must have been the model for the Clintons, got 94 percent of the black vote in 1964. The Democrats have swept the black vote ever since, and never more so than in the elections of Barack Obama: 99 percent in 2008; 95 percent in 2012.

Trump might ask blacks, channeling his inner Sarah Palin: How's that voting for Democrats thing workin' out for ya?

Democrats routinely and almost uniformly (including, now, Hillary Clinton) oppose charter schools and vouchers, which may be blacks' only hope for a decent education. The Democratic Party is a wholly owned subsidiary of the teachers' unions—the American Federation of Teachers and the National Education Association. President Obama himself, *lui-même*, opposed the District of Columbia Opportunity Scholarship Program. It reminded some people of George Wallace's blocking the doorway of the University of Alabama in 1963 in order to avoid integration. Extra-credit question: Which is nobler—to victimize blacks in order (a) to promote racial discrimination, or (b) to buy votes? Discuss calmly.

Democrats routinely and almost uniformly support minimum wage legislation, which almost any high school student not interned in the AFT–NEA public school gulag could tell you causes low-skilled employees (disproportionately blacks) to lose their jobs. Milton Friedman said the minimum wage law was "the most anti-black law on the books of this land."

Democrats routinely and almost uniformly support unlimited immigration, especially of Latinos (whom Democrats hope will vote Democratic in their sleep, perhaps several times). Donald Trump wants to build a wall to keep them out. It seems plausible (at least?) to think low-skilled Latino immigrants take the jobs, housing, and other opportunities that would otherwise be available to low-skilled blacks. (See the piece by Bruce Bartlett at https://tinyurl.com/pqs7dkq.)

And Democrats caused the economic meltdown of 2008, and caused it by pandering to, primarily, blacks. Congress passed what were called "affordable housing goals" which, essentially, required banks to make loans to un-creditworthy people (disproportionately blacks) who couldn't possibly afford them. Peter Wallison has written *the* book on the subject, *Hidden in Plain Sight*. (If you don't have time for the book, you can get the gist of it at https://tinyurl.com/wchakdm.) It is generally agreed that the recession has been harder on blacks than on any other group. So, Mr. Sharpton, how did that policy, a gifted combination of pandering and incompetence, turn out for ya?

Two University of Chicago economists say that "most black men [are] in a position relative to white men that is really no better than the position they occupied only a few years after the Civil Rights Act." The Pew Research Center says that black financial worth has fallen since 1984, and that blacks' home ownership rate is "no different" from what it was in 1976. The lowest unemployment rate blacks ever achieved was 7 percent, back in April 2000. Now it is around 9.2 percent, only a fraction above what it was (9.0 percent) back in December 1973. And all this failure—for that's what it is—occurred while the number of black Americans with certificates from the AFT–NEA gulag was reaching new highs.

The clichéd political question is, "What have you done for me lately?" But blacks might ask the Democrats, "What have you ever done for us?" It was Republicans, after all, who passed the Civil Rights Act of 1964. But the only aspect of that battle that the Democrats, and the media, ever rehash is Barry Goldwater's voting no. Yet blacks continue to vote for Democrats, who keep them out of good schools and out of jobs, spoil their incentives with endless welfare, glorify the out-of-wedlock "lifestyle," and wreck the economy with taxes, regulations, and loony-bin schemes for social leveling.

For all we know, Donald Trump may think he can do something for blacks—but he has to get elected first. The Left will assume he's as anti-black as he is anti-women. And they may be correct. But it turns out that, despite Trump's obnoxious anti-woman rhetoric, the women in his companies think he's a great boss, as reported by the *Washington Post* (perhaps to help him get nominated because they think Hillary can beat him). Maybe Trump treats blacks the same way he treats women, as individuals. In which case, he's a hypocrite—of the Oscar Wilde variety: being good while pretending to be bad. That is certainly a subtlety the American press is not ready to cope with.

But, then again, maybe Trump just thinks black voters are deluded and unreachable. And, given their almost half-century practice of voting for people who advocate and enact policies that harm them, he may be on to something.

The thought raises the question: "How well is American democracy working?"—the same question that will be asked if Donald Trump secures the Republican nomination.

Introductions and Speeches

Introduction of Hon. Edwin Meese
Philadelphia Society Annual Meeting
Washington DC

July 17, 1987

As I was lying awake at the office last week, I heard Dorothy calling to me and Toto, saying, "Come on. We must hurry to the Emerald City. The polls will be closing soon."

She was right. It was late. I had hoped to vote, if not often, at least early, to avoid being influenced by the news media. So off we went, the three of us, I with my copy of *National Review*, Dorothy carrying *The American Spectator*, and Toto nursing lovingly an endless volume of *Mandate for Leadership*. But before we got to the city, we came upon a candidate seeking our support. Senator Edward M. "Teddy" Strawman said he needed our help, because he wanted to be president but he had no brain. We stopped and listened to him for a moment. Sure enough. He told the people gathered around him he wanted to raise the minimum wage, but that a raise would not cause any unemployment. And then he was asked why he wanted to be president, and he had no answer at all. We came to the conclusion that in fact he had no brain, and we suggested that he accompany us to the Emerald City to vote for our candidate.

We hadn't proceeded very far when we came upon another candidate, Senator Gary Tin, who, apparently to avoid an unseemly expression of gender preference, had shortened his name from Tinman. Senator Tin said he needed our help because he wanted to be president, but he had no heart. Pensively, we listened to him as he told the people of New Jersey that he'd rather be in California. We came to the conclusion that indeed he had no heart, and we suggested to him that he accompany us to the Emerald City to vote for our candidate.

Off we went, and came upon, as you all can now guess, a third creature. The cowardly donkey said he needed our help because he too wanted to be president. We listened to him as he said we shouldn't develop SDI because he was afraid it might be destabilizing and provoke the Soviets to a pre-emptive first strike. He said he was afraid to help the freedom-fighters in Nicaragua because the struggle might turn into another Vietnam—and he was afraid even to remember our involvement in Southeast Asia, although he was quick to blame America first for the holocaust in Cambodia. We even watched his handling of the highway bill veto, on which he voted, almost simultaneously, present, yes, and no. We suggested that he too join us on our journey to the Emerald City, and we discovered later in the course of our travels that he was afraid of the dark at night, and afraid again of the light in the morning.

It was late when we finally reached the city, but we had just enough time before the polls closed to visit with one of the nation's foremost wizards of media imagery, Dr. Russell Kirk (no relation). Dr. Kirk asked our companions if they could read. They said no. He said learn. Then he gave each of them three books to read: *How to Win Friends and Influence People*; *A Disquisition on the Art of Flattering Men, Women, and Children*; and *Beyond the Pleasure Principle: A New Agenda for the Democratic Party*. It was now very late. The polls were almost closed—as was my office. Well, we went to the polls, and the rest—if not the preceding—is history, although for some of those candidates and their colleagues it has remained a disturbing dream. For us here, for our country, and for the free world, the election of Ronald Reagan provided the definitive answer to the question, "Did you ever see a dream walking?"

One of the most significant aspects of this dream-come-true was President Reagan's appointment of our speaker, first as counselor to the president, and then as our current attorney general. Said attorney general needs no introduction to you, which is why, perhaps, I have failed to provide one.

Suffice it to say, he is all brain, all heart, all courage, as those who have tangled with him (as well as those who have observed his tangling) can testify. He has tangled with the Senate, and with members of the House of Representatives. He has tangled with the media, and even with the Supreme Court. Indeed, we might call him the

Compleat Tangier. If he has any faults, it is that he is not at all attentive to his personal interests, and that is not a trait that Washington has much understanding of.

Ladies and Gentlemen: It is a great privilege for me to introduce to you one of the heroes of the Reagan administration, the Attorney General of the United States, the Honorable Edwin Meese.

Introduction of George F. Will
Pacific Research Institute for Public Policy
San Francisco, California

April 22, 1998

Ladies and Gentlemen:

Ideally, we would all be at a ball game tonight. Second best is having America's greatest baseball fan to speak to us. He has been writing and speaking to us, *and about us,* for twenty-five years.

Mr. Will and I live in Scandal Town. But you should understand that the major scandal in Washington is not about President Clinton. We all know what he is. As Mary McCarthy said about Lillian Hellman, everything he says is a lie, including the words "and" and "the."

That, as I say, is well known, although it has not *seemed* yet to matter greatly. And that is puzzling, and a little bit frightening—for what it says about us. Because this scandal is less about Bill Clinton than it is about us: who we are; what kind of people we are; how we want our experiment in self-government and civic responsibility to turn out.

As God sent locusts to the Egyptians to test them, so now has he sent President and Mrs. Clinton—late twentieth century pests—to test us. That story in the Bible—early shake and bake, which should excite any fans of death and destruction literature, as well, no doubt as the chairmen of the relevant Agriculture Committees in Congress—is not about the locusts. It is about the Egyptians, whose hearts had been hardened against the Word of the Lord. The Clinton story is about our hearts.

But the Clinton scandal is not the only event happening in Washington that is about us. In fact, the whole American experiment

is about us. It is we who live in the City on the Hill that John
Winthrop, that most knowledgeable and honorable governor of the
Massachusetts Bay Company, spoke about to his fellow stockholders
on the boat coming over from England, and which President Reagan
reminded us of so many times. It is an understatement to say that
Winthrop's fellow Puritan settlers would have been greatly agitated
if the governor had thought it necessary to deny carnal knowledge
of one of his interns.

As I say, everything that happens in Washington is really about us.
The Clinton scandal is about whether *we* believe in the rule of law.
The tobacco bill is about whether *we* believe in individual responsibility. The blood-alcohol anti-drunk driving bill is about whether we
believe in state government. If we think state governments are incapable of formulating rational rules about drinking, why do we think
that we will be better served by people in Washington, who tell lies
from before the time they brush their teeth in the morning until after they floss at night?

That is surely one of the great mysteries of representative government, and I can think of no one better to unravel that mystery
and others like it than our speaker tonight, George Will.

Mr. Will was born in 1941, which makes him a member of the
last generation of Americans to grow up before the pervading influence of television. He was educated at Trinity College, Hartford,
Magdalen College, Oxford, and Princeton University. And, like his father, he taught political philosophy, first at Michigan State University,
then at the University of Toronto, and then at Harvard. Mr. Will,
who appears weekly on ABC's Sunday morning show, *This Week*, has
written a syndicated column since 1974, which now appears in over
450 papers. In 1977, he won a Pulitzer Prize for commentary in his
columns—a not insignificant achievement for a conservative. Any
doubt that Mr. Will is a conservative can be dispelled by a single
paragraph Mr. Will wrote in 1991:

> The moral of the human story [Mr. Will wrote] is that things go
> wrong more often than they go right because there are so many
> more ways to go wrong. Truths increase arithmetically; but
> errors increase exponentially. Most new ideas are false; hence
> most "improvements" make matters worse. That is why wise

people are wary of intellectual fads, and are respectful of [the] received greatness. . . .

That is exactly the way I would have put it—and will if I'm ever asked.

I first met Mr. Will in 1973 when we were both at *National Review* magazine, and like you, I know, I have been a constant admirer of his wit, wisdom, and skill ever since.

Ladies and gentlemen: America's foremost commentator, George Will.

Introduction of Rush Limbaugh
The Heritage Foundation,
President's Club Meeting
Arlington, Virginia

November 9, 2000

Thank you, Ed, for that very kind introduction.

Mr. Justice Thomas, Ladies, and Gentlemen:

August 1, 1988, *might* be described as a mixed day in history. The Soviet Union established diplomatic relations with the tiny, but rich, sheikdom of Qatar. Democrats in Congress ruled out an arms package for the Contras fighting Nicaragua's Sandanista government; and Central Americans rebuffed Secretary of State Shultz's efforts to condemn Nicaragua. An IRA bomb exploded in London killing one British soldier and wounding ten others. And wild gusting winds fanned fires in Yellowstone National Park.

All in all, you might think, not a good day. But it was a better day for you than it was for one Eric Alterman, who wrote a long screed in the *New York Times* that day, in which he complained bitterly about the power of the conservative pundits who were successful, he said, "not by virtue of wit or insight, but because of their ability to merge political views with the entertainment values of television sitcoms."

Alas, poor Mr. Alterman. He had no *idea* how much worse it was to get, or how soon. For starting just a few *hours* after his piece hit the newsstands, something started sweeping across the nation with more force than all the gusting winds fanning the flames in Yellowstone National Park.

August 1, 1988, ladies and gentlemen, was a *great* day: it was the day Rush Limbaugh began hosting his nationally syndicated radio program. And unlike Yellowstone, which was not seriously affected by the fires, American radio has never been the same.

That first day, Rush's audience was about 256,000 people—slightly more than the number of people who still believe Al Gore prefers the truth to the presidency.

Today, Rush's program is carried on six hundred stations and is listened to by more than 20 million people. It is the highest rated national radio talk show in America—making Rush part of the one percent that Al Gore loves to hate.

Rush was born in 1951 into a family with generations of attorneys—my children know exactly how *that* feels. Rush clearly has talent, and if, like his ancestors, he had chosen law and become, say, a prosecutor in Los Angeles, I have no doubt O. J. Simpson would be wearing numbered pajamas.

But Rush decided to cast a wider net, and for the last twelve years has been bringing the truth, the whole truth, and the truth laced with a whale of a good time to the American people. It is a remarkable record, and one that has not gone unnoticed by his friends or, I'm sure, his enemies.

In addition to the radio show, Rush publishes a newsletter for four hundred thousand subscribers; and his two best-selling books, *The Way Things Ought To Be* and *I Told You So*, sold over eight million copies, the latter book setting an American publishing record.

In 1992, and again in 1995, the National Association of Broadcasters awarded Rush the Marconi Award for Syndicated Radio Personality of the Year. And then this year they gave the award to him a third time. This is high praise indeed. It is one thing to win that award when you're new—and people say you're just a fad. It is something else to win it when you are in your thirteenth year and you have been number one for ten straight years, ever since hitting the top.

Rush is the top, and if you listen to him, you know why. He tells it like it is, and he tells it in a way that is not convoluted or convulsed like the prose of, for example, the editorial writers of the *New York*

Times, who told us that if only we would elect Hillary Clinton to the United States Senate, she would outgrow her ethical legacies. I doubt very much that Rush is on record recommending election as therapy for Hillary's ethical legacy disorder.

Ladies and gentlemen: a Greek philosopher said a city should be no larger than the distance that a man's voice could be heard. As I know all of you in this room recall with great fondness, Ronald Reagan, echoing John Winthrop who echoed St. Matthew, often referred to this country as a shining city on a hill. Today through the magic of Guglielmo Marconi's invention, Rush's voice can be heard throughout that city.

Like Ronald Reagan, Rush believes that the best days for our shining city are yet to come. Again and again over the past months, he attacked the credibility of the man in the organic earth tone hues—and reminded people to vote for the truth candidate. Success may have a thousand fathers, but if Bush wins this landslide election, none of the other fathers of the Bush victory can claim to have given fatherly advice on a daily basis to 20 million people.

We are grateful for Rush's efforts, for his unfailing good cheer, and for the sheer joy and enthusiasm with which he cranks liberal baloney through the grinder. For those of us who listen, it is one of life's great vicarious pleasures.

It is also a pleasure the liberal media would like to deny us—if they could do to the First Amendment what they'd like to do to the Second Amendment. They would give anything, *anything*, to silence Rush.

And in that connection, ladies and gentlemen, I have some questions for you:

If they offered to stop the presses at the *New York Times* if we would take away Rush's microphone, I ask you, would we accept their offer? No.

If they offered to stop the presses at the *Washington Post* as well, would we accept? No.

If they offered also to turn off the current at ABC, NBC, and CBS, would we give them Rush? No.

If they threw in CNN and National Public Radio too, would we give up Rush? No.

Ladies and gentlemen: it is a privilege and a pleasure to introduce to you the man you have indicated you value more than all the liberal media combined; the man 20 million people like to listen to each day: our own Rush Limbaugh.

Introduction of Dr. Henry Kissinger
Pacific Research Institute for Public Policy
San Francisco, California

November 9, 2001

Thank you, Sally.

On behalf of the Pacific Research Institute Board, and our president, let me also welcome you to our ninth annual dinner.

Over the years, this dinner has brought us together with some of the world's most remarkable people, like Prime Minister Margaret Thatcher; with great world teachers, like Milton and Rose Friedman and William F. Buckley, Jr.; with American political leaders like Governor Pete Wilson and New Jersey's Bret Schundler; and with some of America's great commentators, George Will and Bill Bennett.

For our dinner this year, we wanted someone who could continue in this tradition.

In a phrase, we wanted a *big draw.*

So the Board of the Pacific Research Institute assembled and came up with the obvious answer—someone who could fill a room and please a crowd. Madonna.

As chairman of PRI, it fell to me to modify that choice, to come up with . . . something a bit unusual (this *is* California). So I did. I suggested—Madonna with her clothes . . . *on.*

The following morning we had our doubts, and so we decided to ask tonight's speaker—one of the nation's leading intellectuals, and probably the world's foremost expert on foreign affairs.

Dr. Kissinger is hailed as the man who labored to send Nixon to China;

Who invented shuttle diplomacy to craft a cease fire between Israel and Egypt;

Who shared a Nobel Peace Prize for his efforts at ending the war in Vietnam;

Of course, Dr. Kissinger is also remembered for having made priceless contributions to American humor.

It was Henry Kissinger who, in the era of radical protest, when asked what he thought of the Indianapolis 500, simply said, "Free them."

It was Dr. Kissinger who, mindful of the constant use of hidden-camera surveillance by the Soviets, picked up a document at a Moscow conference, held it up to a chandelier, and asked, "Could I have two copies of this delivered to my suite?"

We invited Dr. Kissinger in June. It was a good choice—in June.

Now, almost two months to the day after September 11, being able to listen to Henry Kissinger is a fortunate opportunity for all of us.

Dr. Kissinger is known throughout the world as the foremost practitioner of *realpolitik*—a world view that was out of fashion throughout the previous decade. A great nation, it was held by many, had to transcend obsessions as petty as its national interests.

In his Farewell Address, George Washington said,

> The nation which indulges towards another an habitual hatred, or an habitual fondness, is in some degree a slave. It is a slave to its animosity or to its affection, either of which is sufficient to lead it astray from its duty and its interest.

Washington spoke of the nation's "interest," not its friendship.

America, we have been told in recent years, should invest its clout in human rights, in raising the status of women, in spreading democracy. I am sure that Dr. Kissinger will not speak against any of these worthy ideals. But I also suspect he will remind us that if we place the highest priority on *all* our priorities, we will end up accomplishing none of them. And worse, if we fritter away our advantages and power, we will put our nation and our liberty at risk.

These are, admittedly, somber thoughts. But as someone who watched one of the World Trade Center towers collapse, I, for one, want the straight-up voice of realism, not a siren song of extravagant idealism. I confess: I want my interests protected—the interests of my country, and my children, and my grandchildren.

In a sense, all of us were spectators on September 11. Now we are all students of foreign affairs, and concerned about foreign policy in a way most of us have probably never been before.

Under the circumstances, I can think of no one more appropriate to listen to this evening than the speaker we have with us tonight.

Ladies and gentlemen: Dr. Henry Kissinger.

Introduction of Lou Dobbs
Pacific Research Institute for Public Policy
San Francisco, California

December 12, 2002

If you haven't seen Lou Dobbs on television, you probably don't own a television set. Not owning a television set has its own rewards, of course, such as a complete blackout of network programming.

But watching television has its rewards too, one of which is seeing Mr. Dobbs host *Moneyline* on CNN.

Television isn't Mr. Dobbs's only skill, however. He also anchors a financial news radio report, which is syndicated to over seven hundred stations nationwide. Additionally, he writes a monthly column for *Money* magazine, a weekly syndicated column for the Sunday issue of the *New York Daily News*, and a bi-weekly column for *U.S. News and World Report*.

But it is his program *Moneyline* for which he is justly famous. He became the anchor of *Moneyline* the year he joined CNN, and he was instrumental in making it the prestigious business news program it is today. During his tenure at the network, he helped develop CNN financial news, an award-winning leader in television business journalism, and he oversaw the launch of CNNfn and CNNfn.com in December 1995. He managed the network as president of CNNfn and executive vice president of CNN until June 1999.

Mr. Dobbs has won nearly every major award for television journalism, including the George Foster Peabody Award for his coverage of the 1987 stock market crash, and, in 1990, the Luminary Award from *Business Journalism Review* for his "visionary work, which changed the landscape of business journalism in the 1980s." The *Wall Street Journal* named Mr. Dobbs "TV's premier business news anchorman."

Earlier this year Mr. Dobbs got into hot water by calling for a "war against Islamists." "Terror," he said is not the enemy. The enemies are "radical Islamists who argue that all non-believers in their faith must be killed." He made the distinction, he said, "in the interests of clarity and honesty." The distinction between terror and terrorists is worth making. Picking the right word counts, a point Mark Twain illustrated by reminding us of the difference between "lightning" and "lightning bug."

Perhaps Mr. Dobbs learned to make such distinctions at Harvard, where he took a degree in economics. Perhaps he also developed there the sense of injustice that has caused him to write about stripping crooked corporate bigwigs of their ill-gotten gains—perhaps the only punishment the contemplation of which might cause them to be, if not pure in thought, at least pure in deed, to the considerable benefit of stockholders.

Mr. Dobbs has also expressed his concern that the wage gap between rich Americans and average Americans continues to widen. In 1979, he has told us, the average income of the top 5 percent of Americans was around $150,000. Currently, the average income of that group has jumped to around $240,000—a gain of 60 percent. In 1979, the average income for middle-income Americans was $44,000. Today, the average middle-income worker brings home around $51,000—an increase of 15.9 percent.

There may, however, be a starker way of reading the figures. The average annual salary in America has risen about 10 percent over the last twenty-nine years, in real dollars. According to *Fortune* magazine, the average real annual compensation of the top one hundred CEO's went, in the same period, from something like thirty-nine times the pay of an average worker to more than one thousand times the pay of an average worker.

However much we revere Adam Smith's "invisible hand," the magnitude of that disparity should attract the attention of even those who suffer from attention deficit disorder whenever it comes to corporate finance, especially when the hands of the CEOs have been invisibly looting the corporate till.

Mr. Dobbs was quite right to bring the matter to our attention, as he brings so many matters to our attention, with grace and skill.

Ladies and gentlemen: Lou Dobbs.

Graduation Address to Honors Class 02–05
Naval Air Station: Pensacola, Florida

October 8, 2004

Thank you, Commander Miller, for that kind introduction.

Ambassador Oliver, Captain Roberts, Commander Miller;
    Members of the Graduating Class, the Honors Graduating Class;
    Parents and friends of members of the graduating class;
    Ladies and gentlemen:
    It is a great privilege and a great honor to be able to address a graduating class at this Officer Candidate School, and I am truly delighted to be here today to address this graduating class.

There was a story on the radio a few weeks ago, around the anniversary of 9/11, which described the actions of a marine corps reservist who worked in the financial district in downtown New York City. When the marine realized what was happening on that fateful day and understood the need for rescue workers, he acted swiftly, courageously—and cleverly. He nipped into a barber shop and had his hair shaved off so he could blend in with the official rescue workers. He then raced down to Ground Zero and spent the day working with other rescue workers to do whatever could be done. It is a remarkable story of courage and cleverness.

But that is only part of the story. The more remarkable, rest of the story is that while he was assisting in rescue efforts he came across several other marines who had done the same thing—gotten their heads shaved so they too could be accepted as official rescue workers—all of them at considerable personal risk.

That is the spirit that makes the American military the fighting force it is today—the fighting force that our country and the world depend upon.

I know that if I tried to tell all the stories about the courage of the American service men and women, we'd be here until long after hurricane Zelda had made even your drill instructors' uniforms look like winners of an Irish pennant contest. But I want to tell you two more stories.

One is the story California Governor Arnold Schwarzenegger told at the Republican National Convention. Some of you in the graduating class may have seen him—I'm sure you all had a lot of time to watch television during your training here—but I have a reason for telling it.

Gov. Schwarzenegger said he had visited a soldier in the hospital, a soldier who had been badly wounded in Iraq: he'd lost a leg and had a hole through his stomach. What the soldier told the governor was that he was going to get a new leg, and then get some therapy, and then go back to Iraq to fight alongside his buddies.

I tell that story because it is very much like the story that was told to me by General B. B. Bell, the Commanding General of the US Army in Europe. General Bell and I were in France at the American cemetery at Omaha beach, standing next to rows, and rows, and rows of gleaming white grave markers, marking the graves of thousands of American heroes—people like you. We were waiting for the ceremony commemorating the sixtieth anniversary of the D-Day landings at Normandy to begin. General Bell said he had visited a hospital and had spoken with a young soldier who had been wounded in Iraq. The soldier said to Gen. Bell, "I want to go back to my unit in Iraq." Well, he probably said, "I want to go back to my unit in Iraq, SIR!" Gen. Bell told the soldier in soothing tones that he had to get well first and then they would give him a good assignment.

Then, as Gen. Bell told me the story, the soldier said, "Gen. Bell, sir: you don't understand. If I don't get *sent* back to my unit, I'm going to go AWOL and go back to my unit." Gen. Bell told me he said to the attending doctor, "Fix him up and send him back."

Both Gen. Bell's story and Gov. Schwarzenegger's story are testimony to the courage and determination of the American fighting man. But there's someone missing from both stories—someone *not* mentioned. You see, these are also stories about the officers who commanded the units those soldiers served in and wanted to return to. Those commanding officers had been so successful in building a team, and infusing it with team spirit, that the wounded wanted to return to harm's way to serve with their fellow soldiers.

None of you will serve in position of command all the time, but whatever your position is, in whatever unit you find yourself, you should lead, and do your part to infuse that unit with the amazing spirit of camaraderie, brotherhood, and belonging these stories speak of.

It is because of real-life stories like these that the annual Gallup poll on public confidence in American institutions published last June found that the US military is the institution that the American pubic has the most confidence in. You and your colleagues here—and the rest of our armed forces—are members of the most respected institution in our country.

Your basic training here had at least two purposes. One was to allow the navy to discover if you were made of sufficiently stern stuff to be an officer in the most respected institution in the United States. And one was to allow *you* to discover if you were made of sufficiently stern stuff. The navy has tested you and has found that you are indeed worthy, and in a few minutes you will become commissioned officers in the most respected institution in the United States. That is an achievement you can be truly proud of, but your new status carries with it awesome responsibilities.

In his last address, General Douglas MacArthur, one of the most articulate officers in our country's history, a soldier who lived a long life of duty, honor, and country, spoke to the cadets at West Point about courage—and not just physical courage, but mental courage as well—the courage to follow your conscience, not the crowd.

I had the great privilege of serving President Ronald Reagan for eight years in Washington, and I want to tell you two Cold War stories about President Reagan's courage.

The first story is about President Reagan's "Evil Empire" speech. A young speech writer, a friend and colleague of mine, wrote the phrase "evil empire" into a speech about the Soviet Union. He sent the draft up through channels, but a high-ranking, nervous Nellie in the White House—but, this morning, a nameless Nellie—took out the phrase as being too "provocative." President Reagan never saw that draft.

But the young speech writer persisted. He kept putting the phrase in draft after draft of speeches about the Soviet Union. One day, Nervous Nellie was out of town when the speech writer sent up yet another draft containing the phrase. This time, the draft with the phrase got all the way to the Oval Office. The president read the phrase and liked it because he thought it was accurate. The Soviet Union was an evil empire.

The speech, which the president delivered to the National Association of Evangelicals in 1983, became one of his most famous. It was a speech that gave hope to the people behind the Iron Curtain because it assured them that the president of the United States understood the true nature of the regime they lived under and had the courage to confront it without the compromising doublespeak of diplomacy.

The second story concerns another Reagan speech—the speech he gave in Berlin when he said to the Soviet "President," "Mr. Gorbachev: Tear down this wall."

That speech was written by another friend of mine. This time the speech, with the phrase intact, got directly to the president, who right away understood the power of the phrase, and accepted it. But when the State Department and the Department of Defense heard he was going to use the phrase, they went ballistic—so ballistic that President Reagan was forced to ask his staff, "Am I or am I not the president of the United States? And can I or can I not say what I please in a speech?" When they indicated assent, he said, "Good! It stays in." And so it did, the State Department twitching and moaning all the way.

But this is the best part. On the way to the Brandenburg Gate in Berlin where the president would give the speech, a young State Department aide made a last-ditch effort to get the president to take out the phrase. He said, "Mr. President: I hope you're not going to use that phrase, 'Mr. Gorbachev: Tear down this wall.'"

President Reagan looked at him calmly, wagged his head as he often did, and replied, "I'll do the right thing." He went on to give the speech, the most famous speech of his career, the speech that signaled it was closing time for communism.

President Reagan's persistence in the face of hostility not just from the intellectual and journalistic crowd, but from the crowd at his own State Department as well, took immense strength of character—more strength even than surviving Black Saturday or doing a hundred push ups for Gunnery Sergeant Murphy in the Soo-ya. That is the courage General MacArthur was talking about when he addressed the cadets at West Point. That is the courage expected of you.

And so, as a result of President Reagan's vision, courage, rhetoric, and, in the face of tremendous hostility, of his building up the armed forces, including a six hundred-ship navy, communism collapsed, and the fates gave us a moment of peace.

Alas, a moment was all they could spare.

As we think of the grave markers at the Normandy cemetery, or at Arlington National Cemetery, or in the graveyard we pass coming into this naval base, we remember the ominous words of Plato: "Only the dead have seen the end of war."

Of course, we need not harken all the way back to Plato to be reminded of the permanence of war. Alexander Hamilton, one of our most brilliant Founding Fathers, warned his contemporaries— and us—to "wake from the deceitful dream of a golden age" (doesn't that sound like pre-9/11?) and to be suspicious of rival powers; to be willing to fight, and to have the resources to do so.

Today, the navy has fewer than three hundred ships, down from Reagan's almost six hundred. Today we spend only 3.5 percent of our Gross Domestic Product on defense. During the Reagan years, we spent about 6.2 percent of GDP on defense.

Yet today we find ourselves engaged in a worldwide war against terrorists—but scraping along on only 3.5 percent of GDP, and with fewer than three hundred ships.

My guess is that in the coming decade we will conclude that *that* is not sufficient—regardless of who is elected president this November. Consider only China.

The giant sucking sound you hear in world economics is China feeding its boundless growth by importing minerals and raw materials from around the world at a frenzied pace—copper, iron ore, aluminum, platinum, and other commodities. It is a reasonable bet that to protect its supply lines, in the coming years China will build a serious blue-water navy. I hope it is a good bet that the United States will not stand idly by, allowing China's naval force to surpass our own.

But never mind tomorrow. Given the hostility we face *today*, my guess is that the navy you are about to be commissioned in will be a growing navy. Perhaps that is good news. But the ominous implication is that it is entirely possible you will see combat in defense of the cause of freedom.

Then will you be tested in a way you never were during your basic training here. Then will you long for those quite Pensacola afternoons spent taking 'T with your drill instructors in the Rose Garden.

But we know—know, because you have been tested—we know that you have the courage and the fortitude to meet any challenge that comes your way, and to perform as bravely as our troops have performed in Iraq. After all, you are part of the most respected institution in the United States.

And when your great challenge comes, and come it will, you will say, to your staff, or to yourself, to your crowd, and to your conscience: "Am I or am I not an officer in the United States Navy?"

You are the hope of the world.

You are the envy of your friends.

And you are the pride of your parents and your country.

I wish you all the best—fair winds, a following sea, and godspeed.

Introduction of Christopher Buckley
Pacific Research Institute
San Francisco, California

November 16, 2006

Good evening, Ladies and Gentlemen:

I want to welcome you again to the Pacific Research Institute's annual dinner. Our speaker this evening is Christopher Buckley. If that comes as a surprise to you, you may be at the wrong dinner. The California Undertakers Association is having its dinner on the third floor and I know they would feel let down and consider it a grave offense if you ditched them for us.

Mr. Buckley's speaking agency lists a number of topics their people can speak about. Those topics include Business Management and Finance, Celebrating Diversity, Food, Fashion and Fine Living, and a number of others. There was no specific mention of the undertaking trade, although I assume Mr. Buckley could celebrate with the undertakers the diversity of death.

I first met Mr. Buckley when he was thirteen, and it never occurred to me to call him "Mr. Buckley." The age thirteen sticks in my mind because that was about the age my own son was when Mr. Buckley gave him a nine-inch knife for his birthday—although it may have been a thirteen-inch knife for his ninth birthday. I know my wife remembers. Those are the precious moments no parent can forget. Or forgive.

Mr. Buckley is the author of eleven books, most of them best-sellers. His latest novel is *Florence of Arabia*, which he describes as his "first and probably last Middle East comedy."

His others include *No Way to Treat a First Lady, God Is My Broker*, and *Little Green Men*.

The movie version of his 1994 novel *Thank You for Smoking* opened this spring to rave reviews.

His novel *Little Green Men* is being made into a movie starring John Malkovich, directed by Whit Stillman.

Mr. Buckley has also written extensively in the Business Management field, as his speakers agency suggests. He is the author of last year's widely acclaimed business management blockbuster bestseller: *Home Alone: Thinking Inside the Box*—soon to be a major television series on Fox Television.

Mr. Buckley shipped in the merchant marine, graduated with honors from Yale, was managing editor of *Esquire Magazine* at age twenty-four, and at age twenty-nine was chief speechwriter to Vice President George Bush.

He is editor-in-chief of *ForbesLife* magazine, and writes regularly for the *New Yorker, New York Times, Wall Street Journal*, and many other publications.

His awards include the Thurber Prize for American Humor and the Washington Irving Prize for Literary Excellence.

Ladies and gentlemen: please welcome . . . Christopher Buckley.

XV International Meeting in Political Studies and International Summer School
The Treaty of Rome at 50:
The Future of Europe
Estoril, Portugal

June 29, 2007

Thank you, Madame Chairman for that kind introduction.

And thank you, Professor Espada for inviting me back to this distinguished forum.

I seemed to have been assigned no title for this session—which is as risky for you as it is for me. So I thought I would share some thoughts about Europe fifty years after the commencement of the European Project. And I will try to put those thoughts into, if not *the* American perspective, at least *an* American perspective.

The European Project is now fifty years old. Although it may have problems, it has had at least one crowning success—if we are allowed to use the word "crowning" in the post-monarchical era.

To the extent that the purpose of the European Project was to prevent the European countries from going to war against each other again, it has been a triumphant success.

But now that the danger of an intra-European war has disappeared, other issues, the details of the European Project, appear larger: issues such as the shape of its leadership: Should it have a semi-permanent council president, fewer commissioners, and a single foreign policy representative?; and its democracy content: Should bigger states have more influence? What kind of decisions should be subject to majority voting? Should the charter of fundamental rights be legally enforceable? And should a new constitution be voted on by the people? According to an FT/Harris poll, European citizens strongly oppose plans by Europe's leaders to push a reworked constitution without further referenda.

However important all those issues, including democracy, are, the European Project is not focusing on the issue that I think is far more important. The real issue facing Europe, I think, is the future *existence* of Europe, or as they say, of Europe "as we know it."

And how do we know Europe? What is the Europe we know? What is the Europe we know and love? And love despite many differences and disagreements in policy?

Europe is the home of Western Civilization. Europe is the birthplace of the common values of Western Civilization which nurtured what we refer to as the "universal" principles of liberty under law, constitutional democracy, pluralism, and human rights. Western Civilization is the spirit and the habits that gave us Chartres and St. Peter's, Bach and Beethoven, Shakespeare and Copernicus, Magna Carta and the Rights of Man, and the US Constitution. Western Civilization and the transatlantic relationship are the special concerns of the *New Atlantic Initiative.*

It seems to me that the continued existence of Europe is not assured. What will determine the future existence of Europe? That existence will depend, I think, on Europe's survival instincts—and whether and how those survival instincts are translated into public policy and action. And it will depend on demographics.

A question is, does Europe have the will to survive? And does European civilization have the will to survive? And to survive in a world that seems to contain an element of growing hostility? Or did the carnage of the last century exhaust Europe?

We are now fifty years out from the start of the European Project, but we are sixty-three years out from another project, a project that was one of the wonders of the modern world.

Three weeks ago I was in a small French town in Normandy called Colleville-sur-Mer attending the ceremonies commemorating the sixty-third anniversary of the Allied Forces' landing on the Normandy beaches. No one who has visited the American Cemetery there and has seen the rows and rows of simple white grave markers can fail to wonder and marvel at the effort that freed Europe from the tyranny of that day.

I went to the dedication of the new Visitors Center—a dignified stone and glass edifice, with exhibits that seek to explain why more than nine thousand young Americans came to a French beach and died there, thousands of miles from their homes.

Most of them were, from my vantage point, children—much

younger than most of my children are now (one of whom is a lieu-
tenant [j.g.] in the US Navy), and younger than most of the people
in this room.

Why are their bodies buried in France? Because they went there
to save Western Civilization, in a mighty endeavor that President
Roosevelt called "a struggle to preserve our Republic, our religion,
our civilization."

It was that endeavor—surely one of the wonders of the modern
world—that made possible the European Project.

We are also, today, sixty years out from the beginning of another
project of historic undertaking, the Marshall Plan, and it may be
instructive to spend a few minutes reflecting on the Marshall Plan.

The Marshall Plan—and its siblings, NATO, the International
Monetary Fund, the World Bank, and UNESCO—were part of an
effort by the United States to remain engaged in world affairs, which
meant primarily European affairs, after what some considered a
thirty-years war in Europe, one that lasted from 1914 to 1945. Seeing
that part of history as a period of thirty years of war made ensuring
peace all that more important.

Isolationism had almost kept the United States out of World War
II, and isolationism still existed after World War II. Senator Robert
Taft, known as "Mr. Republican," objected to the creation of NATO.
"We have quietly adopted a tendency to interfere in the affairs of
other nations," he said in 1949, "to assume that we are a kind of
demigod and Santa Claus to solve the problems of the world." Why
does that sound familiar?

President Truman's vision, however, was different. Speaking
about the Marshall Plan, he said, "I believe that in years to come,
we shall look back upon this undertaking as the dividing line between the old era of world affairs and the new—the dividing line
between the old era of national suspicion, economic hostility, and
isolationism, and the new era of mutual cooperation to increase the
prosperity of people throughout the world."

The postwar institutions were designed, of course, to help
Europe survive and prosper. But its architects, who thought that
a failing economy in Europe would facilitate Soviet ambitions and
Communist electoral victories, saw the Marshall Plan primarily as a
way of containing Communism. Years later, Theodore White would

write, "The Marshall Plan was the most successful anti-Communist concept in the past fifty years."

The Marshall Plan, drawn up by George Kennan, the author of the doctrine of containment, meshed nicely with the Truman Doctrine, which had been announced on March 12, 1947: that all nations fighting for their freedom could count on the assistance of the United States. For by then the Cold War had begun. Churchill had made his "Iron Curtain" speech; Walter Lippman had published his famous book, *The Cold War*, and a French historian, Georges-Henri Soutou had published a book, in 1943, with the prescient title *The Fifty Years War*. He was off by only four years.

The point I would make—and perhaps it is obvious that an American, or at least this American, would make this point today—is that the statesmen of those days had long-term strategies, designed to ensure survival, not just of themselves, but of their friends, in the face of a threat by a particular enemy. And the statesmen were backed up by an exuberant economy, a muscular military, and a vibrant birthrate.

And, of course, it all happened before television and sound bites.

Jean Monnet, the father of the European Project, wrote about the Marshall Plan saying that it was at that time, "not just a matter of material well-being: it was the necessary basis for national independence and the preservation of democracy." I am not a student of Monnet's and I do not pretend to know what he meant by that, but it strikes me as interesting for two reasons. The European Project as it is currently being managed seems to be intent on suppressing "national independence," and perhaps democracy as well.

As I noted earlier, the European Project may have been successful in preventing the European countries from going to war against each other again. But to the extent that the Project's drift and bureaucracy have been responsible for sapping the will of the people in the several countries of Europe to produce goods, guns, and grandchildren, it has—or perhaps only "may have"—sown the seeds of its own termination.

For without a strong economy, military, and population base—all of which are interdependent—the survival of Europe and European civilization will be difficult.

I would refer you to a short book by Mark Steyn, titled *America Alone: The End of the World As We Know It*, which describes the disappearance, not just decline, of religion in Europe and its complete secularization, the population implosion, and the incredible immigration of largely unassimilated immigrants.

As we discussed yesterday, the birth rates in the European countries are mostly below the rate, 2.1 children per woman, necessary to keep the population stable. No country in Europe reaches that rate. The lowest in Europe is Greece, with 1.29; the next lowest is Spain with 1.32; then Italy with 1.33. France has 1.9, and Ireland has 1.99.

But that's not all. Although the fertility rate in France is 1.9, two out of every five babies born in France are children of Arab or African immigrants. In Germany, with a fertility rate of 1.37, 35 percent of all babies have a non-German background.

The Nobel Prize-winning economist Milton Friedman said an open welfare system and open immigration were incompatible. At least they are incompatible if you want to preserve your culture.

But there is more bad demographic news. According to Paul Belie, since 2004 the number of Germans who have left Germany each year has been greater than the number of immigrants who have moved to Germany. The Germans who left were highly motivated; the immigrants who came were mostly poor, untrained, and uneducated.

"In a survey conducted in 2005 among German university students," Mr. Belie writes, "52% said they would rather leave their native country than remain there. . . . There are two main reasons why so-called 'ethno-Germans' [leave]. Some complain that the tax rates in Germany are so high that it is no longer worthwhile working for a living there. Others indicate they no longer feel at home in a country whose cultural appearance is changing dramatically."

Assimilating immigrants is key to preserving a culture—in Europe, as in America. In America, there is an American ideal that people, native Americans and immigrants alike, aspire to.

But it's not clear there is a European ideal that immigrants can aspire to; while it is clear, I think, that aspiring to become part of one of the nation-states of Europe is not likely, the very concept of nation-state having become politically incorrect. How that squares with what Jean Monnet had in mind when he spoke of "national independence" I do not know.

But I do know that if it is not politically correct to assimilate and become, say, French or Italian or Portuguese, and if at the same time it is not emotionally satisfying to assimilate to become European, then an immigrant in Europe might as well remain whatever he was before he came to Europe—there being no attractive alternative. After all, if Germans are leaving Germany, that is, if Germans are no longer interested in being German, how can we expect immigrant Muslims to become German? I think we cannot.

In the long run, this will cause trouble, especially if the immigrants bring with them a religion that is wholly different from, and maybe hostile to, the religion that gave birth to the values of Western Civilization, whatever may be left of it in Europe. One question is, how long, or perhaps more pertinently, how short, is the "long run"?

The European Project seems consumed with creating rules and regulations. So, while the birth rate declines, and the natives leave, and the immigrants come, and assimilation doesn't take place, Europe is busy making rules about how big a banana must be before it can be sold in European grocery stores.

One has a sense that the grand European Project is like painting the smoke stack of the *Titanic*. I would ask, who is manning the lifeboats of the good ship *Western Civ*?

We are in a struggle for the world today. Indeed, we may always be in a struggle for the world. If Europe cannot preserve itself, how can it assist in that struggle for the world?

I want to make one other point about population. President Bush has asked the US Congress to give $30 billion to The President's Emergency Fund for AIDS Relief over the next five years; and the EU has pledged to increase its aid to Africa to 30 billion euros in the next five years. (By way of reference, incidentally, the assistance given under the Marshall Plan during its four years, $13.3 billion to sixteen countries, would amount to more than a $100 billion today.)

Africa may have AIDS and poverty, but there's one thing Africa does not have: a population *implosion*. Despite Africa's AIDS epidemic and its incredible poverty, the continent as a whole has a population growth rate of about 3 percent. Europe's population growth rate is about 0.3 percent—and that it is positive at all is due to immigration.

Maybe Europe should focus more attention on Europe and the preservation of Western Civilization and less attention on other places. Europe should spend less time worrying about climate change and more time worrying about Europe change. Perhaps the Europeans should create their own Marshall Plan for Europe—given that Europe seems to be losing, literally, its body, as well as its soul. If that remark seems unduly culturally imperialistic, perhaps we can rely for defense on Saint Paul's comment to the Galatians (6:10): "While we have time, let us do good unto all men, especially unto them that are of the household of faith."

In our context, that household is Europe and its Western Civilization with its universal principles. If Europe vanishes as an effective protector of those principles, will they still be universal? Will America alone be able to protect them? And if not, what chance will Africa, and its burgeoning population, have then?

Is it realistic to think Europe will help defend those universal values?

Europe's military, from a US perspective, is not exactly muscular—and that may be a function of its economy, which for a decade at least has been anemic. The European countries do not spend on defense the same proportion of their GDP that the US does. In 2006, France's defense spending was 2.4 percent of GDP; the UK's was 2.3 percent, and Germany's was 1.3 percent. US spending on defense is about 3.9 percent of GDP. At the height of the Vietnam War is was almost 11 percent; it was 6 percent during the 1970s, and about 4 percent during the early 1990s.

Why are Europeans such reluctant warriors? I don't know, but the *New Atlantic Initiative* intends in the coming months to see if we can discover the causes of that reluctance.

Meanwhile, many Americans have a sense that America, with its military might and economic muscle, bailed out Europe and helped produce peace here. And they think Europe is failing now to help midwife peace elsewhere. Is that part of the nature of the French or the Portuguese or the Germans? Or is it part of the nature of a new Europe—a conglomerate that is neither French nor Portuguese nor German?

The central problem the civilized world faces today may be larger that any previous problem—though I am not sure of that.

But I am sure that the politics of today are different. In the era of televised wars and sound bites, even America may not be able to conquer evil alone, or even hold it at bay. It is not that America lacks the material resources: I think America has those. But the American spirit seems to be flagging; America's will is in doubt.

Europe may not be militarily robust, but it could still offer vocal support to America's efforts. I think that would have more than a marginal effect. A US general said a year or so ago that if the US announced it was going to stay in Iraq (by which he meant stay in Iraq with a large military force) for ten years, the enemy would give up. Vocal and moral support from Europe could discipline those Americans who speak ill of America's current efforts who today can count on the silence of the Europeans. And it would tell our enemies that we in the West are united and in this together for the long haul.

Americans were once inward looking: but Americans roused themselves twice in the previous century to shoulder international responsibilities. Is Europe now so engrossed with its own project—now fifty years old—that it will not rouse itself to help America keep the peace?

A few weeks ago at the American Cemetery in Normandy, US Secretary of Defense Robert Gates said, "We once again face enemies seeking to destroy our way of life, and we are once again engaged in an ideological struggle that may not find resolution for many years or even decades."

It seems to me that Secretary Gates's remarks echo resoundingly the spirit and the words of the people who crafted the Marshall Plan—and the military venture that preceded it, an effort to preserve, as President Roosevelt described it, "our religion, our civilization."

Now the US is engaged again, or more accurately, still engaged, in a struggle for the world. The question is, how engaged in that struggle are the people of the European Project?

Is the conglomeration of Europe inimical to greatness in Europe—to the kind of greatness needed when civilization is threatened? It may be that a more localized nationalism is a necessary ingredient to greatness. Has the "national independence" that Jean Monnet spoke about survived? I don't know. Homogenization—or something—seems to have paralyzed many in Europe.

And perhaps we see a reaction to that in the people who want to separate into more distinct political units—Scots, Basques, Bretons, whatever. Like Macaulay, it seems they'd rather have an acre in Middlesex than a principality in Utopia.

I say, yes, indeed. Bring back the nation-state, so that all the people of Europe can sing, in their own idioms of course, that song written by the two Brits, Flanders & Swan, the refrain of which goes:

The English, the English, the English are best.
I wouldn't give tuppence for all of the rest.

Happy Birthday, Europe.

Introduction of M. Stanton Evans
At a party celebrating the publication of
Blacklisted by History: The Untold Story of
Senator Joe McCarthy
The Metropolitan Club
Washington DC

November 20, 2007

It's a great pleasure to welcome you all to this book party for Stan Evans. Stan has been a leader of the conservative movement for many, many years, and an old friend of most of the people in this room.

We are here to celebrate the publication of the remarkable book Stan has just written, *Blacklisted by History: The Untold Story of Senator Joe McCarthy*.

Stan will speak to us about his book, but I'd like to make just a few comments before he does.

First, I'd like to thank Al Regnery and his staff for doing all the organizing of this party. Many or most of you have done these sorts of events and know the work that has to go into them to make them come off. Al did that work and we are grateful.

The McCarthy myth is too strong to be destroyed easily, but there is dynamite in these pages of Stan's magnum opus, dynamite that is now available to scholars and school children who delight in promoting unfavorable causes and tormenting p.c. teachers.

Stan provides the details of the famous Wheeling, West Virginia, speech, but most particularly how the Democrat-controlled Senate was responsible for naming the names.

Stan puts the spotlight on Senator Tydings, and his missing pages and missing files: Tydings makes Sandy Burglar look like small beer. And for his sins Tydings's constituents had the good sense to remove him from office.

Don't miss this book. Read about McCarthy's patience. Learn the true story of the Army-McCarthy hearings. Read about that fraud Joe Welsh. Read about the shameless, and perhaps impeachable, behavior of people in the Eisenhower administration.

And read, at the end, about McCarthy's real legacy: the guys he got; and the changes in governmental practices that were made because of his activities. Stan concludes—I don't think I'm giving anything away—"that it's doubtful that any other American figure, outside the confines of the White House, had more impact on the course of Cold War history."

A number of years ago, Bill Buckley remarked that he would thenceforth no longer discuss the Vietnam War with anyone who had not read Henry Kissinger's *The White House Years*—which is fourteen hundred pages long. I think it wasn't just that Bill was tired of re-fighting the Vietnam War. His point was, if you hadn't read what the expert had to say, why should he (Bill) spend his time discussing the topic with you?

I think that is now true about Senator McCarthy. Henceforth, we can say to any pest who brings up McCarthy, or even "McCarthyism," that we won't discuss the subject unless the pest has read Stan Evans's book.

Stan's book is, I suspect, the last word on McCarthy. *We* don't need another; and the liberals won't bother writing another: they already have "McCarthyism" in the lexicon where they want it. So the last word will belong to Stan.

Introduction of George F. Will
Pacific Research Institute for Public Policy
San Francisco, California

November 12, 2008

Ladies and Gentlemen:

In the circles that the kind of people who attend a dinner like this move, George Will needs little introduction.

If you do not know Mr. Will—by which I mean, have never read him or heard him—you may want to check to be sure you are at the right dinner.

Oh, I understand you may not know how many papers his column appears in (450) or when he began writing it (1974) or when he started his column for the back page of *Newsweek* (1976) or which year it was that he won the Pulitzer Prize (1977).

It's even possible that some of you have never read his book on baseball, *Men at Work*, which spent two months on the bestseller lists in 1989—but if you have a chance to meet Mr. Will, don't tell him that.

In 1977, the *National Journal* called him one of the twenty-five most influential Washington journalists. He is in fact one of the most widely recognized, and widely read, writers in the world.

But if I were Mr. Will, the award I would prize most is the one he received in 1985 from *The Washington Journalism Review,* which named him "Best Writer, Any Subject."

The mark of a skilled writer is the ability to craft a piece on a subject in which you have no interest whatsoever—but a piece so compelling you can't put it down.

That is the kind of piece George Will writes.

If you look at his most recently published collection of columns, *One Man's America,* you will find a piece on Harley Davidson motorcycles, one on Brooks Brothers, another on Starbucks and nail salons—topics that, I suspect, interest few of you . . . until you are seduced by Mr. Will.

I have known Mr. Will since 1973 when we were both on the staff of William F. Buckley's *National Review* in New York, so I have been an avid reader and admirer—and friend—for thirty-five years.

Ladies and gentlemen: George Will.

Introduction of George F. Will
Pacific Research Institute for Public Policy
San Francisco, California

November 9, 2012

A number of years ago, someone called George Will, derisively, "the nation's schoolmaster." Of course, today, the term is almost without meaning. Most schools are run by administrators.

I remember once meeting my own schoolmaster, in his office, on his carpet, in front of his desk. I was eleven. He was a dead ringer for George Will—but three feet taller.

For us tonight, the only relevant datum concerning my meeting is that there was nothing voluntary about my attendance.

Not so of the nation's conversation with George Will. Although, like my schoolmaster, Mr. Will does all the talking, the people listen because they want to.

And the audience is huge. Mr. Will's column appears in over four hundred newspapers—which, today I think, is all of them.

And he appears regularly on ABC's Sunday morning show, *This Week*, which had three million viewers last Sunday. The other 311 million Americans forgot to change their clocks.

My favorite George Will quote goes as follows: "Most new ideas are false; hence most 'improvements' make matters worse."

Since he wrote that, there has been a plethora of new ideas imposed on the body politic. And we might ask, how are those new ideas workin' out for ya?

At the conclusion of WWII, the Emperor of Japan went on national radio and told the Japanese people that "the war situation has developed not necessarily to Japan's advantage."

That is certainly what conservatives think about this week's election, and, my guess is, that is what our speaker thinks as well.

Ladies and Gentlemen: George Will.

Introduction of M. Stanton Evans
At a party celebrating the publication of
Stalin's Secret Agents
The Metropolitan Club:
Washington DC

June 10, 2013

Ladies and Gentlemen:

It is wonderful to see so many of you here to celebrate the publication of Stan Evans's new book, *Stalin's Secret Agents*.

This is the companion volume to *Blacklisted by History*, the publication of which we celebrated a few years ago, and about which Bill Schulz wrote: "Of the hundreds of books on the McCarthy era, Evans has written the best—a nuanced, incredibly detailed work of scholarship."

The important take-away from *Stalin's Secret Agents* is not that spying by the reds was the major issue. The major issue was the influence on policy that the Soviets' agents were able to have.

This book describes that influence, compared to which Whittaker Chambers described spying as trivial.

Stan has some wonderful quotes made at Yalta by that paragon of progressivism, Franklin Roosevelt. Roosevelt was at the top of his game at Yalta, or so we were assured by Chip Bohlen and Averell Harriman.

At Yalta, Stalin urged the shooting of fifty thousand Germans as soon as they could be captured. Churchill was horrified, but Roosevelt, that paragon of progressivism, suggested that perhaps they could compromise by shooting only forty-five thousand.

Later, when Stalin asked Roosevelt what concession he might make to Ibn Saud in dealing with Middle Eastern issues, Roosevelt, that paragon of progressivism, said the only concession he might make was to give Saud the six million Jews in the United States.

Those data may not have been in the history books you read in school, because they weren't known then. They certainly won't be in the history books of the future, because they are inconvenient facts.

Ladies and Gentlemen: This is a wonderful book. Don't miss it.

I want to digress, just for a moment, to note that when we were trying last week to get Simon & Schuster to send us some books, Stan and I decided that if Simon & Schuster had been in charge of the Cold War, we would have lost.

That prompted Stan to tell me a story, which I will insist, on a point of personal privilege, that Stan relate to you this evening.

I think I remarked the last time we gathered here for a Stan Evans Book Party that Bill Buckley once remarked that he would thenceforth never discuss the Vietnam War with anyone who had not read Henry Kissinger's *The White House Years*—which is fourteen hundred pages long.

I think it wasn't *just* that Bill was tired of re-fighting the Vietnam War. His point was, that if you hadn't read what the expert had to say, why should he (Bill) spend his time discussing the topic with you?

That's the way I feel about the Communist period in American history. Henceforth, we can say to any person who brings up McCarthy or Communist infiltration, that we won't discuss the subject unless he has read Stan Evans's books.

Stan's books are, I suspect, the last word on the subject. *We* don't need another; and the liberals won't bother writing another.

So the last word will belong to Stan.

Ladies and Gentlemen: Stan Evans.

Introduction of Allan Ryskind
At a party celebrating the publication of
Hollywood Traitors: Blacklisted Screenwriters, Agents of Stalin, Allies of Hitler
The Metropolitan Club:
Washington DC

February 17, 2015

Ladies and Gentlemen:

Louise and I, and Tom and Dawne Winter, and Jim and Patti Roberts are delighted you could join us this evening to celebrate the publication of Allan Ryskind's new book, *Hollywood Traitors: Blacklisted Screenwriters, Agents of Stalin, Allies of Hitler*.

This is an important book. Ann Coulter describes it as "the book we've been waiting for." Well, that all depends on who "we" are. We may have been waiting for this book. But the Left most assuredly has not been waiting for it.

Allan's book can be seen, I think, as the third book of a trilogy, the first two books being Stan Evans's: *Blacklisted by History*, and *Stalin's Secret Agents*.

This is history that does not appear in history books—certainly not in Howard Zinn's unfortunately widely used textbook on US history. And it is history that most likely never will appear in history books.

Allan's book is about Hollywood communist screenwriters who wrote as much communism into their movie scripts as they dared. And then many of them refused to answer questions posed by the House Un-American Activities Committee. And then they went to jail. And then they were blacklisted by the studios which chose not to hire a lot of communists who would write as much communism into their movie scripts as they dared.

Well, the critics might say, that was a long time ago.

Yes, and no. In 1997, the Academy of Motion Picture Arts and Sciences—pause for a moment to notice the hype of the title: "Academy of Motion Picture Arts and Sciences"—in 1997, the Academy honored the writers who were blacklisted by the Hollywood Studios. And hundreds of lefties gathered to honor these people who were, as Allan shows in his book, agents of Stalin, allies of Hitler. Only in America?

The book is a great read. What distressed me was how many of the villains' names I recognized. There were, however, a few heroes, one of whom was Morrie Ryskind, Allan's father.

Ladies and Gentlemen: Morrie Ryskind's son, young Allan Ryskind.

Index

About the Author

DANIEL OLIVER has been writing political commentary since 1971 when he did his first stint at William F. Buckley Jr.'s *National Review* magazine, the flagship of the Conservative Movement. (Mr. Oliver had been director of research for James L. Buckley's successful campaign for the US Senate in 1970.) His second stint began in 1973, when he became executive editor of the publication. He wrote regularly for the magazine and had a column in the *National Review Bulletin*, an eight-page publication that appeared on the weeks that the fortnightly magazine did not. Before going to *National Review*, Mr. Oliver practiced law in New York City with famed novelist Louis S. Auchincloss. Buckley said it took him only a year to leech the legalese out of Oliver's writing. Mr. Oliver began writing columns regularly in 2004 when his wife moved to Paris to be the US representative (with rank of ambassador) to the United Nations Educational, Scientific, and Cultural Organization. His columns have appeared in *American Greatness, The American Spectator, The American Conservative, The Claremont Review of Book, The Daily Caller, The Federalist, First Things, Fox News, The Washington Times,* and *The Western Journal,* among other publications.

About Mr. Oliver's writing, Pulitzer Prize–winning journalist Anthony R. Dolan* commented: "I am surprised how easily you handle the style, without struggle, it seems to me, which is most unusual for someone whose professional training has been for the most part otherwise. Still the NR experience may have been formative or you may—autodidactically—have been making mental notes while reading the daily paper over the years. Or perhaps you are a born columnist. Whatever (to quote Sen. Dole), it works."

DANIEL OLIVER was born in New York, went to Milton Academy, Harvard College, and Fordham Law School. He served in the US Army from 1959 to 1962. He practiced law in New York City before joining the staff of *National Review* magazine. In 1981, he was

---

*Deputy assistant to President Reagan, director, and chief speech writer, 1981–89.

nominated by President Ronald Reagan to be general counsel of the Department of Education. In 1983, Reagan nominated him to be general counsel of the Department of Agriculture. In 1986, Reagan nominated him to be chairman of the Federal Trade Commission. All three appointments required confirmation by the US Senate. Subsequent to his government service, Mr. Oliver worked for, *inter alia*, The Heritage Foundation. He has served on the boards of several public policy institutions, including Pacific Research Institute for Public Policy, of which he is a former chairman, and Education and Research Institute, of which he is the current chairman. He lives in Washington DC with his wife, Louise V. Oliver, the former US ambassador to UNESCO.